the cooking of
Indonesia and the Philippines

the cooking of

Indonesia and the Philippines

Sensational dishes from an exotic cuisine, with 150 authentic
recipes shown step by step in 700 beautiful photographs

GHILLIE BAŞAN, TERRY TAN AND VILMA LAUS

LORENZ BOOKS

This edition is published by Lorenz Books,
an imprint of Anness Publishing Ltd, Hermes House,
88–89 Blackfriars Road, London SE1 8HA;
tel. 020 7401 2077; fax 020 7633 9499
www.lorenzbooks.com; www.annesspublishing.com

If you like the images in this book and would like to investigate using them
for publishing, promotions or advertising, please visit our website
www.practicalpictures.com for more information.

UK agent: The Manning Partnership Ltd; tel. 01225 478444;
   fax 01225 478440; sales@manning-partnership.co.uk
UK distributor: Grantham Book Services Ltd; tel. 01476 541080;
   fax 01476 541061; orders@gbs.tbs-ltd.co.uk
North American agent/distributor: National Book Network;
   tel. 301 459 3366; fax 301 429 5746; www.nbnbooks.com
Australian agent/distributor: Pan Macmillan Australia; tel. 1300 135 113;
   fax 1300 135 103; customer.service@macmillan.com.au
New Zealand agent/distributor: David Bateman Ltd; tel. (09) 415 7664;
   fax (09) 415 8892

Publisher: Joanna Lorenz
Editorial Director: Helen Sudell
Editors: Emma Clegg and Rosie Gordon
Contributing Editors: Beverley Jollands and Alison Bolus
Page Design: Ian Sandom
Production Controller: Steve Lang
Home Economists: Lucy McKelvie and Katie Giovanni
Photographers: William Lingwood and Martin Brigdale
Stylist: Helen Trent

Publisher's Acknowledgments
The publisher is grateful to the following for permission to publish
photographs: Alamy pp.10bl, 13b, 18b, 22tr, 22bl, 23tr; Corbis p.23bl;
Photoshot pp. 11br, 12b, 36b; Still Pictures pp.14b, 16b, 17t, 19tl, 19tr;
Travel_ink pp. 6tl, 7tl, 8tr, 8bl, 9tl, 9br, 11tr, 12t, 15t, 15b .

Parts of this book were previously published in another volume,
The Food and Cooking of Indonesia & the Philippines by
Ghillie Başan and Vilma Laus.

Ethical Trading Policy
At Anness Publishing we believe that business should be conducted in an
ethical and ecologically sustainable way, with respect for the environment
and a proper regard to the replacement of the natural resources we use.
As a publisher, we use a lot of wood pulp to make paper for printing, and
that wood commonly comes from spruce trees. We are therefore growing
more than 750,000 trees in three Scottish forest plantations near Aberdeen
– Berrymoss (130 hectares/320 acres), West Touxhill (125 hectares/305
acres) and Deveron Forest (75 hectares/185 acres).

The forests we manage contain more than 3.5 times the number of trees
employed each year in paper-making for our books. Because of this
ongoing ecological investment programme, you, as our customer, can have
the pleasure and reassurance of knowing that a tree is being cultivated on
your behalf to naturally replace the materials used to make this book.

Our forestry programme is run in accordance with the UK Woodland
Assurance Scheme (UKWAS) and will be certified by the internationally
recognized Forest Stewardship Council (FSC). The FSC is a non-
government organization dedicated to promoting responsible management
of the world's forests. Certification ensures forests are managed on an
environmentally sustainable and socially responsible basis. For further
information about this scheme, go to www.annesspublishing.com/trees

Notes
Bracketed terms are intended for American readers.
For all recipes, quantities are given in both metric and imperial measures
   and, where appropriate, in standard cups and spoons. Follow one set, but
   not a mixture, because they are not interchangeable.
Standard spoon and cup measures are level. 1 tsp = 5ml, 1 tbsp = 15ml,
   1 cup = 250ml/8fl oz.
Australian standard tablespoons are 20ml. Australian readers should use 3 tsp
   in place of 1 tbsp for measuring small quantities of gelatine, flour, salt, etc.
American pints are 16fl oz/2 cups. American readers should use 20fl oz/
   2½ cups in place of 1 pint when measuring liquids.
Electric oven temperatures in this book are for conventional ovens.
   When using a fan oven, the temperature will probably need to be reduced
   by about 10–20°C/20–40°F. Since ovens vary, you should check with your
   manufacturer's instruction book for guidance.
The nutritional analysis given for each recipe is calculated per portion (i.e.
   serving or item), unless otherwise stated. If the recipe gives a range, such
   as Serves 4–6, then the nutritional analysis will be for the smaller portion
   size, i.e. 6 servings. Measurements for sodium do not include salt added
   to taste.
Medium (US large) eggs are used unless otherwise stated.

Main front cover image shows Prawn Adobo in Coconut Milk – for recipe, see
page 134.

CONTENTS

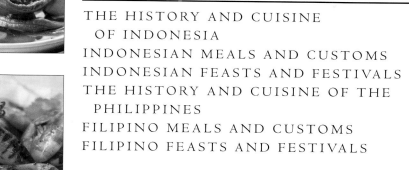

THE INDONESIAN AND FILIPINO KITCHEN

THE RECIPES OF INDONESIA AND THE PHILIPPINES

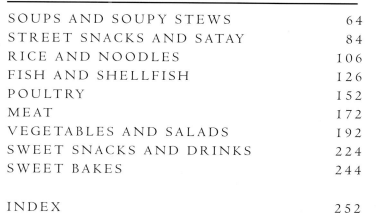

INTRODUCTION

The culinary traditions of neighbouring Indonesia and the Philippines are surprisingly different, for two essential reasons: their histories and their geographical locations. Indonesia's islands lie in the middle of ancient trade routes, and the country's history of colonialism has enriched the cuisine with exotic spices and cooking methods from India, Persia (now Iran) and China. By contrast, an intriguing combination of Chinese and Spanish influences have shaped the food of the Philippines – resulting in a cuisine quite distinct from any other in South-east Asia.

THE ISLANDS OF INDONESIA

Indonesia's more than 13,500 islands of varying sizes, not all of which have names, are sometimes likened to 'a jewelled necklace'. They lie between Australia and the South-east Asian mainland, and the country includes Java, Bali, Sumatra, parts of Borneo and parts of New Guinea. Fewer than 1,000 of the islands are populated, as some are too small or too barren to support successful habitation.

A total of 234 million residents means that Indonesia's population ranks as the sixth largest in the world. However, the distribution of people is very uneven, and one third of the total population of the entire archipelago lives in the city of Jakarta – over 80 million people.

The Indonesian landscape and climate have a significant influence on the food. The islands often suffer from floods and volcanic eruptions, which together produce very fertile soil and a lush green landscape. High humidity makes living there a hot and steamy experience, somewhat akin to being in a greenhouse, although the cooler mountain peaks and high volcanic craters running down the back of most of the major islands provide a welcome relief from these conditions.

The topographical variety leads to the cultivation of many different crops. Rice grows on neatly carved hillside terraces in Bali and Java; cassava grows wild on Mount Merapi's slopes in Java; tea plantations dominate the landscape in western Java; papaya trees grow freely on Sumatra; and the tropical fish caught in the crystal-clear waters off Lombok are many and varied. The less fertile highlands of West Irian Jaya, however, produce only small quantities of sweet potato, while hilly Nusa Tengarra supports little more than corn.

For the best Indonesian food, visit Java, which is home to a wide variety of agricultural produce and many inspired, tasty dishes. In Javan cuisine, a simple plate of rice can be transformed into a feast that smells and tastes delicious. Spices such as turmeric and saffron tell the story of Indonesia's history, and the fiery chilli, which appears on every plate, reflects the warmth of the people.

FILIPINO LANDS AND LIFE

The collection of islands that makes up the Philippines is more compact than those of Indonesia; they lie roughly 800km/500 miles south-east of the Asian continent. The main group of

Top left: A typical Javanese village with thatched houses on stilts, surrounded by paddy fields.

Left: The islands of Indonesia spread across the base of South-east Asia.

Above: A view of Taal volcano in the Philippines, the smallest and one of the most dangerous in the world.

Right: The Philippines – a cluster of islands almost set apart from the rest of South-east Asia.

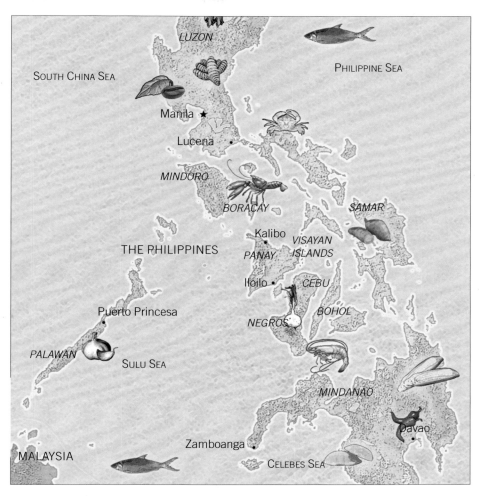

islands, the Visayas, is situated between Luzon to the north, Palawan to the west, and Mindanao to the south. Among the Visaya islands, Cebu and Boracay stand out from the rest for their beauty, with their palm-fringed beaches and their stunning reefs, making them very popular places to visit.

The development of tourism, which can bring mixed blessings to a country, has not, however, reached all of the islands, many of which still remain a traveller's secret paradise. In this diverse ecosystem, there are ingeniously devised rice terraces, spectacular waterfalls, lush tropical jungles, deserted pristine beaches and steep mountains with active volcanoes. On the small island of Bohol, there are also the extraordinary Chocolate Hills: 1,268 nearly identical, neatly rounded hills, each 30–50m/ 98–165ft tall, on which the sun bakes the thick grass to a dark chocolate colour.

A few indigenous tribes still live in the remote hills of the islands, where they uphold their ancient traditions and way of life, but in the more fashionable towns there is the ubiquitous blend of American music, coffee shops and fast food that tends to come with tourism. The inhabitants of these islands are some of the friendliest people on Earth, whose *joie de vivre* and strong sense of religion together influence every aspect of the Filipino culture.

Food is a very important part of life for the Filipinos, who love to eat. A combination of their love of life and their love of food makes for much happy feasting and a generally very positive view of food. The fact that they eat an average of five meals a day, rather than the usual three of the West, means that they seem to be forever eating – and with very obvious enjoyment and impressive appetites!

HOW TO USE THIS BOOK

The introductory pages of this book will allow you to become familiar with the islands of Indonesia and the Philippines – not only with their geography but with their customs, feasts and festivals and, of course, their kitchens. Discover the essential ingredients that cooks of the region have in their store cupboards and the fruits, vegetables, herbs and spices that they buy in their local markets. Cooks all over the world are able to access these exotic ingredients today, and experience delicious cooking and great culinary heritage.

These pages will also show you the basic spice blends, equipment and cooking techniques that you will need to make Indonesian and Filipino food.

A superb collection of 150 authentic and unforgettable recipes completes this guide to the food and cooking of Indonesia and the Philippines.

THE HISTORY AND CUISINE OF INDONESIA

Due in part to their location, the fertile green islands that comprise modern Indonesia have frequently been invaded. They have also traded with nations such as Malaysia, China, India, Persia, Arabia and Spain, as well as some European sea-going nations during the Spice Wars in the 16th and 17th centuries. This regular and long-term contact with foreign countries has had a significant impact on all aspects of Indonesian life, from religious beliefs and agricultural methods to culinary ingredients and cooking techniques – which are all still very much in evidence today.

EARLY ANCESTRY

Archaeological research reveals the indigenous inhabitants to have been hunter-gatherers who subsisted on a diet of fruit, fish, taro and game. From c.4000BCE, repeated migrations from South-east Asia replaced them with a new Indonesian race that was mostly composed of Malays and sea-going Melanesians. It was not until the Dongson civilization spread from Vietnam and southern China around 3,000 years ago, however, that large cultural changes took place. The appearance of the Dongson initiated the spread of rice cultivation and irrigation across the islands, as well as the introduction of the water buffalo as a beast of burden and a

Above: A typical street market in Bima, with local produce displayed in baskets lined with banana leaves.

Above: Lake Bralan, Bali, where the Pura Ulu Danau temple lies at the heart of a lush, flower-filled valley.

source of food. The custom of sacrificing a buffalo was also adopted from the Dongsons and is still followed in Sumatra, Sulawesi and Nusa Tenggara.

By the 7th century BCE, the Indonesian archipelago was home to well-organized societies in which people tended irrigated rice paddies and raised domesticated water buffalo, chickens, pigs and dogs, and rural kitchens were stocked with foods such as bananas, breadfruit, coconuts and yams.

TRADE INFLUENCES

In their early years, the islands that now form modern Indonesia were heavily influenced by the ingredients and cooking methods of China, India, Persia, Arabia and Malaysia. The Chinese traders and immigrants who visited the islands from the 7th century onwards brought ingredients such as noodles, rice and soy sauce, as well as the technique of stir-frying, which has become an integral part of the cuisine throughout the islands. Although Chinese dialects are rarely spoken today, and the government ruled that all original Chinese names had to be converted into Indonesian, there are still reminders of early Sino-Indonesian union in dishes such as lumpia and bak

mie goreng. They can easily be linked with the Chinese dishes of spring rolls and fried noodles, but have had indigenous herbs and spices added.

Chinese products and island spices, such as cloves and cinnamon bark, were traded for Indian, Persian and Arabian goods. The origin of the Indonesian curry, gulai or kare, can be traced back to these traders, since the spices in the dish (cardamom, cumin, coriander and garlic) all came from India. Trading links with these countries also introduced Hinduism and Buddhism to Indonesia, so bringing about a major change to the indigenous belief system. Islam was introduced in the 13th century, spreading from west to east, and was eventually adopted by most of the islands: the satellite kingdoms of the Majapahit were declared independent Muslim states. In spite of the ongoing presence of European sea-going nations during the Spice Wars in the 16th and 17th centuries (see below), Islam remained the dominant religion, spreading to most areas of the island chain. The result today is a Muslim population so large that it claims to be the biggest in the world.

The Spanish explorers of the 16th and 17th centuries brought with them unusual ingredients from the New World, such as corn, pineapples and tomatoes, as well as the

ubiquitous chilli pepper, which quickly became an essential part of many Indonesian dishes.

THE SPICE WARS

Water was of vital importance to life in Indonesia. Oceans, rivers, streams and fertile deltas have affected the lives of the inhabitants as well as the way in which their cuisines have evolved. In fact, produce from waterways formed much of the early Indonesian diet. Water also brought traders and new culinary ideas, in addition to unusual goods from the Middle East and China.

Before the 16th century, Arab sailors who had visited the 'spice islands' of the East Indies (now known as Indonesia) sold spices to merchants at Constantinople, who then took them to Venice, where they were sold on to European merchants, who in turn took them to their own countries – a long and expensive chain. However, as the price of spices rose, these distant islands became ever more desirable to European traders who wanted to make money.

The first to arrive were the Portuguese in 1511. They captured the Malay port of Melaka and made large sums of money by trading there in cloves and

Right: For families in Bali, social and religious gatherings tend to involve gifts of food and flowers.

Left: People fishing off Samur beach in Bali, wearing hats and masks to protect themselves from the sun's glare.

nutmeg. The Spice Wars began when the Dutch reached the East Indies in 1596. By 1607 they had defeated the Portuguese and won control of the clove trade from Maluku as well as occupying the Banda Islands for their nutmeg. The English were drawn into the Spice Wars in 1601, setting sail under the auspices of the East India Company.

EUROPEAN INFLUENCES

The European sea-going nations who were involved in the Spice Wars had limited influence on the culinary scene of Indonesia (although the introduction of tea was a major contribution).

Interestingly, nasi goreng, the egg-topped national fried rice dish, is one of the few dishes to trace its origins to a European country – Holland. Another Dutch influence is rijsttafel (rice table), which came from the village custom of holding a harvest-end feast, but has since evolved into an array of 12–30 side dishes served with rice – often with the misleading claim that it is an example of classic Indonesian cuisine. Indonesia was under Dutch dominance for some time, which accounts for Dutch influence in the cuisines, but the ethnic origins of many dishes remain strongly evident.

The cuisines of other Asian countries have more natural links with Indonesian cooking than those of Dutch and other European countries, but the colonial influences are still important and have added their own part to the story. One can conclude that indigenous cuisines are largely shaped by history, but also enriched by their country's location.

INDONESIAN MEALS AND CUSTOMS

The home cooking of Indonesia is a relaxed affair, and the dishes all share a simplicity at their core. The attitude towards ingredients and preparation is matter-of-fact and open-minded: there are no strict rules, no correct or incorrect ingredients, just an acceptance that most dishes begin with a chilli-laced spice paste. Street food is popular in the cities, and most Indonesians enjoy a snack on the move during the day. This comes as no surprise when you see the amazing range of tempting snacks on offer at stalls and from roving vendors on every street.

BREAKFAST

Indonesians start each morning with breakfast at sunrise, before the day starts to heat up. In the morning you can often see groups of women sitting outside their homes, chatting over bowls of rice topped with chillies and fried shallots. What Indonesians eat varies from region to region. In Java it might be just a bowl of rice left over from the day before, while in Maluku it could be a sago cake served with a cup of tea, and in Surabaya it might be a more substantial rice porridge with chicken. In rural communities, this first meal of the day is informal and snacks are eaten as minor sustenance as dawn breaks.

For a wealthy person in one of the large cities, however, a Western-style breakfast of a bowl of cereal and a cup of coffee is likely to be on the menu, although increasingly for Indonesians, breakfast tends to be a meal on the run, especially among urbanites.

LUNCH AND SUPPER

It is traditional in many households to cook a large pot of rice in the morning, along with three or four dishes, which often include fish or meat, vegetables and a sambal, to go with it. The rice is often par-boiled and drained, then left in the pot to steam until it is fluffy and fully cooked. Doing this means that the cook can keep the rice warm for long periods of time while the other dishes, which are spread out on the table, are left all day for people to help themselves for lunch and supper. Both meals consist solely of what is on the table, which can be eaten in any combination or order as desired. In this type of meal, the rice (or any other staple) forms the main part of the meal, and diners spoon small helpings of the other dishes over it simply to flavour and moisten the grains. By contrast, more wealthy families may regularly eat thick curries, fried or grilled (broiled) meat and hearty fish or chicken dishes.

STREET FOOD

All over Indonesia you can find *warungs* (casual, usually outdoor, food vendors, many operating in simple lean-to stalls) selling everything from cigarettes to rice and curries. These sellers play a very important role that is far more than just selling snack food: they are the pulse of social life; places where friends can meet and chat over some noodles or rujak; and a convivial stop on the way home on market day. Eating throughout Indonesia is a completely relaxed and informal experience, which means that *warungs* offer a home-from-home experience, but without the cooking or washing up! They epitomize the whole tradition of eating out, which is such a part of life in Indonesia that it is woven into the very fabric of the food culture.

Above: Sticky coconut crêpes are a popular street snack in Indonesia.

Left: Indonesian meals usually include rice and lots of other small dishes.

Most city-dwellers will eat at least one meal a day from a street seller, though for different reasons. For business people, the reason is that they are often simply too busy to cook, while country folk who have moved to the city often live in very basic accommodation with no kitchen, so they cannot cook for themselves. Luckily for both, there is a wide variety of snacks available all day long from the *warungs* and *kaki-limas* (roving vendors: literally 'five feet' – three for the cart and two for the vendor). The *kaki-limas* often specialize in just one type of snack, such as nasi goreng, or pisang goreng, which are sweet, sticky, deep-fried bananas.

ETIQUETTE AND HOSPITALITY

If you are visiting an Indonesian home, your host will treat you with great respect, but you may find certain practices disconcerting at first. For instance, you may be invited to eat alone while your hosts sit and watch you. This is seen as a gesture of hospitality, showing that you are the priority, but it can be unnerving. Accept whatever food is offered with gratitude, but do not eat so much that there is not much left for the family. On large social occasions, wait until the host has motioned to you that you can start. The eldest member of a family will usually serve him- or herself first, but a guest may be allowed to jump the queue.

Indonesians usually like to eat with their hands, so the tradition of chopping ingredients into bitesize pieces before cooking them is highly practical. Use only your right hand to scoop up rice and other ingredients, and also this hand for passing dishes around the table. (The left hand is strictly reserved for another bodily function, so to use it at the table would be a tremendous *faux pas*.) If you are left-handed, you will need to learn how to use your right hand for eating very quickly if you are to avoid causing offence. If hands are not appropriate, such as for a meal with a sauce, you will be given a fork and spoon to make eating easier. When you have finished, compliment the cook, then clean your teeth with a toothpick while covering your mouth with one hand.

Above: It is customary for Indonesians to eat with the right hand rather than with Western-style utensils.

Below: A colourful street market, with women carrying baskets of produce on their heads, in Bali.

INDONESIAN FEASTS AND FESTIVALS

In Indonesia, Islamic holy events, such as Ramadan or Idul Adha, are marked either by fasting or by eating traditional foods, such as goat. By contrast, the Hindu communities traditionally prepare large feasts to celebrate family births, marriages and deaths, as well as making elaborate food offerings to present to their deities.

RELIGIOUS OFFERINGS

Islam, Hinduism, Buddhism and Animism (the belief that everything has a soul, even inanimate objects such as rocks and vegetables) are practised with great enthusiasm, and the hunger of souls takes precedence over the hunger of the people. Festivals in other religions involve preparing food for the people to eat, but Indonesian special dishes are instead treated as reverent offerings to their different gods.

Rice lies at the essential heart of Indonesian life. Not only is it their staple food, which is central to every family meal, with the numerous dishes served alongside being mere accompaniments, but it is also held in high regard as the offspring of the goddess Dewi Sri. At the end of the fasting month that marks Ramadan, there is an hour of sunset prayer, known as *magrib*, when people come together to eat. Large amounts of sweetened tea are drunk with impressive quantities of food. This is a time when the food is for the believers, and not just for the gods.

The appeasement of the deities is of great importance to Hindu culture, most particularly in Bali, where their culinary needs are paramount. For instance, Galungan is a time when the souls of ancestors are said to come back to Earth to spend time with their families. Outside every home *penjors* (very tall, curved bamboo poles, each one decorated with banana and coconut leaves as well as fruit and flowers, rice and other tidbits) are erected in honour of the god of the mountain – Hyang Giri Pati. Offerings are also placed in shrines at the foot of the *penjors*. With spirits fêted and bodies and souls fed, harmony is believed to be maintained throughout the land.

Above: Families in Seminyak, Bali, gather on the beach to celebrate many occasions, from births to religious festivals.

SELAMATANS AND OTHER FEASTS

Throughout its history, many religions have influenced Indonesia, and ritual celebrations are common affairs. Food is such an integral part of these festivities that there is even a name reserved for a meal prepared for a lot of people: *selamatan*. Such a meal is usually held at home to mark a family occasion, such as the birth of a child, a birthday, moving to a new house, the harvest, circumcisions and deaths. *Selamatans* will include a combination of meat, chicken and egg dishes, which are placed around the *tumpeng* – a

pyramid of yellow rice, the tip of which is offered to the eldest guest.

Meat is always served at celebratory feasts, especially cooked in traditional dishes such as rendang (slow-cooked buffalo or beef in coconut milk). While 90 per cent of the population of Indonesia is Muslim, and so does not eat pork, the Hindu island of Bali is an exception, and here feasts may revolve around a spit-roast pig.

Family weddings can range from a small domestic affair to a large feast, depending on the wealth of a family. A feast may last for several days and consists of a large buffet-style spread, which usually includes a spit-roast pig or goat. In Java, the bride feeds the groom by hand to symbolize her new role in life. Here there is also a feast for the seventh month of pregnancy, which involves seven dishes and seven hard-boiled eggs, which are skewered and placed in the main rice dish. If the feast is elaborate and beautifully presented, it is thought to predict the birth of a girl, whereas a less extensive collection of dishes will indicate a boy.

Left: A young Hindu boy in traditional dress for Kuningan at the end of the Galungan Festival.

MUSLIM FESTIVALS

For most Indonesians, the main celebrations are Ramadan, the Muslim month of fasting, which ends with Eid al-Fitr, and Eid al-Adha (or Idul Adha, the Day of Sacrifice).

During the month of Ramadan, the devout must not eat or drink anything in the hours between sunrise and sunset, and many street vendors and other eateries shut for this period as a mark of respect. Once the sun has set, however, drums beat to call the faithful to prayer, and heaps of rice, along with meat and vegetable dishes, are brought out and eaten in company.

The end of the month of fasting is called Lebaran or Eid al-Fitr, and this is an occasion when many Indonesians go to see their families to ask forgiveness for any errors, and to drink sweetened black tea and sticky rice cakes. Ketupat (small coconut-leaf packets of steamed rice) are hung up as decoration and goodwill symbols.

Another important date on the Muslim calendar is Eid al-Adha, which commemorates Ibrahim's willingness to sacrifice his son Ishmael. Because God spared Ishmael, substituting a sheep in his place, it is traditional in Muslim cultures all over the world to sacrifice a sheep or goat to mark the event, and the meat is then shared among the family or wider community to be cooked in various ways. Eid al-Adha occurs 70 days after Eid al-Fitr; the animals that are marked for sacrifice are much in evidence as they are taken live to the market in the family car, in the backs of pick-up trucks or strapped on to the backs of bikes.

The Sekaten fair commemorates the prophet Mohammed's birthday, and huge cones of rice blended with many other ingredients, known as Gunangan Nasi, are taken to Kasunanan Palace in Surakarta. These are then blessed and distributed among the visitors around the Grand Mosque, to give prosperity and happiness in the coming year.

Right: A procession of Hindu women in Bali carry carefully stacked and very elaborate food offerings for the gods.

HINDU FESTIVALS

Bali is particularly famous for its celebrations, when spicy regional dishes are cooked for the lively and colourful events on the Hindu calendar. These festivities include Kedaso, the festival of the tenth full-moon, and Penampahan, a festival of purification, when the gods are appeased with sacrificial pigs.

Wherever a deity may live, there you will find offerings of fresh fruit and food cooked specially for the gods. These offerings are frequently beautifully presented and can include impressive towers of fruit, small amounts of rice prettily held in banana-leaf pouches, and rice cakes made in fancy shapes. Whether you come across offerings in a rice paddy, a bus station or just a doorway, you must step around them carefully and move on, leaving them untouched. Daily offerings of rice, flowers and incense to the deities are also scattered along the edges of rice paddies to keep any demons away, and there is often a shrine to Dewi Sri, the Hindu goddess of rice and harvest, who is presented with fresh fruit and flowers.

Other food offerings, which may include home-grown vegetables and chickens, are made to mark the anniversary of the founding of a local temple. The people spend much of the day making rice cakes and decorations and preparing fruits, which they then assemble into stacks up to 1.8m/6ft high. Later, immaculately dressed women proceed to the temple with the beautiful foods carefully balanced on their heads. When the gods have eaten their fill, the leftovers are given to the community. At such celebrations, the gender roles are clearly defined: the men do the cooking and the women prepare the spices.

Other celebrations include Pager Wesi, where Hindus celebrate Sang Yang as the creator of the universe with offerings of food. At the Kasada festival, Javanese farmers of the fertile lands around Mount Bromo volcano process and throw food offerings, from fruit to livestock, into the crater for the deity.

THE HISTORY AND CUISINE OF THE PHILIPPINES

Surrounded by oceans and criss-crossed by rivers and streams, the Philippines are flanked by the South China Sea on the west, the Pacific Ocean to the north, the Celebes Sea to the south and the Sulu Sea to the south-west. It is inevitable, therefore, that the cuisine has drawn inexhaustibly from the ocean. Climatically, the islands enjoy an almost entirely tropical ambience where fruits and herbs grow to sweet magnificence. Most ubiquitous is the humble kalamansi, a diminutive native lime with a delicious tartness, used in everything from drinks to marinades, dips and casseroles.

A CULTURAL MELTING POT

Filipino cuisine has maintained vibrant indigenous elements from many countries. The islands have a long and turbulent history of colonization by various nations, including China, Spain, America and Japan. It was the 400-year period of Spanish rule, however, which had by far the biggest impact on the cultural and culinary landscape, and which first drew the disparate island communities together under one banner. Today, this profound influence is much in evidence in the food, cultural and religious beliefs of this predominantly Catholic archipelago, although some traces of the legacy left by other nations can also be detected.

EARLY INFLUENCES

Prior to the *conquista* by the Spanish in the late 1500s, the native people of the Philippines had existed as a series of tribes based on a subsistence economy and animistic beliefs. This pagan world of the South Seas was akin to their sea-faring cousins, the Polynesians, and was completely distinct from the Hindu, Buddhist, Sinified or Islamized world of Asia, which included the islands of neighbouring Indonesia.

The islands were colonized by the Chinese for a brief period in the 11th century, and were visited throughout history by Chinese, Indian, Malay and other traders. These traders settled on some of the islands and married local girls, adding to the developing pool of culinary knowledge. The Malay influence is still evident among the Moros of the Luzon and the Bicolanos, both of whom enjoy hot, spicy food in rich coconut milk sauces. By 1565, the era of the Hispanic-speaking Filipinos had begun. During this period, after a history of being bypassed by its neighbouring cultures, the Philippines suddenly became a worthy destination for leisure and trade. With all the food and jewels arriving from places like India, Cambodia and Japan, Manila emerged as the Port of Asia and was finally regarded as Asian.

SPANISH INFLUENCES

During the 400 years of Spanish rule, the Philippines were used as a production base for sugar and other agricultural crops, as well as a significant trading port within the Spanish Empire. The cultural and physical landscape of the Philippines was transformed by the Spanish, who brought with them not only the Catholic religion, but also corn, sweet potatoes, tomatoes, chillies, cacao, tobacco, papaya, pineapples, guava and avocados from the New World, and cheeses, sausages, hams and olives from Spain. As well as food the Spanish brought art, architecture and engineering and, most important of all, they introduced water buffalo and the plough. Where there had once been recurrent famine on islands such as the Visayas, corn and sweet potatoes now became staples, and the region was able to trade rice, sugar, tobacco, coffee, hemp, spices, indigo, pearls, cotton, tortoiseshell, betel nut and jute.

The character of *la cocina Filipina* was cast during this period, resulting in an interesting blend of Spanish, Malay and Chinese traditions. The Spanish influence is clearly evident in both the ingredients and the names of many dishes, including arroz caldo (colonial rice soup), pochero (beef and chorizo stew with plantain and chickpeas), leche flan (Filipino crème caramel) and the popular tortilla made with potatoes or bitter melon. Even when Chinese cooking methods were widely adopted, their provenance was disguised by Creole names, such as pancit guisado (stir-fried noodles) and lumpiang frito (fried spring rolls).

The tremendous strength of the Spanish culinary influence was due to the guisado, a simple process of sautéing ingredients to garnish the food that every proud Filipino cook swears by. This practice has resulted in the

Left: A Filipino fishing village among palm trees in Palawan. Coconuts and fish are part of the staple diet.

Above: Rice field terraces and a rural village at Batad, Luzon Island.

creation of many of the classic dishes including adobo (chicken and pork cooked with vinegar and chickpeas), guisadong ampalya at itlog (Spanish-style omelette with bitter melon) and tinolang manok (chicken and ginger broth with papaya). Armed with these new techniques and their own indigenous ingredients and knowledge, these simple-living people were thrust into a world of haute cuisine under their Spanish rulers, who demanded the familiar foods of their homelands as well as elaborate menus considered worthy of visiting royalty and other guests, who would dine in European style with fine wines and sherry.

It is unsurprising, then, that by the 19th century, the Filipinos had become such skilful cooks that whole towns and provinces became renowned for their local culinary art. Entire peoples, such as the Pampango and Visayan, were considered gourmets, and this attracted visitors to their regions from all over the world.

MODERN FILIPINO CUISINE

The United States took over the Philippines in the late 1800s and gave them independence after the end of World War II. The Americans brought their education system with them, resulting in a high literacy rate in English, although Tagalog is the national language, and Spanish is still spoken, too. The American culinary influence was minimal; the main effects of Amerian rule have been the national use of spoken English; the well-known global fast food outlets selling fried chicken and burgers which are common; and the Westernized youth cultures of music and fashion.

With so many outside influences fused within the Filipino culture, it is not easy to work out the exact origins of a few dishes. A typical example is escabéche, pickled fish in sour sauce that borrows freely from the South American template of ceviche, but has mingled with elements of Chinese cuisine to resemble deep-fried fish in a sweet and sour sauce. Thanks to the course of its chequered history and colonial rulers, the Philippines have

evolved and developed many regional cuisines and individual dishes that are quite unique to the islands, such as bistek – steak with onion rings, braised in soy sauce; lumpia, similar to spring rolls; a sour soup called singaging; and lechon, barbecued pig, often served with liver sauce.

Above: A woman buys salt from a trader at City Market, Baguio.

FILIPINO MEALS AND CUSTOMS

The food culture of the Philippines is generally a healthy one that is based on a lot of rice, fresh fish and a wide range of seasonal vegetables, which include both indigenous ingredients and those that were brought over by settlers. A typical Filipino day will include an average of five meals – breakfast; morning *merienda* (snack); lunch; afternoon *merienda* and dinner. There are numerous feasts throughout the year, all of which give the Filipinos every excuse to indulge their passion for making and consuming large amounts of delicious food.

MEALS AND MERIENDAS

As in the rest of South-east Asia, rice is the staple food of the Philippines and is served with almost every dish. Fried rice is popular for breakfast, served with dried fish or longaniza, the local spicy pork sausages, spiked with black pepper and garlic. Fried eggs are popular for breakfast too, as are continental-style breads, coffee and hot chocolate. Although the morning *merienda* is referred to as a snack, it can range from something as simple as a few slices of refreshing watermelon to a substantial bowl of stir-fried noodles, spring rolls or even an assortment of savoury sandwiches and sweet, sticky rice cakes.

Lunch and dinner tend to be big meals in the Philippines. Among the wealthy, these meals may include four or five courses, comprising a soup, followed by fresh fish and then a meat dish, fresh fruit and finally, if dining Spanish-style, a rich, sweet dessert. Between lunch and dinner there is yet another *merienda*, which consists of sandwiches, cakes and tea, but also spring rolls (lumpia), noodles (pancit) and a few local sweet dishes made from coconut milk, glutinous rice, pineapple or other tropical fruits.

REGIONAL VARIETIES

There is enormous geographical diversity within the Philippines, from the mountains and coastal regions of Northern Luzon to the innumerable islands of the Visayas and Mindanao. Bicol lies at the southern-most tip of Luzon Island and the abundance of coconuts is reflected richly in Bicolanos cuisine. The Pangasinans of Luzon are adept at curing fish from the briny providence of the Pacific Ocean and Philippine Sea, both on their doorstep. The Tagalogs use vinegar and fruits with abandon, while fermented fish paste, hot chillies and spices are the hallmark of Mindanao cooking, drawn from the cuisines of Malaysia and South-east Asia because of their close proximity. All the cuisines have been inevitably, and wonderfully, shaped by land and sea.

TRADITIONAL INGREDIENTS AND TECHNIQUES

Roasting, steaming and sautéing are the traditional methods used for cooking fish and meat. Fish is also marinated in sour flavours which are sourced naturally from fruits such as tamarind, guava and kalamansi limes. Salty flavours are derived from the national fermented fish sauces, patis and bagoong, and from Chinese soy sauce, whereas the sweet notes come from blocks of natural palm sugar (jaggery), which is grated or melted for use. Meat, although much sought after, is eaten less frequently because of its cost. However, when it comes to fiestas and family celebrations, no expense is spared and every imaginable meat dish is cooked.

At a meal, food is often laid out buffet-style in a skilful and colourful display. The indigenous Spanish-influenced dishes are often quite heavy on the stomach, but interspersed among them are lighter dishes, such as prawns (shrimp) and vegetables in a tamarind-flavoured broth, and tangy seaweed and papaya salads. Thanks to the Spanish, bread plays an important

Left: Typical Filipino meals are based around rice, here served with fish, crab and vegetable dishes on banana leaves.

Left: Young pigs are roasted on spits in a Manila street. Pork is one of the most popular meats on the islands.

ETIQUETTE AND HOSPITALITY

In some of the outlying islands and rural areas of the Philippines the traditional custom of eating with the fingers still persists but, in the cities, the Filipinos usually eat Western-style with plates and cutlery. Filipinos usually eat with a spoon and fork, holding the latter in their right hand and using it to put food into the spoon in their left hand.

Filipinos are particularly hospitable people, and visitors to the islands are often treated to a fabulous range of cooked dishes and fresh fruit, which may well be served on simple bamboo tables in the shade of roofs made from woven banana leaves. The Filipinos are extremely family-minded, and very respectful towards their elders. As a visitor to the islands, one should greet the eldest in a group of Filipinos first, with a handshake. If you have been invited to eat at a Filipino home, aim to arrive about 15 minutes late and dress smartly, bringing a small gift with you. These are small formalities in an otherwise relaxed tradition.

Below: Adobo chicken and pork, flavoured with coconut vinegar, is a typical Filipino dish.

role in Filipino meals, where it is called pain de sal and is made with salt, sugar and wheat flour to produce a spongy baked bun that is dipped into mugs of hot coffee or tea.

Apart from the baguettes of Vietnam or the Western loaves of Hong Kong and Singapore, the appearance of bread in the Philippines is quite unusual for South-east Asia, where rice tends to be the staple that is served with every meal. To drink, water is usually served alongside the food, although wine goes well with dishes that are not too spicy.

The names of many Filipino dishes denote the cooking style or the ingredients used in the dish. For example, adobo, a dish originating from Mexico and now, arguably, the national dish of the Philippines, always refers to pork or chicken, or a combination of the two, cooked gently in vinegar, ginger, garlic and black pepper. Sinigang, adapted from delicate Japanese soups, refers to meat or fish simmered in a sour-flavoured broth, which is often garnished with the flowers of the tamarind tree. Kinilaw is a dish of fresh fish or shellfish marinated in vinegar or kalamansi lime juice and spices, and inihaw refers to a dish of grilled (broiled) meat or fish.

Cities like Manila and Cebu are particularly renowned for both the variety and excellence of their dishes and restaurants, where almost every regional cuisine is available. In Pampanga, the specialities are tocino (honey-cured pork) and longaniza (sausages), and the cuisine of the Bicol region, based on chillies and coconut milk, is famous for its spicy flavour and rich, creamy sauces, exemplified by dishes such as laing (taro leaves simmered in spiced coconut milk) and bicol express (a fiery pork dish).

FILIPINO FEASTS AND FESTIVALS

The Philippines is the only country in Asia that is predominantly Christian; principally Catholic thanks to her 400-year long Spanish colonial era. With the faith came religious festivals and festive dishes, which are mainly of Spanish origin but with a native twist. Only in western Mindanao are most people Muslim and eschew the eating of pork, which is otherwise the main meat throughout the islands.

RELIGIOUS BELIEFS

Although Hinduism reached the distant outpost of Bali, it never spread as far as the Philippines. Similarly, Buddhism was carried across much of South-east Asia but did not get as far as the Philippines. In fact, the Philippines managed to escape most of the spreading religions, including the cults and philosophies of China and the Shinto and Zen beliefs of the Japanese.

Islam did arrive in the Philippines in 1475, but it only really reached as far as Mindanao, a lush volcanic island in the south. The Muslim minority of the Philippines celebrate the festivals of Ramadan and Idul Adha with fasting and feasting in the same way as other Muslims in Asia.

FIESTAS AND PATRON SAINT DAYS

There are plenty of occasions to celebrate in the Philippines, as the festivals range from religious and communal get-togethers to the full-blown, week-long Mardi Gras, Ati-Atihan, which rivals the carnival in Rio de Janeiro for vibrancy and takes place in towns such as Kalibo, Badan and Makato, starting on the third Sunday of January. Another Mardi Gras-style festival takes place in Iloilo City and celebrates the patron saint, Santo Nino, with a procession of outrageous costumes, dancing and lots of feasting. In October, there is a wonderful food festival in Zamboanga city. With street parties, food fairs, open markets, dancing and a regatta with traditional sailboats, this is a loud and colourful extravaganza.

Every town in the Philippines has a patron saint, and each town has a feast day to celebrate the anniversary of its founding. This means that there is always a fiesta somewhere in the Philippines. Floats are decorated with flowers and images of the village royalty, and people dress in historical costume and hold dancing competitions. Special dishes, such as adobo (chicken and pork cooked with vinegar and ginger), are prepared and shared among neighbours to signify the gathering together of a community.

HOLY DAYS

Christian festivals and holy days, such as Christmas, the Lunar New Year, Lent and Easter, are also flamboyant occasions, and are celebrated with a great deal of feasting. Many of the festive foods on these occasions are

Left: A vibrant street procession at the Ati-Atihan carnival in Kalibo.

Spanish in origin, and include savoury favourites, such as pochero (beef and chorizo stew with plantain and chickpeas), and sweet dishes, such as leche flan (Filipino crème caramel). Chinese-inspired noodle dishes, such as pancit guisado (stir-fried noodles), pancit luglog (noodle soup) and pancit molo (a Filipino version of wonton soup), are also popular festive dishes. For All Saints Day on 1 November, families gather at the local cemetery to give the crypts a fresh coat of paint and to feast on the favourite dishes of the deceased, snacking and celebrating long into the night by the gravesides, to the sound of guitars.

Christmas celebrations start on 16 December and go through to the first Sunday in January (Epiphany). The food rituals at Christmas manifest in a no-holds-barred feast on *Noche Buena* (Christmas Eve), when turkey, ham, stuffed chickens and other Western viands are cheek-by-jowl with lumpia, noodles and native kakanin dishes such

as puto, suman and bibingka, a baked rice or tapioca cake enriched with coconut milk. Not surprisingly, bibingka is derived from an Indonesian tapioca cake called kueh bingka. Puto is freely borrowed from the Indian and Sri Lankan putu, a rice flour pancake. Kakanin is actually the generic term for all native desserts deriving from the word kanin, which means 'cooked rice'. Whatever the festival, kakanin creations take centre stage but in daily meal practice, Filipinos usually eat desserts during *merienda*, an in-between snack time, and rarely after main meals. It is at Yuletide that kakanin reach their sweet glory, most made with a base of sweetened rice flour. Wealthy Filipinos sometimes choose to have spaghetti as a special meal for Christmas, as pasta is regarded as a status symbol.

New Year welcomes the abundance of produce in the coming year. To mark the occasion, Filipinos prepare satay and fruit salads, which include more expensive fruits, such as grapes and

Above left: Revellers crowd a bus during the Santo Nino festival, in which communities dress up, dance and make as much noise as possible.

Above: A Christmas tree in Manila.

apples, and there are lantern processions and fireworks in every village. Easter is the main Christian festival in the Philippines, and it is the one that Filipinos look forward to most, since everyone goes to the beach with lots of food to share. During Holy Week, when the Filipinos fast for five days, they are only allowed to eat fish and vegetables in the morning and evening. Between 12 noon and 5p.m., they must fast, and at no time during the five days can they eat meat. With such dietary restrictions on a nation that constantly thinks about food, the feasting on the Sunday, the Day of the Resurrection, is inevitably spectacular. There is always a suckling pig roasting on a spit, and many other pork dishes.

THE INDONESIAN AND FILIPINO KITCHEN

The culinary cultures of Indonesia and the Philippines have both been greatly influenced by the cuisines of settlers from India, China, Thailand, Spain, Holland, England and other regions. However, they retain their own distinct characteristics — where Indonesian food is often delicate, with coconut and chilli flavours, Filipino cuisine tends to be rustic and hearty.

ESSENTIAL FLAVOURS

In South-east Asian cuisine, it is vital that ingredients blend harmoniously on the plate, yet retain their distinct flavours. The presence of five principal flavour notes – salty, bitter, sour, spicy and sweet – plays an important role in every Indonesian and Filipino meal.

CLASSIC INDONESIAN INGREDIENTS

A typical Indonesian kitchen will revolve around the *sembako*, the nine essentials: rice, sugar, eggs, meat, flour, corn, cooking oil, salt and gas fuel.

The Indonesian kitchen boasts many fragrant spices that are gradually becoming more available to westerners: galangal, lemon grass, turmeric, kaffir lime leaves, the twisted pandanus (screwpine), cinnamon bark, cumin and coriander seeds, and cloves (although in Indonesia these are more likely to be used in scented cigarettes than food).

In parts of Indonesia where there is a history of Arab and Indian traders, such as Sumatra, many different local spices are used, but generally it is the chilli that is all important: an Indonesian dish without chillies in it, or accompanying it, is almost unimaginable! In fact, the Indonesians' love of chillies means that they appear throughout a meal: in the bumbu at the start, chewed between mouthfuls during the meal, then in a sambal at the end. From their dominance of the cuisine, one would think that

chillies are indigenous, but in fact they are a New World ingredient, which arrived in the 16th century.

Palm sugar (jaggery) is the primary sweetener, though cane sugar is used sprinkled over fried bananas or in tea.

The sour notes that are often detected in local recipes tend to emanate from tamarind, which is sold in dried or paste form in the markets, and is used liberally to cut through the oiliness of a dish.

Banana leaves are used for wrapping food that is going to be steamed or roasted, for wrapping soya beans and yeast together to make tempeh, or as a serving vessel or plate.

The flesh and water from freshly picked coconuts are free, and widely used in home kitchens, though coconut milk and other products can be bought. The oil from coconuts is often used for cooking, imparting a rich flavour.

FILIPINO STAPLES

The long period of Spanish rule has meant that the food of the Philippines differs from that of the rest of South-east Asia, primarily in that it does not rely heavily on local herbs and spices. The exception to this is the coconut- and chilli-based food of the Bicolano people of the Luzon. The Bicolano share the Indonesian love for chillies, and coconut milk, in fact they love chillies

Above: An Indonesian woman cooks in a rustic kitchen setting, Sumatra.

so much that they are prepared to tolerate the regular typhoons and extreme weather as long as the chilli plants remain standing in the ground!

Generally in the Philippines, ginger, onion and garlic are the main base ingredients in a cuisine that combines the cooking methods of the colonial Spaniards with the traditional ingredients and the dishes of the native island people.

The Spanish/Filipino style cuisine makes the most of an interesting blend of local ingredients, which are often sautéed and casseroled using Western utensils and equipment. Chillies do not feature as extensively as they do in Indonesian cooking, though they are used in some dishes, and hot Thai chillies, or finger chillies as they are known, are offered to chew on, or will be chopped finely and added to the coconut vinegar that is splashed on to everything and used as a dip.

An interesting feature of the rustic cuisine is the use of innards and oxtail (as well as insects such as crickets). The usual Asian herbs and spices do not feature heavily in Filipino kitchens, with cooks relying far more on garlic, ginger and bay leaves. The Filipino preference for sweet and sour flavours is revealed in combinations of coconut

Left: Shrimp paste is fermented in the sun for two weeks.

vinegar or kalamansi lime juice with palm or cane sugar, as in the national dish, adobo (chicken and pork cooked with vinegar and ginger), which originally hailed from Mexico.

When Filipinos mention their beloved vinegar, they mean coconut vinegar (suka) made from coconut palm sap, which is cloudy white. They prefer cooking with coconut oil for its flavour, or with groundnut (peanut) or corn oils for frying.

PASTES, SAMBALS AND SAUCES

Pungent pastes and fiery sambals are key aspects of Indonesian food. The first step of many dishes is to make a bumbu, which is a base paste made from crushed cumin, coriander seeds, cardamom, turmeric, shallots, garlic, ginger, lemon grass, cinnamon and chillies, which has coconut milk or stock added to it to make a paste.

Shrimp paste, terasi belacan, is made from small shrimp that are rinsed in sea water and then dried, salted and dried again, pummelled into a paste, then left for two weeks to dry out. It adds an essential salty and fishy taste to almost every dish. A popular paste for seafood, poultry and meat dishes in Bali and Java is gede, made by pounding garlic, shallots, galangal, chillies, lemon grass, turmeric, candlenuts and the ubiquitous shrimp paste.

Left: The ubiquitous hot, fresh, red chillies are piled high at a local vegetable market in Surabaya, Java.

Above: Satay stalls are very popular at open-air markets in the Philippines.

Sambals are considered essential to the enjoyment of an Indonesian meal. They are particularly good for livening-up grilled (broiled) or deep-fried fish and for tempering the taste of roasted goat. The base ingredients are always chillies, garlic, shallots and salt: variations include shallots, sugar, tamarind, galangal and shrimp paste (sambal badjak), lime juice, lime rind, chillies, salt and vinegar (sambal jeruk) or chillies, lime and shrimp paste (sambal terasi). The word sambal also refers to something fried with lots of chillies, such as sambal cumi-cumi (squid cooked in a hot chilli sauce), which is then served with yet more sambal on the side – not a dish for the faint-hearted.

The Filipinos have their own version of shrimp paste, which is called bagoong. The fermented bagoong is sold in bottles in which you can see the tiny shrimp or anchovies floating inside. The sauce is a cloudy greyish colour with a pungent, often unpleasant smell and is an acquired taste. While the national fish sauce, patis, is splashed in and over almost every dish, bagoong is more often kept for particular dishes, such as pinakbet (aubergine/eggplant, bitter melon and okra stew).

The Spanish-influenced Filipino cooking often uses marinades as a starting point. Ingredients are frequently marinated in coconut vinegar, ginger and garlic before being cooked, while raw ingredients such as oily fish and shrimp are cured in lime juice and coconut vinegar, as in the favourite national dish kinilaw (Filipino cured herring).

Like sambals, dips and sauces are important to both cuisines, and are thought to be crucial to the whole enjoyment of a particular dish rather than an optional condiment. For example, without coconut vinegar dipping sauce, the Filipino spring rolls, lumpia, would be regarded as naked and plain, just as the popular bakmie goreng (Indonesian stir-fried noodles) and nasi goreng (Indonesian stir-fried rice) both rely on the ever-popular kecap manis, a thick, sweet soy sauce, for their essential flavour. When it comes to street food, these traditions adapt to modern tastes, and tomato ketchup appears increasingly in the Westernized stalls and bars.

FINISHING TOUCHES

On every island of Indonesia and the Philippines, cooks regard garnishes and other finishing touches as extremely important. Crispy fried shallots, spring onions (scallions), sprigs of coriander (cilantro) and even fried eggs may be added to the dish at the end of cooking, but this does not mean that they are for decoration only: they are very much part of the dish as a whole and should not be left out.

SWEET SNACKS AND DRINKS

Along with most other culinary cultures of South-east Asia, the Indonesians prefer to eat fresh fruit at the end of a meal and sweet snacks during the day. This is because the meal is intended to be a balance of the five key flavour notes – salty, bitter, sour, spicy and sweet. The Filipinos, on the other hand, enjoy a dessert at the end of a meal, as well as at any hour of the day.

SWEET LOCAL FLAVOURS

As an island steeped in Hindu-Buddhist history, strewn with ancient temples and bubbling volcanoes, Java could evoke many poetic words, but there is only one to describe the palate of its inhabitants and that is 'sweet'. The local palm sugar (jaggery) is used in both the savoury and sweet dishes of this region, more than any other part of Indonesia. Special sweet snacks include kelepon, green rice-flour dumplings filled with palm sugar, and geplak, sticky rice cakes made with palm sugar and coconut. The Filipinos share this sweet tooth, adding liberal amounts of palm sugar to their steamed rice cakes and sticky, fried bananas. The Filipinos have the added attraction of European-style, Spanish-influenced puddings, such as the ever-popular leche flan (Filipino crème caramel with orange).

Above: Barquillos, Filipino 'cookies'.

In spite of the Spanish influence, some native sweet dishes have survived, including suman, a sweet snack which can be made from rice, cassava or bananas, which are steamed in the hollow of a bamboo stem or wrapped in banana leaves, and served with fresh grated coconut and sugar. Another traditional Filipino sweet snack is buko (the name refers to the local sweet coconut), which must be made with the tender flesh of young coconuts, as the internal coconut water and flesh are combined together with sugar and then frozen until it resembles a refreshing and delicate sorbet.

In Indonesia, many of the traditional sweet snacks are made from glutinous rice, sweetened with sugar and flavoured with fragrant leaves, then steamed in tiny packages woven from palm fronds. The concept of ending a meal with something sweet is alien to the Indonesian culture, where sweet snacks are enjoyed at any time of the day. With the Spanish and American influences on their modern culinary customs, the Filipinos indulge in both: a sweet snack at any time of day and a pudding to end the meal.

TROPICAL FRUITS

Fresh fruit, on the other hand, is usually eaten at the end of the meal in both countries. With the abundance of tropical treats, the choice is always inspiring – watermelon, pomegranates, apples, pineapples, mangoes, jackfruit, star fruit (carambola), mangosteens, snakeskin fruit, rambutan, sapodilla, passion fruit, sweet bananas and guava.

Generally, all these fruits are eaten fresh when ripe, but some are chosen when still immature to be chopped up for salads, such as rujak, a crunchy, fruity salad served with a spicy sauce.

Above: Black sticky rice pudding (bubuh injin).

Above: Palm leaf flavours many sweet rice dishes.

Above: Fiesta coconut rice cake (suman).

BEVERAGES

The Indonesians enjoy many fruit drinks but, as the nation is predominantly Muslim, the home-made spirits and alcoholic beverages are consumed to a minimal degree. Among the many delectable and refreshing tropical fruit drinks and syrupy iced drinks is the delightfully refreshing es ketimun, made with shredded cucumber, sugar syrup and lots of ice. On a daily basis, most Filipinos drink fresh juices such as passion fruit and a refreshing soursop juice. Kalamansi limes are used to make a cordial, and the buko coconut is sought after for its delicious liquid.

In tea and coffee, Indonesia excels. Originally set up by the Dutch, the tea and coffee plantations are a feature of the stunning landscape tapestry of rice paddies. The majority of Indonesia's tea produce is black tea, three-quarters of which is exported, but there is plenty left to satisfy the tea-drinking nation. Generally, tea is served black with sugar. Other teas include green tea and ginger tea, which is a popular morning beverage, particularly for peasants before they go to the fields.

Right: Fresh, spicy ginger tea (bandrek) is good for the digestion.

Above: Both ripe and unripe fruit are used.

Black tea is generally drunk among the Chinese communities and served in Chinese restaurants. A ginger-infused tea is drunk to aid the digestion, apart from in the cool air of the hilly regions where it is drunk at breakfast early in the morning.

Indonesia is also the third largest coffee producer in the world. Its coffee plantations are found in the highlands of Java and Bali and in central Sulawesi

and Sumatra. To drink coffee Indonesian style, you need to think of it as a pick-me-up, rather than a pleasant after-dinner digestive. You can ask for milky coffee (kopi susu), which is served with sweetened condensed milk, or have black coffee (kopi tubruk), which is chewy, gritty and sweet.

Coffee is traditionally reserved for special occasions in the Philippines and is offered to guests as a form of hospitality. However, traditions are changing and the current trend among students in the cities is the coffee house scene, where they can enjoy good coffee and browse through books.

A popular cocoa drink (cacao) is made by pounding the cocoa bean and infusing it in boiling water, sweetened with sugar.

Many Filipinos enjoy fermented drinks, in particular the sweet coconut wine, tuba. Throughout the islands, buckets hang from the leaves of palm trees which have been cut to release the sap. As the sap collects, bubbles form and the liquid ferments into a wine that is believed to have aphrodisiacal qualities. Other fermented drinks include local wines made from rice, coconuts and bananas, and the powerful spirit, lumbanog, made from coconut, raisins and other fruit.

ESSENTIAL RECIPES

BALINESE SPICE PASTE

The founding spirit of Balinese cooking, base gede can be used as paste or a marinade in meat, poultry and fish dishes.

SERVES SIX TO EIGHT

INGREDIENTS
  2 shallots, finely
    chopped
  2 garlic cloves,
    finely chopped
  25g/1oz fresh galangal,
    finely chopped
  25g/1oz fresh
    turmeric, chopped
  4 fresh red chillies,
    seeded and chopped

1 lemon grass stalk,
  chopped
5ml/1 tsp ground
  coriander
2.5ml/½ tsp ground
  black pepper
30ml/2 tbsp palm or
  vegetable oil
10ml/2 tsp terasi
  (Indonesian
  shrimp paste)
10ml/2 tsp palm
  sugar (jaggery)

1 Using a mortar and pestle, grind the shallots, garlic, galangal, turmeric, chillies and lemon grass to a coarse paste. Beat in the coriander and black pepper.

2 Heat the oil in a small, heavy-based pan, stir in the paste and fry until fragrant and just colouring. Stir in the terasi and sugar and fry for 2–3 minutes, until darker in colour. Remove from the heat and leave to cool. Store in a lidded jar in the refrigerator for up to 1 week.

Per Portion Energy 158kcal/654kJ; Protein 6.6g; Carbohydrate 8.9g, of which sugars 7.5g; Fat 13.6g, of which saturates 1.3g; Cholesterol 25mg; Calcium 126mg; Fibre 0.8g; Sodium 355mg.

SHALLOT AND LEMON GRASS SAMBAL

In Indonesian kitchens, sambal matah is a master blend with multifarious uses as a marinade, curry paste and topping.

SERVES FOUR TO SIX

INGREDIENTS
  2.5ml/½ tsp black
    peppercorns
  10g/¼oz terasi
  20 shallots, thinly sliced
  5 garlic cloves, sliced
  6 lime leaves, shredded

10 fresh red chillies,
  thinly sliced
4 lemon grass stalks,
  2cm/¾in of root end
  very finely sliced
1 tsp salt
45ml/3 tbsp lime juice
1 tsp sugar
75ml/5 tbsp vegetable oil

1 Crush the peppercorns using a pestle and mortar until grainy.

2 Toast the terasi briefly over a live flame.

3 Combine all the ingredients except the oil in a mixing bowl and blend well. Heat the oil and fry the sambal over a low heat for 8–10 minutes until the oil seeps out again.

Per Portion Energy 126kcal/520kJ; Protein 2.9g; Carbohydrate 7.5g, of which sugars 5.6g; Fat 9.6g, of which saturates 1.1g; Cholesterol 8mg; Calcium 51mg; Fibre 1.2g; Sodium 405mg.

CHILLI AND SHRIMP PASTE

There is a saying in Indonesia: 'If your eyes do not water, the food is not good', which gives an indication of this highly popular paste's fieriness. This, like many other Indonesian pastes and spice blends, should be approached cautiously at first, but is bound to become a favourite condiment.

SERVES FOUR

INGREDIENTS
15ml/1 tbsp palm, groundnut (peanut) or vegetable oil
2 shallots, finely chopped
3 garlic cloves, finely chopped
4 spring onions (scallions), finely chopped
8 fresh red Thai chillies, seeded and finely chopped
10–15ml/2–3 tsp terasi (Indonesian shrimp paste)

1 Heat the oil in a small wok or heavy-based pan. Stir in the shallots, garlic, spring onions and chillies and fry until fragrant and beginning to colour.

2 Add the terasi and continue to fry for about 5 minutes, until dark and blended. Remove from the heat and leave to cool.

3 Spoon the spice paste into a jar, cover and store in the refrigerator for up to 1 week.

Per Portion Energy 46kcal/191kJ; Protein 2.6g; Carbohydrate 2.2g, of which sugars 1.3g; Fat 3g, of which saturates 0.4g; Cholesterol 13mg; Calcium 44mg; Fibre 0.5g; Sodium 111mg.

KALAMANSI SAUCE

This popular Filipino dipping sauce can be served with anything but is particularly good with fish and rice dishes – try it with grilled prawns (shrimp) at your next barbecue party. It gives a clean and simple tang to food, and takes only a few seconds to prepare.

SERVES FOUR

INGREDIENTS
juice of 2 kalamansi limes
60ml/4 tbsp patis (Filipino fish sauce)

1 Put the lime juice in a small bowl. Add the patis and beat together until thoroughly blended.

2 Spoon the sauce into a screw top jar, seal and store in the refrigerator for up to 1–2 days. The sauce may be used chilled or at room temperature, and is best eaten sparingly as a dip for grilled (broiled) food.

Per Portion Energy 8kcal/33kJ; Protein 0.5g; Carbohydrate 1.5g, of which sugars 1.4g; Fat 0g, of which saturates 0g; Cholesterol 0mg; Calcium 4mg; Fibre 0g; Sodium 1068mg.

TAMARIND AND LIME SAUCE

This popular hot and sour dipping sauce is usually prepared for eating with freshly grilled fish or steamed shellfish. If you cannot find kalamansi limes for this or any recipes in this book, simply use the best limes you can buy – they should be glossy and plump with a zesty scent.

SERVES FOUR TO SIX

INGREDIENTS
  juice of 2 kalamansi limes
  30ml/2 tbsp tamarind
    paste
  2 spring onions
    (scallions), white parts
    only, finely chopped
  2 fresh red chillies, seeded
    and finely chopped

1 Put the lime juice in a small bowl. Add the tamarind paste and mix together. Add a little water to thin the mixture until it is of dipping consistency.

2 Stir in the spring onions and chillies.

3 Spoon the sauce into a jar, cover and store in the refrigerator for up to 1 week.

Per Portion Energy 6kcal/23kJ; Protein 0.6g; Carbohydrate 0.6g, of which sugars 0.6g; Fat 0.1g, of which saturates 0g; Cholesterol 0mg; Calcium 10mg; Fibre 0.2g; Sodium 6mg.

COCONUT VINEGAR SAUCE

This spicy dipping sauce is good with various foods, such as steamed shellfish, spring rolls and fried chicken, which makes it perfect for a buffet or drinks party.

SERVES FOUR TO SIX

INGREDIENTS
  60–75ml/4–5 tbsp
    suka (Filipino
    coconut vinegar)
  3 fresh red chillies,
    seeded and
    finely chopped
  4 spring onions
  (scallions), white parts
    only, finely chopped
  4 garlic cloves, finely
    chopped

1 Spoon the suka into a small bowl. Add the chillies, spring onions and garlic and mix well together. If you prefer a really fiery dip, you could add an extra chilli, but this quantity provides plenty of heat for most people.

2 Spoon the sauce into a jar, cover and store in the refrigerator for up to 1 week. To serve, decant the vinegar sauce into small dishes for dipping spring rolls or fried and grilled (broiled) finger foods.

Per Portion Energy 21kcal/85kJ; Protein 1.8g; Carbohydrate 2.2g, of which sugars 0.7g; Fat 0.3g, of which saturates 0g; Cholesterol 0mg; Calcium 14mg; Fibre 0.6g; Sodium 4mg.

INDONESIAN PEANUT SAUCE

Also known as bumbu sate, this is a very popular dipping sauce for fried and grilled meats and steamed vegetables.

SERVES FOUR

INGREDIENTS
30ml/2 tbsp groundnut
   (peanut) or vegetable oil
1 shallot, finely chopped
2 garlic cloves,
   finely chopped
150g/5oz/¾ cup plus
   2 tbsp unsalted peanuts,
   finely ground
15ml/1 tbsp terasi

(Indonesian shrimp paste)
15ml/1 tbsp palm
   sugar (jaggery)
15ml/1 tbsp tamarind
   paste
15ml/1 tbsp kecap manis
   (Indonesian sweet
   soy sauce)
5ml/1 tsp chilli powder
300ml/½ pint/1¼ cups
   water

1 Heat the oil in a heavy-based pan, stir in the shallot and garlic and fry until golden brown. Add the ground peanuts, terasi and sugar and continue to fry for 3–4 minutes, until the peanuts begin to colour and release some of their oil.

2 Stir in the remaining ingredients, bring to the boil, then simmer for 15–20 minutes until the sauce has reduced and thickened. Remove the pan from the heat and leave the mixture to cool, then blend in a processor to form a smooth sauce. Spoon into a jar, cover and store in the refrigerator for up to 1 week.

Per Portion Energy 309kcal/1284kJ; Protein 14g; Carbohydrate 10.9g, of which sugars 7.5g; Fat 23.6g, of which saturates 4.2g; Cholesterol 19mg; Calcium 77mg; Fibre 3g; Sodium 431mg.

FRIED GRATED COCONUT

Indonesians rarely have a meal without this condiment on the side. Use freshly grated coconuts for a superior flavour. You should be able to buy coconuts readily from Asian supermarkets or your local grocer.

SERVES FOUR TO SIX

INGREDIENTS
15ml/1 tbsp vegetable oil
2 lemon grass stalks,
   2cm/¾in of root end
   very thinly sliced
3 fresh red or green
   chillies, thinly sliced

5 shallots, thinly sliced
4 garlic cloves,
   thinly sliced
175g/6oz freshly
   grated coconut
5ml/1 tsp salt
5ml/1 tsp sugar

1 Heat the oil in a wok and fry the lemon grass, chillies, shallots and garlic over a low heat for 2 minutes.

2 Add the coconut and stir-fry for 10 minutes, tossing and turning constantly, until the coconut is light brown and the flavours are well incorporated.

3 Add the salt and sugar and stir to blend thoroughly. Leave to cool and store in an airtight jar for up to 2 weeks.

Per Portion Energy 147kcal/606kJ; Protein 1.6g; Carbohydrate 3.2g, of which sugars 2.5g; Fat 14.3g, of which saturates 10.9g; Cholesterol 0mg; Calcium 9mg; Fibre 3g; Sodium 334mg.

CUCUMBER AND PINEAPPLE RELISH

Acar is the generic term for pickles in Indonesia. Some will keep for a while, but this one must be eaten within a day or two.

SERVES FOUR

INGREDIENTS
1 cucumber, peeled, quartered lengthways and seeded
2.5ml/½ tsp salt
45ml/3 tbsp terasi (Indonesian shrimp paste)
6 fresh red chillies
45g/1½oz dried shrimps, soaked in hot water until soft
½ sweet pineapple, peeled, eyes and thick core removed
juice of 3 limes
5ml/1 tsp salt
5ml/1 tsp sugar

1 Slice the cucumber flesh into diamond shapes, each 1cm/½in wide. Sprinkle with salt, toss well and set aside for 20 minutes.

2 Toast the terasi over a live flame for 2 minutes until it is slightly charred and pungent, then grind with the chillies using a pestle and mortar until fine. Squeeze the moisture from the cucumber, handfuls at a time, into the mix. Set aside.

3 Cut the pineapple into small chunks. Grind the dried shrimps until coarse with a pestle and mortar. Mix all the ingredients in a large bowl and adjust the seasoning to taste. Serve the relish as a side dish with coconut rice or curries.

Per Portion Energy 105kcal/446kJ; Protein 13.3g; Carbohydrate 11.9g, of which sugars 11.9g; Fat 0.8g, of which saturates 0.1g; Cholesterol 114mg; Calcium 298mg; Fibre 1.5g; Sodium 1715mg.

LIVER SAUCE

This is a liver pâté, almost, no doubt with Spanish origins but cooked in a Filipino way. It is generally served with roast pork or chicken, but may be spread on toast for a highly-flavoured snack.

SERVES FOUR

INGREDIENTS
450g/1lb pig's liver
15g/1 tbsp fine salt
175ml/6fl oz/¾ cup water
5 garlic cloves, crushed
15ml/1 tbsp vegetable oil
6 shallots, sliced
50ml/1¾fl oz/¼ cup white wine vinegar
50g/2oz sugar
2.5ml/½ tsp black pepper
60g/4 tbsp fine breadcrumbs

1 Roast the liver with half the salt at 200°C/400°F/Gas 6 for 25 minutes, or until cooked through, then slice into several pieces.

2 Process the liver and half the water in a blender until roughly chopped, then add the garlic and blend to a smooth paste.

3 Fry the shallots in the oil until soft, add everything except for the breadcrumbs, and bring to a gentle boil. Simmer for 8 minutes, then add the breadcrumbs and stir until thick.

Per Portion Energy 260kcal/1097kJ; Protein 26g; Carbohydrate 25.9g, of which sugars 14.3g; Fat 6.6g, of which saturates 1.5g; Cholesterol 293mg; Calcium 36mg; Fibre 0.6g; Sodium 1681mg.

BALAYAN FISH SAUCE

Bagoong, when used judiciously, really makes a dish, and just a little spoonful of this fish sauce complements many different savoury foods. Try serving it with grilled fish or meat.

SERVES 10–12

INGREDIENTS
15ml/1 tbsp vegetable oil
5 garlic cloves, crushed
3 shallots, diced
2 cherry tomatoes, sliced
150g/5oz bagoong
    (Filipino shrimp sauce)
2.5ml/½ tsp sugar
120ml/4fl oz/½ cup suka
    (Filipino cider vinegar)

1 Heat the oil and stir-fry the garlic until golden brown, then add the shallots and tomatoes and fry until soft. Add the bagoong and sugar and stir well to blend.

2 When the sugar has completely dissolved, add the suka and simmer for 10 minutes.

3 Remove and store in a jar for serving with savoury dishes. This sauce will keep in the refrigerator for up to 3 weeks.

COOK'S TIP
If you find bagoong too strong, use the Indonesian equivalent, terasi (shrimp paste).

Per Portion Energy 379kcal/1590kJ; Protein 56.7g; Carbohydrate 8g, of which sugars 6.6g; Fat 13.6g, of which saturates 1.7g; Cholesterol 505mg; Calcium 1218mg; Fibre 1g; Sodium 4334mg.

SWEET AND SOUR SAUCE

Serve this sauce poured over fried poultry, or use it as a base for any sweet and sour recipe. It is a very familiar flavour to lovers of Chinese food, and really enlivens savoury rice-based meals if used as a condiment.

SERVES 6–8

INGREDIENTS
300ml/½ pint/1¼ cups
    water
30ml/2 tbsp sugar
45ml/3 tbsp tomato
    ketchup
15ml/1 tbsp lime juice
30ml/2 tbsp plum sauce
10ml/2 tsp cornflour
    (cornstarch)

1 Combine all the ingredients except the cornflour in a small pan and bring the mixture to a slow boil.

2 Blend the cornflour to a paste with a little water, add to the simmering mixture and cook, stirring well, until it is the consistency of pouring cream, adding more water if needed.

3 Adjust with more water if it is too thick. Use as required, or store in the refrigerator until needed.

Per Portion Energy 284kcal/1209kJ; Protein 1.1g; Carbohydrate 74.1g, of which sugars 64.4g; Fat 0.1g, of which saturates 0g; Cholesterol 0mg; Calcium 27mg; Fibre 0.4g; Sodium 749mg.

EQUIPMENT AND UTENSILS

Once, Asian kitchens were smoky sanctums with the aura of pungent wood smoke and strange cooking implements. The term 'dirty kitchen' applied to these old-fashioned cooking quarters, an area usually separate from the house. Contemporary lifestyles may dictate the need for high-tech appliances, but a few tools used in both countries are richly evocative of the agrarian way of life.

CLEAVER

This heavy-bladed knife has more uses than it is given credit for. Originating in China and traditionally fashioned from iron – tempered steel is the modern norm – it has the weight and leverage that slices through solid bone. It slices, crushes and scoops in one fell swoop. Its blunt edge acts as a tenderizing tool much like a meat mallet. The ideal type is a single piece of tempered stainless steel, weighing in at 500g/1lb and measuring 30cm/1ft from the end of the handle to the blade tip. One or two small paring knives are all you need by way of additional cutting tools.

COCONUT GRATER

There is nothing quite like grating your own shreds from fresh coconuts. Many specialist stores sell a version made of a wood-mounted sheet of heavy aluminium or brass and one fashioned from a whole piece of thick bamboo. They also come shaped from one piece of aluminium with four legs.

Above: The traditional coconut grater is a robust wood and brass structure.

MORTAR AND PESTLE

Fundamental to the process of grinding and pounding is the familiar mortar and pestle (it's called *almirez* in the Philippines and *lesong* in Indonesia), which came originally from India, transplanted to most of South-east Asia. The pestle grinds dry spices, nuts and other hard ingredients to a cream. When you buy a new mortar, make sure it has high sides so that ingredients do not jump out.

WOK

An implement that is the result of thousands of years of evolution, a wok or *kwali* or *kawali* serves for frying, braising, steaming and boiling. Cast iron ones, when seasoned with oil and cleaned, are best. Non-stick woks only last about a year before the special coating wears out. Stainless steel and aluminium woks conduct heat too rapidly.

When a trivet is placed in a wok and a lid is used, it becomes a steamer. Wok tools such as strainers for deep-frying, lids and long chopsticks often come as a set. Woks come with either one or two handles, the former being used more by chefs for tossing stir-fried dishes.

WOK BRUSHES

An original Chinese design that has not changed for centuries, these are simply little makeshift brushes of a bound cluster of fine strips of bamboo or rattan for cleaning out woks.

TERRACOTTA POTS

Known as *palayok* in Tagalog and *belangah* in Indonesian, these are very much in use as the ideal utensils for cooking anything with vinegar, typical of many Filipino dishes.

CLAY OR SAND POTS

Traditional Chinese clay pots have one handle. Those with a wire mesh frame are not meant for cooking on direct heat; they are gently heated and dishes cooked conventionally are transferred to them to be served at table. Originally meant for herbal and medicinal brews, they are now common everyday utensils for stews and braised dishes.

SCOOPS AND LADLES

In metal, porcelain or coconut shell, these are useful for many specific

Above: Bamboo is fashioned into many kitchen items. This is an unusually-shaped steamer basket for cooking rice.

purposes. Coconut shell ladles look rustic and are pleasant to use. Some believe that they impart a special flavour to food, especially curries. It is more common today, however, for cooks to use stainless steel ladles, which are durable and easy to keep clean.

WOVEN BASKETS

Bamboo is an extremely versatile material shaped into myriad forms and sizes for steaming, serving, ladling and storing. Rural folk are adept at fashioning palm and other pliant natural leaves into trays and baskets for winnowing and drying – for example, coconut palm fronds are rigid enough to be fashioned into plates and bowls, and their spines become skewers for satay. In Indonesia, Thailand and Laos, woven bamboo baskets containing rice are placed above metal pots to act as steamers.

Above: Brushes for cleaning woks are traditionally made from bundles of bamboo or rattan.

STEAMERS

Traditional Chinese bamboo steamers, dating back centuries, come in many sizes. As the material is porous, steam can escape and prevent condensation that can turn dishes mushy. They are totally organic and require only simple rinsing to clean. Modern variations include electric and microwave versions.

BANANA LEAVES

Regarded as wrappers and throwaway plates, banana leaves are organic and more aromatic than foil. When made pliable after being blanched, they wrap all manner of foods for grilling (broiling), baking and steaming while imparting their distinctive perfume.

LOTUS LEAVES

Of Chinese origin, dried lotus leaves have become popular as alternatives to banana leaves for steaming, but they are too delicate for direct heat. Fresh lotus leaves are not easy to obtain, but impart a lovely perfume to food.

COOKIE CUTTERS

In Indonesia especially, small brass cookie cutters come in different shapes: stylized flowers, paisley and abstract designs. They are particularly useful for punching out shapes for identical, perfect batches of rice cookies.

TWEEZERS AND CRIMPERS

Made of brass or iron, these little tweezers crimp and pinch designs on small cakes and cookies. Some come with tweezers at one end and a serrated roller at the other for making designs like leaves and other floral patterns.

WOODEN CAKE MOULDS

Small abstract or floral designs are carved from a block of wood for pressing in rice and flour mixtures that are then knocked out gently for baking. Others are simple devices with heart-shaped or round designs that are pressed on to tart and cookie dough.

Above: Two wooden cake moulds, used to shape cookie dough before baking.

CAKE PRESSERS, CUTTERS AND SCOOPS

In hard aluminium and mounted on wood or with a metal handle, pressers are meant for pressing down yam and

Above: A tweezer and crimper with a selection of cookie cutters.

radish cakes or glutinous rice bases with sweet toppings for steaming. Cutters, either plain or serrated, are used for making linear or curvy cuts of rolled dough or other cooked, soft bakes and jellies. Small oval scoops are made extra thin for lifting soft and delicate silken tofu so that it doesn't break up.

JELLY MOULDS

Mostly made from metal or plastic these days, jelly moulds are used for the very popular sweet jellies and agar agar items. Designs range from fish, pineapple and turtle shapes to traditional ridged ones. Being mainly small, they are easy to unmould with a gentle tap on the sides.

NOODLE STRAINERS

Traditional noodle strainers are made of brass or aluminium wire mounted on a bamboo handle. They are used for straining and scooping noodles and vegetables out of hot oil or cooking liquid. This is a particularly useful item for deep-frying spring rolls and other popular snacks and appetizers.

Left: A single-handled wok is good for stir-frying; a double-handled wok is better for steaming and deep-frying.

Above: A wire mesh noodle strainer is a traditional kitchen implement that is still regularly used in modern kitchens.

COOKING TECHNIQUES

The technique most employed by the Indonesian cook, as a preparation for the main cooking, is the grinding and then sautéing of spice pastes in a wok or small pot. There is a strict order of what goes in first: hard, dry herbs such as lemon grass, garlic and candlenuts are ground first, to provide a 'cushion' for wet ones such as onions and chillies, so that bits don't fly out of the mortar. The sautéing step imparts the intrinsic flavour to many dishes. The watchwords are 'when the oil separates', meaning the spices are adequately fried and ready for the next step.

Both Indonesian and Filipino cooks fry their spices for the same reason – to extract the rich flavours in which to bathe meats, poultry and vegetables. Aromatics such as shallots, garlic and onions are used with abandon and then blended with fermented seafood sauces such as terasi, bagoong and patis for an intoxicating blend of tastes and aromas.

STIR-FRYING

Used for the most basic and simplest of dishes, stir-frying is a method that has evolved over centuries in China and is indispensable for a whole range of dishes that need to be cooked quickly.

In both Indonesia and the Philippines, the pre-blanching of vegetables to preserve their colour and crispness is almost *de rigueur*, and results in exquisite textures. Intense heat and constant motion ensure that food cooks in minutes. This is where the *kawali* or *kwali* (wok) reigns supreme.

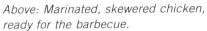

Above: Marinated, skewered chicken, ready for the barbecue.

MARINATING

When not initially fried, spice blends still impart flavour to many foods – from fruits to meat – as a tenderizing and fragrant marinade. The Indonesians tend to find simple boiled or roasted meat bland. Local meat like buffalo, goat and pork may not be of particularly good quality and thus needs to be tenderized with marinades.

Filipino vinegar called suka is a favourite marinade seasoning that underscores dishes calling for tartness, a characteristic in Filipino dishes such as sinigang. Vinegar has great affinity with soy sauce, sugar and other indigenous ingredients such as annatto seeds, kalamansi lime and black pepper. Once blended, the mixture is fried with vegetables, meat or seafood and this has a 'pickling' effect.

STEAMING

The classic method of cooking rice in Indonesia is to steam it in a cone of woven bamboo, inserted over a metal or

Left: Stir-frying is a quick and healthy method of cooking vegetables.

Above: Dim sum, breads and desserts are often steamed rather than baked.

clay pot of boiling water. In the Philippines, a traditional bamboo steamer that came on the backs of early Chinese migrants would be used. However, rice is now more often cooked in an automatic rice cooker, which is widely considered a must-have in modern homes. Many other foods, including breads, fish and desserts, are gently cooked in a traditional bamboo steamer over a pan of water on the hob. This keeps food moist and locks in flavour.

SLOW-COOKING AND BRAISING

With the unhurried pace of life in some areas, slow-cooking methods evolved as much for the need to soften tough meat fibres as for spices to be steeped. Simmering or braising is common to all kitchens and is usually done in a wok in Indonesia. In the Philippines, a conventional pot is used for dishes that reflect Spanish influences in the preparation of stews and soups. The national dish, adobo, consists of seasoned and marinated pork, chicken or other ingredients that are slow simmered on the hob, and may be browned in the oven or frying pan afterwards to get deliciously caramelised and crispy edges on the pieces of meat or vegetables. This achieves results that are similar to casseroling, but the latter is cooked in an oven. Either method is used extensively in rural areas, the tradition being that the meal will be ready on the workers' return from the fields.

GRILLING (BROILING) OR BARBECUING

The modern deep-fat fryer found in Western kitchens is rarely used and grilling (broiling) is the universal method of cooking that comes closest to deep-frying. In Indonesia, any roasting is usually done by placing food in a covered clay pot set over a wood fire for long cooking. Charcoal grilling, on the other hand, is widely practised in homes, restaurants and by itinerant hawkers. In the Philippines, roasting and charcoal grilling are techniques employed in kitchens throughout the land, whether urban or rural in nature.

WRAPPING

Throughout the islands, banana leaves are revered as the means to perfect flavours, and wrapping things in them is a craft as ancient as the land itself. The leaf is resilient, pliant and aromatic, so the food it wraps comes away with a distinct perfume that is hard to categorize. The wrapped ingredients may be cooked either by steaming or grilling. As a 'green' material, it has few peers for versatility, sustainability and sheer flavour, and there is an endless supply in the urban and rural areas of both countries.

Below: Spiced fish wrapped in a banana leaf steams to perfumed perfection on a traditional bamboo rack, which is positioned over a water-filled wok.

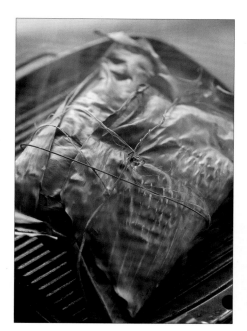

Above: Wrapping food in leaves before grilling helps flavours develop.

RICE

This grain has been a staple crop throughout most of tropical Asia for many generations, and it is around a communal bowl of comfortingly hot, fluffy white rice that most meals are built. For good reason, rice is regarded as the 'staff of life' and some superstitions connected to its power still hold sway. Rice agriculture is bound up with reverent rites and near mystical rituals, in which offerings are made to the rice deity. In every rice-eating household, there is invariably a large barrel or tin in which the raw rice is stored. This must never be completely emptied as it is bad feng shui. As the last few grains are reached families hurriedly top the container up to the brim for fear of attracting bad luck or negative energy.

The 'rice bowl' areas in Indonesia are concentrated in Java, Sumatra and Bali. In the northern Luzon region of the Philippines the terraced rice fields of Banaue go back thousands of years. The Ifugao tribe here still maintain and cultivate them as they have done for centuries. These terraces are an architectural marvel, rising like stairways up almost vertical hillsides that can top several thousand metres in height.

Below: Terraced rice paddies in Sumatra, Indonesia.

No one knows for sure why these rice fields were built so high up and against such fatiguing odds. Perhaps the Ifugao, once farmers in the plains, may have been driven into the hills by invaders, but the remarkably unchanged terraces are still there and still worked. They are truly a beautiful and almost mystical sight.

In times past, freshly harvested rice was pounded in an enormous pestle and mortar and then winnowed to remove the husk and bran before it could be cooked. Commercial milling of rice began in the mid-19th century and today, most processing is done mechanically except in family-owned small holdings.

In the Philippines, rice is valued for its subtle differences in varieties, as much for basic taste as for versatility. For instance, fragrant and aged grains called wag-wag become extremely fluffy when boiled or steamed, a property much valued throughout the regions. Young green rice is ground and roasted to form a powder called pinipig, used mainly in cakes or sprinkled on drinks. The mature grains are given an entirely different treatment, soaked overnight and ground into a thick paste called galapong. The resultant springy texture is much loved in steamed cakes and putus.

Above: Jasmine or Thai fragrant rice has tender, aromatic grains. It is widely available in supermarkets in the West.

RICE DISHES

There are only two methods of cooking rice for basic sustenance: boiling and steaming. But the precious grain is by no means confined to being boiled and eaten unadorned. Once cooked thus, it can be used as the basis of many other dishes. Indonesian cooking especially has elevated rice to delicious heights, matched by few others for spicy ingenuity. Rice with fragrant spice pastes rich in lemon grass, garlic, chillies and ginger; rice tinted a glorious yellow with turmeric, enriched with groundnut (peanut) oil and coconut milk, tossed with seafood, meats and vegetables – it is a glorious palette of flavours, colours and textures.

In the Filipino kitchen, rice is cooked normally but a thin layer is deliberately left at the bottom of the pot to become a crispy crust (tutong). This is then scraped off and fried the next day as a breakfast staple.

Given that rice comes in many different forms – long grain, short grain, sticky, jasmine (fragrant) – the preferences in both Indonesia and the Philipines vary greatly from region to region, from village to village and even from family to family. In general, jasmine is preferred for everyday meals when eaten plain. Good quality jasmine rice has a subtly delicate scent, with dry, thin and firm grains that are translucent when raw. Boiled or steamed, the texture should be firm and still retain some bite. The colour should

be a pristine white and when you rake it with a fork, it should fluff up nicely. Long grain rice tends to be reserved for more important occasions, ceremonial meals and ritual offerings, when spices such as saffron or turmeric are added to impart a golden colour and a delicate scent.

LONG GRAIN RICE

There is some confusion with reference to the types of rice, but there is one simple explanation based on usage. Short grain or pudding rice is for desserts and long grain is for meals with savouries. Basmati, Patna (Indian long grain), Thai fragrant and sweet (Japanese or short grain) rice are not brand names but denote where they come from. They are in effect variety names.

Basmati has the longest grain of all in proportion to its grain size, and peculiarly becomes longer and not wider when cooked. Basmati rice, with its distinctive, nutty flavour, while indigenous to India and Pakistan, is also grown in Indonesia and the Philippines. The town of Cianjur in West Java is reputed to produce the best long grain.

SHORT GRAIN RICE

When a meal calls for rice gruel, known as congee in the Philippines and among the Indonesian Chinese, short grain rice is preferred. Chinese families originating from the Swatow province in Eastern China eat a traditional meal with this watery porridge. It is served with a wide range of pickles, stir-fries and simple dishes. The Indonesian name for this gruel is bubur.

GLUTINOUS RICE

Sticky or glutinous rice can be either short or long grain and the glutinous reference is something of a misnomer. Rice contains no gluten at all; it is the high starch content that gives this rice its sticky, glutinous texture. Usually destined for sweet snacks and desserts as the starch compacts when cooked, glutinous rice is also popular in some regions to soak up spicy curry gravies

and palm sugar (jaggery). All types of rice contain a certain amount of starch, and all are gluten-free.

In the more urban spots such as Jakarta and Manila, varieties imported from Thailand and Malaysia, whether long grain or jasmine, are eaten widely. These tend to contain relatively high levels of starch; hence the produce of these regions is known as 'sticky rice' or 'glutinous rice'. There are two kinds of starch in any cereal grain: amylase and amylopectin. Sticky rice is high in the latter, and when the rice is cooked, these molecules form a gel, enclosing water within their strands.

Glutinous rice comes in both long and short grain varieties. The grains have to be soaked for several hours, sometimes overnight, before cooking. For festive dishes such as saffron or turmeric rice for Indonesian rituals and weddings, it is turned out as savoury offerings, often perfumed with rose water, cinnamon and cloves. It is rarely boiled and eaten plain as part of a meal, unless for a special occasion such as the Dutch-inspired Rijstaffel in upmarket hotels in Indonesian cities. Fundamentally, glutinous rice mainly lends itself to the making of dumplings, puddings and festive sweets.

In contrast to normal long grain rice, the highly polished, glutinous rice grain

Above: Black and white glutinous rice.

is an opaque white colour when raw, and turns translucent when cooked. Although the texture of cooked glutinous rice is quite firm, it is nevertheless sticky and clumps together like a lump of dough. It is this doughy characteristic that makes it popular as a wraparound for a range of filled rice dishes. In Indonesia, lemper is a favourite snack of sticky rice filled with spicy meat or seafood. Where Chinese people celebrate the Chinese Dragon Boat festival, also called the Dumpling Festival, triangular dumplings are made with glutinous rice encasing spicy meat or mung bean paste. They are boiled for several hours and eaten as a snack.

BLACK GLUTINOUS RICE

This unpolished, wholegrain glutinous rice is almost exclusively used for sweet dishes. When soaked in water and cooked, the grains turn a deep reddish-purple. In Indonesia this is called ketan hitam, and cooked with coconut milk and palm sugar. It must be soaked for several hours or overnight before cooking. Black sticky rice is available in some Asian markets.

GROUND RICE OR RICE FLOUR

Used in making all kinds of sticky sweets and cakes, ground rice is also a thickener, used similarly to cornflour or arrowroot. Rice flour is made by grinding the raw grain very finely. Long grain and medium grain rice flour is used to make dough for fresh and dried rice noodles, as well as for dumplings, crêpes and buns. Glutinous rice flour, sometimes called sweet rice flour, is reserved for sweet pastries, pancakes and cakes. Do not confuse this with rice powder, which is much finer and is used in delicate bakes. All types are available from Asian stores and should be kept in an airtight container.

RICE PAPERS

Originally unique to Thai and Vietnamese cuisines, delicate triangular or circular rice papers and wrappers have been adopted by Indonesian and Filipino chefs. Rice papers are now used widely as a skin for spring rolls. Made from rice flour, water and salt, they are brittle to hold. They need to be soaked briefly in hot water until they are soft and pliant. Lift each wrapper out with a chopstick and spread it on a chopping board before topping with filling. Once rolled up, they can be eaten as they are or deep-fried. Dried rice papers are available in Asian stores and some supermarkets.

RICE WINE AND VINEGAR

Local rice wine is used a lot in the Philippines but less so in the Muslim regions of Indonesia, where people nonetheless eat fermented rice in desserts called tapai, disregarding its alcoholic content.

The clean-tasting vinegar is used widely by Filipinos, who prefer it to normal vinegar as it has a delicious aroma and is less acidic. Rice vinegar defines adobo, the famous Filipino stew.

PREPARING AND COOKING RICE

Many people find difficulty in preparing soft, fluffy rice. There are actually few fundamental rules. Most rice grains are cooked using the absorption method, except glutinous rice, which is soaked and steamed. The timings and amounts of water given here relate to white rice. Brown rice needs a longer cooking time.

Washing rice

Traditionalists will insist that rice goes through 'seven changes of water' but most of the rice bought in supermarkets today requires minimal washing to whirl away traces of husks or discoloured grains. However, long grain rice does benefit from rinsing in cold water to reduce the excess starch, so that the cooked grains are light and fluffy and separate easily.

1 Put the rice into a bowl and cover with cold water. Swirl until the water becomes cloudy, then leave to settle.

2 Drain the rice in a sieve (strainer) then return it to the bowl and repeat until the water is clear.

Soaking

Some chefs soak rice before cooking. This is said to make the rice intensely white. Also, increasing the moisture content of the grains means that the cooking water can penetrate more effectively, resulting in fluffier rice.

After rinsing the rice, leave the grains in the bowl and cover with cold water. Leave to soak for half an hour. Drain the rice through a sieve, rinse it under cold running water, then drain again.

If you are using brown rice, soaking it for two hours in warm water prior to cooking activates the enzymes and optimizes its nutritional content.

Cooking by absorption

Rice soaks up a lot of water as it cooks – 450g/1lb of uncooked rice will absorb up to 600ml/1 pint of water, making enough to feed four moderate appetites.

The proportion of water required and the cooking time will both vary slightly with different grains, so it is wise to follow the instructions on the packet if you are cooking an unusual variety. Put the measured grains and water into a heavy pan and cook the rice until all the water has been absorbed. The old method is to add enough water to come up to two joints of the index finger from the top of the rice.

Steaming rice

Rice that is to be steamed should be cooked in a covered, flat vessel such as a shallow pan or bamboo steamer with just enough water to cover it. Test if the rice is cooked by eating a few grains.

1 Fill a wok one-third full with water. Place a bamboo steamer, with the lid on, over the wok and bring the water underneath to the boil.

2 Lift the lid off the steamer and place a dampened piece of clean muslin (cheesecloth) over the rack. Put the rice in the middle and spread it out a little. Fold the edges of the muslin over the rice, put the lid back on the steamer and steam for about 25 minutes, until the rice is tender but still firm.

Using an automatic rice cooker

Once the preserve of the Japanese, rice cookers are now one of the most popular ways of cooking rice. Simply wash and drain the rice, place it in the inner cooker bowl with the requisite amount of water, and switch on. When the rice is cooked, the steamer will switch itself off. It works by weight, with the inner pot resting on a springboard. When all the water is absorbed, the rice cooker switches off automatically.

Cooking in a microwave

Prepare the rice as for a rice cooker but do not cover the pot as the water will boil over. For 250g/9oz rice you will need 300ml/½ pint water, though long grain rice may need a little more.

NOODLES

Ubiquitous in Indonesia and the Philippines, noodles came by way of China several centuries ago and are now firmly within the mainstream of both schools of cooking. Noodles are consumed in great quantities as snacks and main meals. If the main dish doesn't contain rice it will consist of noodles. They are eaten at all hours of the day, in soup for breakfast, simply stir-fried for a filling snack, or incorporated into main dishes with meat, fish and vegetables.

It is no wonder that most food stalls in Indonesian villages and towns serve both staples in many combinations. The common name for noodles in Indonesia is mee or mie as in mee (mie) goreng or spicy fried noodles. It also pops up in richly sauced dishes such as mee rebus (boiled noodles in spicy gravy), mee Siam (a derivative from Siam, the ancient name for Thailand), and mee soto (spicy soup noodles). In the Philippines, noodles are pancit (stir-fried) in many varied forms; fried, boiled, dry, or used in soups. In Indonesia, bakmie goreng (fried noodles) is practically a national dish, as is the aforementioned pancit in the Philippines.

Noodle stalls are found throughout Indonesia and in the dozens of *warungs* or hawker centres; each fields many stalls selling the different types. A favourite in Indonesia is laksa, a rich, coconut milk-based noodle dish with lashings of chilli paste and aromatic laksa leaves. In the Philippines, most noodle stalls sell versions and adaptations of Chinese style dishes in soup or fried.

Noodles are made from either rice or wheat flour, and the everyday ones fall into several main types. Mee are made from wheat flour, sometimes with egg, and are either thin and long or flat, much like tagliatelle pasta strands. Wheat noodles come in a wide range of types, many from China, and are usually sold dried, in packets.

Rice noodles also come in a variety of shapes. Long, flat noodles are called rice sticks or kway teow in the Chinese Swatow dialect. There is a very thin noodle variously called translucent vermicelli or glass noodles, sohoon in Indonesian and sotanghon in Tagalog. This type of noodle, however, is made from mung bean flour.

FRESH RICE NOODLES

Many daily markets and supermarkets in Indonesia and the Philippines sell rice noodles, supplied fresh by local manufacturers. They are sometimes frozen but mainly chilled, in packets. Some wet markets in rural areas stock them loose in basins and customers simply ask for them by weight.

FINE RICE NOODLES

Commonly called rice vermicelli, there are several types of varying thicknesses, all sold dry. Most come from China or Thailand, but increasingly local manufacturers in Indonesia and the Philippines are producing instant noodles in self-contained snack pots.

RICE STICKS

Though not in widespread use, dry rice sticks are useful because of their long shelf-life. They are gradually becoming more popular among busy people who do not have time to buy the fresh variety daily. They are simply briefly boiled or blanched, depending on the type. Generally much thinner than the fresh variety, they are ideal for soups but tend to break up easily when fried.

WHEAT FLOUR NOODLES

Generally pale yellow, these come either dried to be reconstituted or fresh to be blanched before use in stir-fries or curries. There are three distinct types: factory produced dried skeins of yellow noodles that have to be boiled for a few minutes or longer depending on the type; freshly made and semi-dry noodles, usually with a light coating of flour, that need only to be blanched; and fresh yellow noodles that need very light cooking.

Some producers oil their fresh yellow noodles, and these must be blanched thoroughly to remove the grease. Dry noodles, like rice sticks and vermicelli, double in bulk when reconstituted but fresh ones remain the same.

Some wheat noodles contain egg and resemble Japanese udon. They are often referred to as Shanghai-style noodles, and are usually sold fresh. They are firmer and denser than rice noodles and are used in stir-fries and soups. Fairly new to the market is a more nutritious variety where the dough is blended with spinach, which colours the noodles pale green.

Left: Noodles of various shapes and textures, made from rice, mung bean or wheat flour, are popular in broths and stir-fries.

MUNG BEAN NOODLES

Called by many names, including transparent noodles, translucent vermicelli, cellophane or glass noodles – these are made from mung bean flour and are always sold dry. They reconstitute rapidly when soaked in warm water and have the peculiar characteristic that they keep their crunch no matter how long you cook them. Usually sold in small skeins, they have a neutral flavour that soaks up seasoning very well, and are often simply cooked in stock.

HAND-TOSSED NOODLES

A recent import from north China, hand-tossed noodles are made fresh in restaurants, more as a theatrical event than to meet consumer demand – something like hand-tossed pizza. It takes years of practice to be able to knead wheat flour into a firm but elastic dough, then pull and stretch it repeatedly until fine threads appear before your eyes. Most restaurants that offer this dish charge a premium price for it, as only a limited amount of these ultra-fresh noodles can be made each day.

Preparing rice noodles

Fresh rice noodles need to be blanched briefly in hot water and drained before use in soups or stir-fries. Vermicelli, on the other hand, need only to be soaked for about 20 minutes.

Dried rice noodles double in bulk when rehydrated. Once prepared this way, they should not be cooked for too long or they turn mushy and break up. About 150g/5oz of reconstituted noodles are sufficient for one portion, as each bowl will also contain vegetables, meat or seafood.

TO MAKE FRESH RICE NOODLES

A variety of dried noodles are available from Asian stores and supermarkets in the West, but fresh ones are quite different and if you do want to make them, it's not that difficult. For a snack, fresh noodle sheets can be covered in sugar or honey, or dipped into a sweet or savoury sauce of your choice. Alternatively, you can cut them into wide strips and gently stir-fry them with garlic, ginger, chillies and nuoc mam or soy sauce – a popular local snack.

As a guide, to serve four you will need about 225g/8oz/2 cups rice flour and 600ml/1pint/2½ cups water. You will also need a wide pot with a domed lid, or a wok lid, a piece of thin, smooth cotton cloth (such as an old clean sheet) and a lightly oiled baking tray.

Preparing the batter

1 Place the flour in a bowl and stir in a little water to form a smooth paste. Gradually pour in the rest of the water, whisking all the time to make sure there are no lumps. Beat in a pinch of salt and 15ml/1 tbsp vegetable oil. Set aside for 15 minutes.

2 Meanwhile, fill a wide pot with water. Cut a piece of cloth a little larger than the top of the pot. Stretch it over the top of the pot (you may need someone to help you), pulling the edges down over the sides so that the cloth is as taut as a drum, then wind a piece of string around the edge, securing the cloth with a knot or bow.

3 Using a sharp knife, make 3 small slits, about 2.5cm/1in from the edge of the cloth, at regular intervals. If you need to top up the water during cooking, pour it through these slits. Check that the cloth remains very taut throughout cooking.

Cooking the noodle sheets

1 Bring the water in the pot to the boil. Once it is bubbling and steam is rising through the cloth, stir the batter and ladle a portion (roughly 30–45ml/ 2–3 tbsp) on to the cloth, swirling it to form a 10–15cm/4–6in wide circle.

2 Cover the pot with the domed lid and steam for 1 minute, until the noodle sheet is translucent. To remove it, carefully insert a spatula or round-bladed knife under the edge of the noodle sheet and gently prize it off the cloth – if it doesn't peel off easily, you may need to steam it for a little longer.

3 Transfer the sheet to the oiled tray and repeat with the rest of the batter. As they accumulate, stack the sheets on top of each other, brushing the tops with oil so they don't stick together. Cover the stack with a clean dish towel to keep them moist.

4 Cut the noodle sheets into ribbons with a pasta machine or pizza cutter.

COOK'S TIP

You may have to top up the water through the slits. The cloth might need to be tightened over the pot, otherwise the batter will form a pool in the centre.

BREAD

You will rarely see bread on the traditional Indonesian table, barring households of Dutch and Portuguese descent. Filipino breads are a mix of Spanish, Chinese and indigenous bakes. The islands were administered through Mexico for the best part of 200 years and Filipino cuisine has adopted Mexico's baked breads and assorted yeasty buns. By the early 19th century, the Chinese had come to trade and introduced their steamed breads.

In the 1890s, the Spanish-American War erupted and the islands became American territories. Filipino kitchens were once again open to change and American-style bakes such as pizzas, baguettes, pies and other daily breads were adopted and adapted to suit indigenous tastes.

TYPES OF BREAD

Wraps and flatbreads, used for folding around meat and poultry, are distinctly Spanish: enchiladas (wheat flour wraps), ensaimadas (cheese rolls), churros (bread sticks), tortillas (corn bread) and a range of different pan (bread), both sweet and savoury, are all found in Filipino cuisine. The French baguette, which arrived via the kitchens of Vietnam and Cambodia and latterly through Malaysia and Singapore, is also a popular staple. Today there are bakeries in every town centre that sell different breads, including Chinese steamed and baked buns filled with young coconut, red bean paste and almond paste, rolls filled with cheese and cream, and the ubiquitous British sandwich.

Indian breads like putos and chapatis and Middle-Eastern pittas, all relatively recent arrivals, are relished by Filipinos, even though the Indian community in the Philippines is relatively small. Naan and chapati are now commonplace items, in part thanks to the fairly recent trend for thousands of Filipino women to seek work in Malaysia and Singapore – which resulted in bread imports from these two countries, where Indians had settled some 200 years ago. Chapatis are the basic unleavened bread of the sub-continent that resemble Mexican tortillas. They are eaten with Filipino dishes such as adobo and casseroles.

TO MAKE CHAPATIS

You do not need any special equipment to make chapatis, as they can be cooked in a griddle or large frying pan.

MAKES TEN TO TWELVE

INGREDIENTS
  250g/9oz wholemeal
   (whole-wheat) flour
  115g/4oz plain (all-purpose) flour
  pinch of salt
  200ml/7fl oz/scant 1 cup warm water

1 Sift both the flours with the salt into a large bowl and make a well in the centre. Add the water, a little at a time, and stir with a wooden spoon until the dough comes together and forms a ball that is soft and pliant but not sticky.

2 Rinse your hands in cold water and dry them before kneading so that the dough stays cool. Knead the dough until all the flour is absorbed and nothing sticks to the sides of the bowl. Place the ball of dough on a lightly floured board. With the heel of one hand, knead it lightly but thoroughly.

3 Fold and knead again for 10 minutes. Reshape the ball of dough and return it to the bowl. Cover with a damp cloth and leave to rest at room temperature for half an hour.

4 Knead again once or twice and divide the dough into 10–12 even pieces. Use a knife rather than tearing and stretching the dough. Roll each piece into a round ball. Flour the board if necessary to make rolling easier.

5 With a rolling pin, flatten each chapati into an even circle about 15cm/6in in diameter. Stack the rounds as you finish them and cover the stack with a clean damp cloth to prevent drying out.

6 Heat a large, preferably nonstick, frying pan or griddle. Cook each chapati until bubbles appear on the top, then flip it over. This should take no more than a minute or two.

7 Cook the other side for 40 seconds and remove the pan from the heat. With a pair of tongs, lift the chapati and hold it over the naked flame for a few seconds. It should puff up nicely. Keep the bread warm while you cook the other rounds, and serve them warm and fresh with curry.

VEGETABLES

Raw, stir-fried, braised, pickled or salted, vegetables are worked into every meal in some manner in the Philippines and Indonesia. Almost every meal includes a vegetable side dish or a spicy salad, pickled or as raw leaves to serve Ulam-style. It is intrinsic within both cuisines that a meal must be balanced with vegetables, protein and starch. Texture is also important, so 'salads' might include such ingredients as fruit, meat, shellfish and tofu.

AUBERGINES (EGGPLANTS)

Technically fruits, although eaten as vegetables, aubergines (or brinjals as they are known in Indonesia) came originally from India and Thailand. The most common aubergine is long and thin, in shades of pale green and purple. This is the most popular variety, as the flavour is sweet with very little bitterness. Incredibly versatile, it is added to stews, curries and stir-fries, and the flesh absorbs all the delicious spices and flavours of the dish.

Aubergines are never eaten raw in Indonesia or the Philippines. When choosing, look for smooth, unblemished skin and firm flesh. There are also smaller varieties that range from green to purple and yellow, or are small and round, that are much loved by the Indonesians. These streaky pale green and cream-coloured aubergines are usually halved and added to curries. The tiny, green pea aubergines are also popular throughout South-east Asia. The size of garden peas, these aubergines grow in clusters and have a slightly bitter taste with a pleasantly crunchy texture. They are available in Asian stores and some supermarkets.

BAMBOO SHOOTS

Technically a giant grass, bamboo has many important uses. The long, thin stems or 'trunks' are used for making baskets, furniture and even as containers for rice to be roasted in and split open afterwards. Bamboo trunks are also artfully shaped and made into kitchen utensils, such as steamers, strainers and chopsticks. The leaves (usually dried) are used as wrappers for

Chinese dumplings or steamed rice dishes, imparting their own unique flavour to the dish.

The small shoots that are dug up just before they emerge from the ground are very tasty. Fresh, pickled or dried, bamboo shoots are popular throughout both Indonesia and the Philippines, and are a key ingredient in spring rolls and stir-fries. With older shoots, the outer sheath is stripped off and the tough base removed. Once peeled, the pale yellow inner core is sliced and boiled for at least half an hour before it is edible. The smaller, pale yellow or creamy-white, fresh young shoots need only be blanched briefly. They have a wonderful texture and flavour and are delicious added to stir-fries, curries and soups. Dried shoots, mainly from China, require long soaking before use. Fresh shoots are available in Asian stores, but cans of ready-cooked shoots preserved in brine can be bought in most stores.

Above: Bamboo shoots need to be peeled and sliced before use.

YARD-LONG BEANS

Sometimes referred to as 'snake beans' or 'chopstick beans', these long, green beans are the immature pods of black-eyed beans (peas) and can measure up to 60cm/2ft in length. Generally they are cooked in curries, boiled or stir-fried with sambal or chilli paste, garlic and ginger. Pencil-thin and dark or light green in colour, they are available fresh in Asian markets.

Above: If you cannot find long beans, use French or green beans instead.

GOURDS AND SQUASHES

Frequently used in Filipino and Indonesian cooking, gourds and squashes are often stuffed and fried, steamed or boiled, and sliced for stir-fries and curries.

Above: The bitter melon looks like a knobbly cucumber.

Bitter melon

This gourd is considered nutritious and medicinal, as it contains high levels of quinine. Before cooking, the gourd needs to be slit lengthways to remove its red seeds and inner membrane. The outer shell is then sliced into half-moons and stir-fried, blanched or pickled or added to curries. If you want to remove some of the bitterness, sprinkle a little salt on the slices, leave for 10 minutes and then squeeze out the moisture.

Bitter melons are sold fresh in most Asian stores. A firm, green bitter melon should be allowed to ripen a little before use and will keep for 3–4 days, but a soft yellowish one should be used within a day or two.

Luffa squash

Dark green with ridges running lengthways, luffa squash has sweet and spongy flesh and is usually harvested when it's about 30cm/1ft long. The outer skin is tough and inedible and has to be removed to reveal the soft, white flesh. Generally, it is sliced and used in stir-fries, omelettes and soups, much the same way as you would cook a courgette (zucchini). Luffa squash is available in Asian markets. Unlike cucumber or young, tender courgettes, luffa is never eaten raw. Keep fresh luffa in the refrigerator, but do not store it for too long, as within 2–3 days of purchase it will start to go limp. Luffa are also known as Chinese okra, silk squash and sponge gourd.

WINGED BEAN

This unusual vegetable is widely used as a salad vegetable and also stir-fried with spices in both countries. When not overcooked they have a desirable crunch. Cut into small pieces, they have an interesting four-winged shape with small edible seeds in the centre.

MUSHROOMS

Available fresh, dried or canned, mushrooms are used in soups, stir-fries, stews, broths and braised dishes.

Straw mushrooms

Also called bulb mushrooms, straw mushroom caps look like tiny brown eggs. The whole mushrooms are often used in braised dishes for visual appeal and texture. Once peeled, they reveal small dark-brown caps and stocky, cream-coloured stems which look lovely in clear broths. Very delicate in flavour and texture, straw mushrooms are available dried, fresh and in cans. Canned mushrooms must be drained and thoroughly rinsed before use.

Oyster mushrooms

In the wild, oyster mushrooms grow in clumps on rotting wood. The caps, gills and stems are all the same colour, which can be pearl grey, pink or yellow. The flavour is mild, with a hint of seafood. Oyster mushrooms are popular in soups and stir-fries, and they are also used in noodle and rice dishes. They seldom need trimming. Large ones should be torn, rather than cut into pieces. The soft texture becomes rubbery if they are overcooked, so always add them to dishes at the last moment. Buy oyster

mushrooms that smell and look fresh, avoiding any with damp, slimy patches and discolouring. Store in a paper bag in the vegetable compartment of the refrigerator, and use as soon as possible after purchase. They do not keep for more than 2–3 days.

Chinese black mushrooms

Sometimes known as Chinese shiitake, these pungent mushrooms are usually sold dried. Light brown in colour with white markings on the surface, they have thick-fleshed caps which can grow to about 5cm/2in in diameter and have a meaty flavour and a chewy texture. Once softened in warm water for about 30 minutes, the stems are removed and the caps are added to stews, stir-fries and fillings. Chinese black mushrooms are available in Asian supermarkets.

Above: Chinese black mushrooms are sold dried or canned.

PULSES

Used in both sweet and savoury dishes, pulses are a mainstay of the cuisine.

Red beans

Dried red beans, also called aduki beans, are some of the smallest available. In both countries, they are usually soaked, boiled and mashed as a stuffing for sweet cakes. They are often boiled and used as a sweet base in the iconic Filipino dessert known as halo halo and ais kacang (shaved ice with beans and syrup) in Indonesia, sold by hawkers or dessert stalls. They are also

cooked as a sweet drink with rock sugar or sweet winter melon slices as a favourite after-meal drink.

Beansprouts

Ubiquitous throughout Asia and China, beansprouts can be eaten raw but are usually added to stir-fried noodles for their crunch. The most common sprouts come from mung beans and soya beans. They are similar in appearance, except the soya bean at the head of the sprout is almost twice the size at about 2cm/¾in long. The stems of both are white, but soya bean heads are pale green, while those of mung beans are yellow. Soya beans are sturdier and stronger in flavour, whereas mung beans are delicate and watery. Both types are nutritious, rich in vitamins and minerals.

Fresh sprouts can be stored in the refrigerator for up to 2–3 days. Packets of mung beansprouts are available in most supermarkets. Soya beansprouts can be found in Asian stores and some health stores.

Above: Soya beansprouts are available in many supermarkets.

Soya beans

These yellow beans are about twice the size of corn kernels and play a big role in the Chinese-influenced kitchens of Indonesia and the Philippines, apart from the obvious soy sauce. Fermented and made into yellow bean paste, soya beans are the basis of many sauces. Sweetened with palm sugar (jaggery), they are a popular dessert and drink ingredient.

ORIENTAL GREENS

Versatile and full of nutrients, oriental greens are very popular in both cuisines.

Pak choi (Bok choy)

This perennial, green, leafy cabbage is popular throughout Asia. The ribbed, white stems are juicy and crunchy; the dark green leaves are succulent and tasty. The tender stems of small cabbages are rarely eaten raw but often stir-fried with prawns (shrimp) or added to noodles. The leaves, which are

Above: Pak choi is excellent in stir-fry dishes as well as salads.

mostly composed of water, require little cooking and lose a lot of volume in the process. It is a good idea to cook the leaves and stems separately, as the stems take slightly longer. These fresh greens are available in Asian stores and supermarkets.

Chinese leaves (Chinese cabbage)

Often confused with the above, there are almost as many names for this member of the brassica family as there are ways of cooking it. In the West, it is generally called Chinese leaves, but it is also known as Chinese cabbage, Napa cabbage (mainly in the USA) and sometimes celery cabbage. In the Philippines and Indonesia the names for pak choi tend to be used for this vegetable, which is available all year.

Chinese leaves have a delicate sweet aroma with a mild cabbage flavour that becomes even more subtle when it is cooked. The white stalk becomes less crunchy when cooked. It is a very versatile vegetable and it can be cooked in stir-fries, stews, soups, or eaten raw in salads. It will absorb the flavours of

any other ingredients with which it is cooked and yet retain its own characteristic taste and texture. Restaurant chefs blanch the vegetable in boiling stock, which enhances the flavour, before frying, or blanch the leaves to soften them for wrapping around minced (ground) pork and fish as a festive dish. Chinese leaves can be stored for up to 10 days in the refrigerator. Don't worry if there are tiny black specks on the leaves. This is normal and will not affect the flavour.

Mustard greens

Also known as Chinese cabbage, mustard greens look a bit like a head of lettuce such as cos or romaine, except that the leaves wrapping the heart are thick. The leaves are sharp and robust in flavour but, once blanched, they lose some of their bitterness. A classic stir-fry addition when poached with egg white and crab meat, fresh mustard greens are available in Asian markets and will keep for several days in the salad compartment of a refrigerator.

Preserved mustard greens

In the Philippines and Indonesia, salty preserved mustard greens are as common as the fresh variety. They are eaten with many Filipino meals and Indonesian seafood curries, or sliced and added to soups or omelettes. They are available in Asian markets, usually canned or vacuum-packed.

Above: Mustard greens are larger and curlier than pak choi.

Water convolvulus

Also called water spinach, swamp cabbage or morning glory, this attractive leafy green vegetable is traditionally grown in swamps or ponds, near rivers and canals, although it does grow on dry land too. In Indonesia it is essential in the spicy salad called rujak, and is often added to spiced fish or prawns and wrapped in banana leaves for steaming or barbecuing. Somewhat rare in the West, water convolvulus is occasionally available in some Asian markets and supermarkets. It is highly perishable and must be used promptly.

Preparing water convolvulus

1 Slit the hollow stalks right down their length to check for creepy-crawlies! Separate them from the leaves and split lengthways.

2 Trim off the end bits that usually have a few rootlets. Slice into 7.5cm/3in pieces.

3 Tear off leafy stems or cut into similar lengths so each stem has a few leaves. Individual leaves, if they are small, tend to shrink too much when cooked. Wash and drain thoroughly before cooking. Store in a plastic bag for up to 2 days refrigerated.

TUBERS AND AQUATIC ROOTS

These vegetables are quite unlike root vegetables used in Western cuisine.

Cassava (Tapioca)

Also known as manioc or tapioca, cassava is a large tuber similar in shape to a sweet potato, but longer, with skin like firm brown bark. The creamy-coloured flesh of the root is starchy and often used for sweet, sticky puddings such as bibingka in the Philippines or kueh bengka in Indonesia. Cassava can be steamed and tossed with desiccated (dry unsweetened shredded) coconut or simply eaten as a sweet snack, or mashed and sweetened with palm sugar (jaggery) and coconut milk as a baked pudding. It has a subtly sweet, almost buttery flavour, sometimes with nuances of almond and new potato. Cassava must never be eaten raw. Fresh cassava tubers are available in Asian markets.

Tapioca flour

This silky flour is made from the starch of the cassava root. Primarily, it is used to thicken sauces and desserts, but it is also used to make fresh rice papers. The flour is available in Asian stores.

Mooli (Daikon)

Apart from being white, this vegetable looks very similar to a large carrot. Also known as Oriental white radish, or mooli in Hindi, it is crisp and juicy with a slightly fiery edge. It can be eaten raw or cooked and it is a popular vegetable throughout the two countries. Daikon can be found in Asian markets.

Jicama

Resembling a large turnip, this root vegetable has a delicate sweet taste with a crunchy texture, similar to water chestnut. Simply peel before use and cut into chunks or slices for soups, salads and stir-fries. Jicamas can be found in most Asian stores.

Lotus root and seeds

The lotus plant, or water lily, with its delicate flowers, is quite unique, and edible in its entirety. The stamens are infused to make a fragrant tea; the seeds are dried and boiled for use in festive sweets and cakes; the large leaves are used for wrapping sticky rice and steamed snacks; the stems are peeled, sliced and added to salads, soups and braised dishes. Lotus roots are tan-coloured with a pinkish hue. The roots taste similar to water chestnuts. When sliced, they reveal small holes which hold the seeds. Chinese tradition says that the nourishing lotus root aids blood circulation and increases virility. The roots, stems and seeds of the lotus plant are available, fresh, dried and preserved, in most Asian stores. If dried, all of them need to be soaked overnight before being cooked.

Above: The texture of a jicama is like a cross between an apple and a potato.

Taro

This root vegetable, known as taro or yam is either small and egg-shaped or about 13cm/5in long and barrel-shaped. Both varieties have short hairs and white purple-flecked flesh. The larger variety is firm with a nutty flavour; the smaller is creamier and sweeter.

Taro roots are available in Asian stores as well as in some supermarkets.

Above: Taro is a rough-skinned tuber.

Indonesian cooking also features the tender stalks of young taro for curries. They absorb the flavour and sauce of the dish. In the Philippines, taro leaves, also called gabi but natong, are also widely eaten. All over the country, you can see food vendors laden with bunches of the leaves with slender stalks that go into many traditional dishes. The most famous is the Bicol classic of Laing, pinangat, in which the leaves are cooked with coconut milk to make a stew with meat or fish.

Ube

This pretty root is often confused with taro but is a yam and uniquely Filipino. It is a delicious flavouring for ice cream and is used as a topping for halo halo. Filipino stores sell frozen ube chunks.

Below: Fresh lotus roots, which are in fact rhizomes, look like linked sausages. The papery leaves and light-coloured seeds are also widely used.

FRUIT

Traditionally, fruit is eaten at the end of a meal to cleanse the palate or aid the digestion, while desserts and cakes are nibbled and indulged in as snacks. A wide variety of fruits are available in Indonesia and the Philippines.

BANANAS

The banana plant looks like a tree but is actually a perennial herb. Every year, it grows a new 'trunk' and, after it has borne blossom and fruit, it dies back to its roots. The fruit grows in bunches (hands). Most are yellow-skinned and pale-fleshed, but there are some with orange flesh and others with green-striped skins and pink flesh. The sweetest tend to be short and stubby.

After coconuts, bananas are possibly the most widely used fruit in the Philippines and Indonesia. In the former, they even have grand names like Baston or Cavendish, and these are exported around the world. Latundan is flattish with white flesh; Lacatan is long and slender with sweet yellow flesh; Senorita is one of the smallest at 8cm/3in, and the Saba is like a plantain and has to be cooked. At Filipino food centres a popular snack is Banana-Q, a peeled and skewered Saba banana cooked on a barbecue. In Indonesia, a favourite snack is pisang goreng (battered and fried bananas) or jemput jemput, mashed bananas mixed with rice flour and fried. Many desserts call for bananas, fresh or fried, while a number of savoury dishes require the leaves or blossom of the banana plant.

Below: Banana leaves are useful for wrapping food.

Above: The purple banana blossom may be eaten as a vegetable.

Banana leaves

You don't need foil, baking parchment or clear film (plastic wrap) when you've got banana leaves. They can be used as plates, table mats or be shaped into bowls and cups. The leaves are often used as wrappings for pâtés and sweet and savoury sticky rice cakes. Banana leaves are available in Asian and African supermarkets, sold both fresh and frozen.

Banana blossom

The lovely deep purple flower of the banana tree is enjoyed throughout South-east Asia as a vegetable, especially in Indonesian salads. In the Philippines it is often called banana heart on account of the purple casings of the buds, which make it look like a large heart. Only the inner yellow blossoms are used; they are fabulous sliced, blanched and tossed with coconut cream, cooked prawns (shrimp) and chilli and shrimp paste sambal. To prepare the inner blossom, slice it finely and soak in water with a squeeze of lemon or lime juice to prevent it discolouring. The blossoms can be eaten raw but have a slightly bitter taste. The purple outer husks are inedible.

COCONUT

The coconut is the most commonly used fruit for both sweet and savoury dishes throughout the Philippines and Indonesia – indeed,

Above: The brown, hairy stone of the coconut contains the water and flesh.

throughout all of tropical Asia. Ripe fruits are hulled, shredded and squeezed for a clear white milk that is essential in Indonesian curries and Filipino stews (called guinataan). The soft, jelly-like flesh of the young nuts makes a tasty snack or forms a sweet base for tropical drinks.

Coconut palm leaves are woven into baskets and mats, or used to wrap rice for boiling and serving with satay. The spines are cut into lengths for satay skewers, and the husks and fibres are used as mattress stuffing, fuel, or for making ropes.

The whole coconut that we buy is only the stone (pit) of the actual fruit; the husk and fibres are removed in the country of origin. When buying a coconut, the hard shell should be brown and hairy. Shake it and you should hear the sound of the coconut water inside. To extract this liquid, pierce the eyes on top of the coconut and pour it out. The coconut water should be clear and taste sweet. It is generally drunk or used to tenderize meat. Once you have extracted the water, place the coconut on a flat surface and use a heavy object like a cleaver or hammer to hit it all the way round. Pull the shell apart, pry the flesh out with a knife, and peel the brown skin off the flesh so that it is ready to use. If you have difficulty cracking the coconut, place it in a fairly hot oven for about 15 minutes, until it cracks. The flesh is often easier to extract from the shell using this method.

Coconut milk

This is the equivalent of dairy cream in Asia, and fundamental in most curries and puddings. It is used to enrich sauces and soups, especially in Indonesian cooking. Coconut milk is also boiled with red or green beans, bananas and mangoes and sweetened with palm sugar (jaggery) for a popular dessert called penghat in Indonesia.

When you squeeze coconut flesh without water, you get an initial cream called 'first milk' that is used for desserts. The second milk comes from adding a little warm water to yield a thinner liquid, used mainly in curries. (If thin coconut milk is allowed to settle in a bowl a little cream will rise to the top, and may be skimmed off for use.)

Fresh coconut milk does not keep well and is usually made daily. It can turn rancid very quickly in hot weather and is best refrigerated if you are not using it immediately. It keeps for up to 2 days if chilled.

Canned coconut milk is now widely available, and you can purchase powder or blocks of cream from Asian markets, health stores and supermarkets. These are essential store cupboard items for enthusiasts of South-east Asian cuisine. Follow the package instructions for use.

Above: Red-skinned mangoes are eaten as a fruit or in desserts, and green-skinned ones as a vegetable.

Coconut oil

By boiling coconut cream gently until the liquid evaporates, coconut oil is made. In the Philippines, coconut milk is simmered for a long time until oil rises to the top and a cheese-like, delicate brown precipitate forms at the bottom. This is called latik and is used to flavour or top many Filipino dishes and desserts. The oil is used by Indonesians for rich curries but is a saturated fat that turns solid very quickly.

Green coconut water

The coconut water used for cooking is extracted from young, green coconuts. Mild and sweet, it is used in a number of braised dishes and cakes. Although you can use the coconut water from ripened coconuts, it is best to look in Asian markets for a young coconut. It will be cylindrical in shape with a conical top and a white, spongy shell, as the green outer skin will have been removed.

MANGO

Originally from India, the mango is much loved in Indonesia and the Philippines. The sweetest varieties are thick, round and tapered at one end. The skins are yellow, pale orange or green depending on the type, and ripened ones are eaten mainly as a fruit. There are also green mangoes that never change colour and are used mainly as salad vegetables when sliced finely or shredded. Imported mangoes from India and Thailand are available all year round. The sweet, juicy, yellow or orange flesh is thirst-quenching, with a delightful aroma of pine, and is a good source of vitamin A. Different types of mango are widely available. To eat mango, cut a slice from the side and score the flesh into squares, then invert the skin and slice cubes of flesh away from the rind.

Making coconut milk

While most wet markets sell grated coconut for making milk, or cans of milk, it is easy to make.

1 Grate the flesh from a fresh ripened coconut, or shred it in a food processor.

2 Put the grated flesh into a bowl and knead thoroughly. Squeeze out the creamy 'first milk'.

3 Pour roughly 600ml/1 pint/ 2½ cups warm water over the shreds. Stir and leave to steep for 30 minutes. Line a sieve (strainer) with muslin (cheesecloth) over a bowl and ladle the coconut into it.

4 Gather the muslin in your hands and squeeze out any excess liquid. This is the 'second milk'.

DURIAN

This large fruit, encased in a spiky armour-like skin, is creamy, dense and pungent. If you can put up with the strong, cheesy odour, the delicious yellow flesh has nut and honey overtones, quite unlike any other fruit, and is considered an aphrodisiac. Durian is a much sought-after fruit during the season, from May to October. It is an expensive fruit and only available in some Asian markets. The best ones come from Malaysia and have butter-soft flesh with a slight bitter edge. Thai durians tend to be woody and dry. Avoid any fruits that have split.

Preparing durian

Using a wooden wedge that has a thin, tapered end, force it down along each natural ridge between the rows of spikes. The prickly shell will split open easily to reveal large seeds coated in pulp. The pulp can be tugged, or sucked and licked clean from the large seeds. If not eaten straight away, freeze the durian flesh in air-tight containers so as not to impart its strong smell to other foods.

Above: Jackfruit is large and plentiful. It features in many popular savoury and sweet dishes.

JACKFRUIT

Large and spiky, jackfruits look similar to durian but have short stubs instead of spikes. When sliced open, a jackfruit reveals a cluster of yellow fruit, each encircling a large seed. The texture is delightfully crunchy and the taste is similar to ripe mango.

There are two distinct types: nangka, which can weigh in at 5kg/11lb and grow as large as two rugby balls, and chempedak, which is less known in the Philippines but widely grown in Indonesia. The taste of chempedak is more fragrant, with nuances of pineapple and

apricot, and the flesh is creamy and chewy at the same time. Packed with vitamins, jackfruit is enjoyed on its own as well as mixed with other fruits in tropical fruit salad. Peel the fruit like a pineapple, pull away the fruits attached to a central stalk and they separate easily. Eat the flesh and reserve the seeds, which can be boiled or roasted and eaten as a snack. Peeled, whole, canned green jackfruit are available in some Asian markets.

Above: Knobbly kalamansi limes are widely used in South-east Asian cuisine.

LIME

Fresh green limes are used for their juice, much like lemons in Mediterranean cooking, or pickled and dried for use in sambals and chutneys. Tossed in marinades and dressings, they impart a slightly fragrant, citrus taste. Kaffir limes yield aromatic lime leaves integral to Indonesian cooking. The rough-textured rind is grated and added to many savoury dishes. The fruit

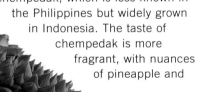

Above: A durian and its large seeds.

is highly prized in sambals and curries. Both varieties and the kaffir lime leaves are available in Asian markets and some supermarkets.

LYCHEE AND LONGAN

Both lychees and longans are native to the sub-tropical regions of South-east Asia, and they require heat and high humidity to ripen well. They belong to the same family, although the smaller and less fleshy longan is sometimes regarded as the inferior relative. Lychees have terracotta-pink, bumpy skins, rather than the smooth, brown ones of longans, but both are easily peeled to reveal gleaming white, occasionally pink, juicy flesh covering a shiny, coffee-coloured seed. Clusters of fresh lychees and longans are sold on their stalks in the markets and supermarkets of Asia. Sweet and fragrant, they are usually eaten as a refreshing snack. Fresh longans can be found in some Asian markets, and lychees are readily available in Asian markets and most supermarkets. They keep well in the refrigerator and are delicious chilled. Lychees and longans are also sold in cans, preserved in their own juice or in syrup.

PAPAYA

This ripe, yellow-skinned fruit, with its sweet, flame-coloured flesh, is also known as paw paw. It is full of vitamins and honey-sweet. When a savoury recipe calls for papaya, it is a different variety that is required. Large and round, or pear-shaped, this papaya has a dark green skin with light green flesh and white seeds. High in iron, this tart fruit is enjoyed as a vegetable, peeled and finely sliced, or shredded, in salads. Both types of papaya can be found in Asian markets and some supermarkets. Choose fruit with firm, unblemished skin, not bruised or shrivelled. Ripe papayas do not last very long. Slit them open, scoop out the seeds and enjoy the flesh with a squeeze of fresh lime.

PINEAPPLE

Grown throughout tropical regions, pineapples vary in size, juiciness and sweetness. Often pineapple slices are sold with a little salt and chilli powder to sprinkle on them. Ripe pineapples are mainly eaten as a fruit, but are an important ingredient in Indonesian sour curries, especially with fish and shellfish. Pineapples are readily available; when choosing, look for a firm, puckered skin, with a good orange colouring and a good fragrance.

Preparing pineapple

To prepare fresh pineapple slices, first slice off the leaves, then use a sharp or serrated knife to cut off the skin in vertical strips about 1cm/½in thick. Make diagonal cuts all along the fruit, removing any black eyes. Slice the whole fruit lengthways into four quarters and remove the hard, pithy core. Finally cube or slice and serve.

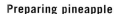

RAMBUTAN

Shaggy-haired rambutans look like tiny red sea urchins. There are a number of varieties, varying in sweetness and coloured with streaks of gold, orange or

Above: Rambutans have a distinctive skin covered in soft spiky hairs. They are available fresh or prepared in cans.

green. The hairy shells are easy to open and encase a translucent white fruit with a stone (pit) in the middle, similar to the lychee and longan. Cool and sweet, these fruits are available in some Asian markets.

STAR FRUIT

Also known as carambola, this pretty fruit is mildly floral tasting and similar in texture to an Asian pear but juicier. With a smooth shiny skin, the fruit has an attractive star shape when sliced through the centre. In both countries, the ripened yellow fruit is enjoyed as a snack or pulped for its refreshing juice. The green immature fruit is sliced finely and served as a tangy vegetable, salted and dried as a pickle ingredient, or tossed in salads. Star fruit is available in some Asian markets and from good supermarkets.

Above: Bright yellow star fruit is used in snacks, drinks and savoury dishes.

Above: Papayas, often known as paw paws, are one of the most attractive tropical fruits.

SOUR STAR FRUIT

These small, sour fruit, also known as belimbing, are related to the carambola that grows profusely all over the Philippines and Indonesia. Found widely in high altitude regions, it is variously called camia, cucumber tree and tree sorrel. The thumb-sized fruits grow in clusters and impart a zesty, tangy flavour to seafood curries and salads. The leaves are crunchy with a faint bitter edge, and are very popular in the Philippines. They are not widely available in the West, but may be found in Thai and Filipino markets and those

---

How to prepare sour star fruit (belimbing) pickle

1 Remove the small stalks at the ends of the fruit. Remove the pith.

2 Cut up the fruits or mash lightly until you get a coarse paste.

3 Sprinkle liberally with salt and set aside to sweat for an hour.

4 Using a muslin cloth, squeeze out the moisture and toss with two chopped red chillies, 5ml/1 tsp sugar and 15ml/1 tbsp vinegar.

5 Sprinkle with 30ml/2 tbsp chopped nuts and serve as a relish.

---

that specialize in South-east Asian ingredients. Some Filipino stores sell a salad leaf called sour spinach or alas doce, which is a member of the sorrel family that comes closest to belimbing leaves. Otherwise young spinach leaves may be substituted.

SAPODILLA

These kiwi-fruit sized fruit originate from Central America but are widely grown in Indonesia and in some regions of the Philippines. Variously called chiko or chiku, they have a light, slightly fuzzy skin that when peeled reveals a soft, tan flesh with black pips. The flesh is luscious like a soft pear and tastes of burnt sugar. Sapodillas are available from some Asian grocers and markets.

GUAVA

A native of Brazil, the guava was taken by the Portuguese to the Philippines in the 17th century, and gradually spread across the tropical countries. It is also grown widely in Indonesia and there is a profusion of different types, which may be round, ovoid or pear-shaped, and weigh from 25–350g/1–12oz. The thick outer skin ranges from white to pale green, pink or red; the flesh may be white, yellow or pink and contain many small seeds. Guavas have a sweet aroma ranging from rose blossom to mango, and are eaten mainly as a dessert fruit. They are available from most Thai and Indian markets and some supermarkets.

MANGOSTEEN

Grown mainly in hot, humid tropical countries, mangosteens are virtually unknown outside tropical Asia. The handsome fruits are like large berries, the size of apples, with a smooth, rich-looking, red-purple thick rind, partially covered with the flower sepals that remain attached as the fruit ripens. Inside the rind the pulp is chalky white and divided into five to seven segments. The large segments contain a seed but the smaller segments are seedless. The flesh has a delicious perfume. Mangosteens are eaten as dessert fruit.

Right: Mangosteens have a white flesh with a delicate flavour and are best eaten raw.

Above: Sapodilla, with its orange, fuzzy skin, looks similar to an apricot.

SOURSOP

Often mistaken for durian, soursops are grown widely in humid tropical countries. The fruits may weigh as much as 3kg/8lb, and are borne on thick, woody stalks. The thick skin is dark green with rows of soft green stubby spikes – hence the durian reference. The fruit is very soft, white and creamy and very juicy, ranging from tart to sweet flavours. Buried within the flesh are many shiny, black seeds. A rich source of vitamin C, they are often puréed for the juice. They are available in South-east Asian and Chinese markets.

CUSTARD APPLE

Originating from tropical America, the custard apple was introduced to the region by the Portuguese via Madagascar. It thrives in lowland tropics and sub-tropics and is known as a nona kapri in Malaysia. This means the 'nona from Africa', borrowing from the botanical name *Anona longifolia*. The fruits are heart-shaped, buff or green in colour, and each about 10cm/4in in diameter. The skin is thin and may have small bumps depending on the variety. The creamy white flesh surrounds a fibrous central core. Small black seeds are embedded in the flesh, which has a custard-like consistency and is slightly astringent, but sweet when ripe. It is readily available in Indian and South-east Asian markets.

TOFU

Far from a 'poor man's meat', tofu or soy beancurd is enjoyed globally today, and stirred up into great tastes by Filipino and Indonesian cooks. Protein-rich and low in calories, tofu is devoid of cholesterol. It also provides essential amino acids, vitamins and minerals for good health. It is made by combining soya bean milk with a coagulant such as gypsum powder to form curds which are then pressed together into blocks. Some find it too bland, but this very quality makes tofu great for absorbing other flavours. The firmer type can be added to stir-fries, and when fried it has a wonderful texture. It may also be used as a container for various stuffings, and adds healthy bulk to soups, braised vegetarian dishes and spring roll fillings.

FRESH TOFU

Soft white blocks of fresh tofu are packed in water and are available in most Asian markets. The UHT varieties in cartons are also available in many supermarkets and come in two types – soft or firm. Generally, the soft silken texture is better for soups and steamed dishes, whereas the firm variety is best in stir-fries and fillings. Tofu is best used straight away, but, if it is kept submerged in water that is changed daily, it can be stored for 3–4 days in the refrigerator.

Above, clockwise from top: Fried, silken and firm tofu, all varying in degrees of firmness and suited to stir-fries or soups.

Above: Cubes of fermented tofu.

FRIED TOFU

Made by deep-frying firm tofu until a brown skin forms, this is used in many dishes and salads, and as an alternative to meat. It has a delicious, slightly chewy texture and a flavour rather similar to omelette. The Indonesian iconic dishes of tahu goreng and gado gado both feature fried tofu prominently. Both are dressed with shredded vegetables and bathed in a rich, spicy peanut sauce. The tofu absorbs the flavour of the sauce well and retains its firm texture.

PRESERVED TOFU

Cubes of fresh tofu can be preserved in salty water or brine for several months. Before use the tofu should be thoroughly rinsed in water and drained. Used sparingly (because of their strong taste), cubes of preserved tofu add extra flavour to stir-fries and other vegetable and meat dishes. Preserved tofu can be found in most Asian stores.

TOFU SKINS

These are made by lifting the skin as soy milk is boiled and drying it flat to form brown, wrinkly sheets. The skins are often used in manufacturing vegetarian meat substitutes, as the texture is very similar to cooked meat. If the skins have been stored for any time, they tend to become stiff and crack easily when handled. If this happens, they have to be moistened slightly with a damp towel before being used as spring roll wrappers. Many Indonesian and Filipino spring rolls are made with tofu skin as a festive wrapper.

TOFU WAFERS

Light brown pieces of slightly sweetened, dried tofu can be fried to make a 'crackling' to top stir-fried noodles or add to vegetable stews. In Indonesian cooking, such garnishes are an extremely important feature – often giving a dish its essential flavour or texture.

FISH AND SHELLFISH

The coastal waters off the Philippine islands and the Indonesian archipelago are alive with a variety of tropical seafood. Both countries are also blessed with a network of river systems that start from the mountain ranges and run through the jungles to finally join the sea. In every town and village, there are usually wet markets that feature fishmongers selling absolutely fresh fish.

Fish is an important source of protein, vitamins and amino acids. Calcium is also plentiful in small fish such as anchovies and sprats. Most coastal communities depend more on fish than meat for their daily diet.

Fish market stall holders traditionally bought their fish at the crack of dawn from fishermen, straight from the fishing boats. These days, this practice is more organized and buying from large fish wholesalers is the norm.

Much seafood ends up in noodle dishes in both countries. Filipino pancit and Indonesian laksas all feature seafood prominently. Up until the 1950s, refrigeration was rare and all fish bought had to be cooked on the same day. This still applies in many rural areas in both Indonesia and the Philippines, and has trained the local taste buds to expect extremely fresh ocean produce.

Below: Carp is one of the hardiest of all fish, and has meaty flesh that varies in taste according to how it is cooked. It is often wrapped in banana leaves and steamed with herbs.

Above: Fresh catfish is versatile and easy to use. It is often sold on Indonesian street stalls, grilled and served with vegetables.

CARP

A powerful swimmer, the carp leaps like a salmon and migrates in shoals. There are numerous species of carp, all of which have different names. Not all carp are good to eat, as some feed in shallow, muddy waters which can affect the taste. The common variety in Indonesia is known as ikan mas, and is bred in areas including West Java and South Sumatra. It is only eaten fresh, never dried, and is sometimes sold live at the wet market in plastic bags filled with water.

CATFISH

Primarily freshwater fish, catfish are so called because of their barbels, used for feeling along the river beds, which look like whiskers. Free of scales and small bones, catfish are easy to prepare, but the quality of their flesh varies as they are bottom feeders and feed off live and dead prey. In Indonesia, deep-fried catfish is popular, particularly at food stalls, where it is served with a spicy sauce made from chillies, peanuts and tomatoes, in a dish called pecel lele.

EEL

Adult eels are at their plumpest when they have turned silver with almost black backs. Females weigh three times as much as males, so a female silver eel is highly prized. Eels should be bought alive, as they go off quickly once dead. Ask the fishmonger to kill and skin them for you and to chop them into 5cm/2in lengths. You can prepare them yourself after killing them with a heavy blow to the head, but it can be a slippery task that is better left to those with experience.

HERRING

While the common name is herring, these fish are also known as sprat or rainbow sardine. Generally growing to about 15cm/6in, with a dark green back and silver belly, they have very fine bones. They are extremely tasty when fried and eaten with a chilli dip. Larger herrings can be gutted and filleted before cooking.

Above: Milkfish is hugely popular in Indonesia and the Philippines.

MILKFISH

Generally about 1m/3ft in length, with a symmetrical shape, the milkfish (known locally as bangas) is an extremely important fish in Indonesia and the Philippines. It is farmed extensively. Young milkfish live at sea for two to three weeks and then migrate to fresh and brackish water before returning to the sea for reproduction. They are collected from rivers and raised in ponds, then sold fresh, frozen, canned or smoked. In taste and texture the milk fish is similar to sea bass or mullet.

RED GROUPER

Red grouper, known as lapu lapu in the Philippines, are farmed and caught wild. They have bright orange skin with uneven spotting. The pure white flesh has a good texture and flavour, and the fish has become very sought after and expensive. Generally the fish are over 1m/3ft in length. They are usually sold live, or very fresh, at wet markets.

Right: Sea bass has a delicate taste that works well with classic South-east Asian herbs and spices.

SEA BASS

A fine fish, sea bass have variable but always striking coloration, from silvery to light brown to orange with large-edged blue spots. They have a sleek shape rather like a salmon, and can grow to a length of 90cm/36in and weigh up to 7kg/15½lb. The white flesh is firm and delicately flavoured and tastes best when simply steamed.

SNAPPER

One of the most important groups of local fish, snappers are highly esteemed and easily recognized by their straight ventral profile with pointed snout. These snap when they are caught, hence their name. Most are brightly coloured, ranging from deep red in the larger species to shocking pink, silver and yellow, usually with lines and spots. They have a delicate flavour and are usually cooked in curries or fried whole.

SNAKEHEAD

This eel-like fish is highly prized for its meaty flesh and full flavour, and features in Cantonese fish and rice vermicelli soup (yue tau mifun). The fish are usually sold live. They have a near-black, slippery skin and are often mistaken for fat eels. Very popular in north Malaysia, they turn up in many guises, in curries, grilled (broiled), fried or flaked for relishes.

STINGRAY

Although the normal variety is relatively small, about 30cm/12in across its widest part, stingrays can also grow to enormous size, weighing as much as 200kg/450lb.

Above: The red grouper is called Lapu Lapu by Filipinos, after a local hero.

They may be coloured from sandy to dark brown, or marked with numerous spots, but a better recognition point is their whip-like tail. Grilled or fried, they have a similar flavour and texture to skate.

THREADFIN/TASSEL FISH

Probably the most expensive fish and quite rare, these fish have a delicate sweet flesh reminiscent of cod or halibut. They are large, up to 120cm/4ft long, and are mostly sold as steaks or cutlets. They are silvery-green above with a creamy belly and the name refers to the four threads on each pectoral fin. Some species have black dorsal tips to their fins and green tassels.

WOLF HERRING/DORAB

Specimens up to 60cm/24in long have been caught in deep waters off Asian coasts but the market variety is usually around 45cm/18in long.
The fish has a bluish-green back with silvery sides that go grey when it has been dead a while. The large upturned mouth looks fierce but the flesh has a sweet flavour, and the numerous bones cannot spoil the excellent taste and flaky texture.

SQUID

Along with octopus and cuttlefish, squid are members of the cephalopod family. Torpedo-shaped and flanked by two fins, eight short and two long tentacles, the entire body is edible and enjoyed throughout the region. Squid is easy to prepare and can be cooked in a variety of ways, such as stir-fried with spices.

Preparing squid

1 Check the squid is fresh and intact. Rinse it well in fresh water.

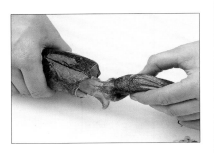

2 Grip the head in one hand, the body in the other, and tug the head out of the body sac, pulling most of the innards with it. Grip the top of the backbone and pull it out. Rinse the inside of the sac and pat dry.

3 Sever the arms and tentacles from the head and innards and put beside the sac. Discard the rest, including the skin.

If stir-frying squid, slit the prepared sac from top to bottom and turn it inside out. Flatten it on a board and score the inside surface lightly with a knife, pressing just hard enough to make a crisscross pattern. Cut lengthways into ribbons, which will curl when cooked briefly.

CRAB

Whenever possible, Indonesians and Filipinos enjoy lobster and crab, including the meaty blue crab found off Palawan, the island famed for the giraffe and zebra brought in by Marcos for his private zoo. However, due to the expense, lobster and crab are often reserved for special occasions, when they are steamed with oyster sauce, or deep-fried and served with a chilli sambal in Indonesia or spiked coconut vinegar in the Philippines.

There are several varieties of crab, the most common being mottled or flower crabs, named on account of the pale blue mottling on their shells. They are about the size of an adult palm, smaller than the large grey mud crabs. They make very good eating, especially in the well-loved Singapore dish of chilli crab.

Above: The blue mottled crab is very popular in Indonesia and the Philippines, and has plenty of meat.

Preparing crab

Usually sold live, crabs tend to become comatose when chilled for a few hours. Make sure the crab is dry, with no sign of water sloshing around in the shell, which should be firm and contain no cracks or holes. Turn the crab belly up and remove the soft V-shaped flap on

Above: Prawn tails turn salmon-pink when they are cooked. The shells must be removed before they are eaten.

the belly. Pull the top shell off, scoop out the soft, yellowish coral and reserve. Discard the feathery gills and snap off the legs and claws. The larger claws should be cracked but not entirely broken, so the flesh can be easily extracted when cooked. Rinse the body and cut into two or more pieces. Alternatively, steam the crabs whole until they turn deep pink throughout.

PRAWNS (SHRIMP)

In spite of the abundance, much of the prawns (shrimp) and squid that are caught in Indonesian waters go to international markets as they is too expensive for locals to afford. However, the tiny shrimp that are not exported are very cheap and are sold in vast quantities in the local markets, destined for a delicious dish of nasi goreng (Indonesian fried rice) or stir-fried water spinach (kangkung). They are also fermented and dried to make the pungent shrimp paste, terasi, which is added to many spice pastes and sambals. In South Sumatra and Kalimantan, the locals enjoy a regular supply of large, juicy river prawns which are often chargrilled with spices.

Prawns have a sweet flavour and turn pink or orange when they are cooked. Buy fresh raw prawns if possible, choosing specimens that are a translucent grey colour tinged with blue. Juicy and meaty, the bigger prawns are often grilled (broiled) whole, or added to stir-fries and curries; the small ones are

Above: Gigantic gigas oysters are now rare in the waters off Indonesia and the Philippines, due to over-harvesting.

dried and added to stocks to enhance the flavour. The small freshwater ones are more delicate and are often steamed briefly, or cooked live in the famous dish called drunken prawns.

SAND LOBSTER

The sand lobster looks like an immature lobster, and has a broad head and tiny claws. Most of the meat is contained within the body section and has much the same delicate, luxurious flavour as normal lobster. When sand lobsters are plentiful, Nonya cooks often use them in place of prawns for spiced or steamed seafood dishes.

MOLLUSCS

Freshly caught molluscs are always sold live and deteriorate rapidly, so cook them as soon as possible after buying. When you are shopping for bivalves such as mussels, clams and oysters, check that they contain sea water and feel heavy for their size. Do not buy any that have broken or gaping shells. When you give them a sharp tap, they should snap shut. If they don't, discard them immediately. Molluscs must be eaten within a day of purchase, but will keep for a few hours in the refrigerator. Put them in a bowl, cover with a damp cloth and keep them in the coldest part of the refrigerator (at 2°C/36°F) until use.

Right: Cockles and mussels are popular bivalves that are farmed and caught wild in Indonesia and the Philippines.

Cockles

These small bivalves are very popular at seafood stalls and are simply boiled and eaten with pungent chilli and vinegar sauces or stir-fried with bagoong in the Philippines. They may contain mud and sand but they will expel this if left overnight in a bucket of sea water or salted water.

Mussels

These are either green lipped or brown with a pale yellow flesh. They are simply steamed or cooked in Chinese wine with garlic and ginger. When buying mussels, allow 450g/1lb per person, as the shells make up much of the weight.

Oysters

Mainly imported from Australia or New Zealand, oysters are more of a Western treat in upmarket seafood places. Those used in omelettes are a smaller variety, or barnacles are sometimes used instead. Oysters can be kept for a couple of days, thanks to the sea water contained in their shells. Store them cupped side down. Never store shellfish in fresh water, or they will die. Ready-frozen bivalves should not be kept in the freezer for more than 2 months.

Scallops

Served steamed with ginger and garlic, scallops make an elegant appetizer. As an exception to the rule about buying fresh molluscs, scallops are often sold already opened and cleaned.

Preparing molluscs

1 Keep the molluscs covered with a damp cloth in the refrigerator until ready to use.

2 Scrub under cold water, using a stiff brush to remove any grit.

3 Tap each shell sharply with a knife. Discard any that do not close. Cook according to recipe, discarding any molluscs that have not opened during cooking.

DRIED AND FERMENTED FISH

Many Indonesian and Filipino cooks still turn up their noses at store-bought stock or seasoning powders, and prefer to boil handfuls of dried shrimps, ikan bilis (sprats or anchovies), cuttlefish or dried scallops to make the requisite stock for noodles and other dishes. Small dried fish and crustaceans are by no means restricted to such a role and are also enjoyed as crunchy snacks or side dishes, chillied or spiced.

DRIED ANCHOVIES

Commonly found in all Chinese and Thai shops, dried anchovies are integral to the cooking of both countries. Sold whole, generally, these finger-length fish are used as stock for seafood dishes, or fried until crispy to be served as a side dish with peanuts and coconut rice. Tossed in a rich chilli sambal, they make a delicious condiment.

Above: Dried anchovies are often munched on as snacks.

DRIED PRAWNS (SHRIMP)

Originating from south India and Sri Lanka, these prized dried shellfish are used in myriad ways, notably in dishes such as Filipino bagoong and Indonesian trasi. They have a rich, salty flavour and a chewy texture, and have to be soaked or boiled briefly to release their distinctive taste. Dried prawns are an important seasoning in many spice blends, especially those meant for seafood curries. They are also added to sambals and condiments. They come in many sizes, some so tiny as to look like

little commas, others 2.5cm/1in long. Matt pink or light tan in colour, they are available in all Asian markets. Stored in an airtight jar, they will keep for months.

DRIED SQUID

An ingredient used in Indonesia and less in the Philippines, dried squid is used as a crunchy addition to Indonesian salads or soaked until soft for Chinese dishes. Grilled (broiled) or roasted, dried squid lends a smoky sweetness and a strong amber colour to soup stocks. When soaked in water with borax powder, the squid turns gelatinous and is sliced up and added to stir-fries or soups. Dried squid are available in most Chinese markets.

SALT FISH

Different types of fish are dried and salted, but the most popular are threadfin.They are generally fried to be eaten with congee (rice porridge) by the Chinese, or added to Filipino and Indonesian stews and stir-fries. Salt fish is available in Asian food markets.

SHRIMP PASTE

Fermented shrimp paste is called terasi in Indonesia and bagoong in the Philippines. Terasi is a traditional condiment essential to practically all Indonesian cooking, and in the Philippines bagoong is used in most savoury dishes. Shrimp paste may be bought in blocks or jars and should be kept refrigerated or in an airtight tub.

Above: Dried squid has a subtle fishy aroma, but a strong flavour.

Using dried prawns
• Used in stocks, dried prawns should be soaked in warm water for 20 minutes or briefly blanched in boiling water if needed as a salad dressing ingredient. This plumps them up and releases their flavour.
• Grind in a pestle and mortar until coarse or fine as required, then toss with lime juice and chilli paste as a pungent dip, or as a flavouring for fried rice.
• Deep-fry them and mix with sliced dried chillies as a crunchy condiment and topping.

Preparing shrimp paste
Shrimp paste can be used straight from the packet if it is to be ground with other herbs and spices and fried, but it should be toasted to temper its raw taste before using in sambals, dressings and salads.

1 Cut off a lump of paste and shape it into a 1cm/½in cube. Mould it on to a metal skewer.

2 Rotate the cube over a low to medium flame, or under an electric grill (broiler), until it begins to char a little along the edges. Ventilate your kitchen to let the strong smell dissipate, as it can linger.

3 Alternatively, wrap the paste in a piece of foil and toast in a hot pan, turning occasionally, or wrap it in a small plastic bag and microwave for 20–30 seconds.

POULTRY

As poultry is so popular in Filipino and Indonesian cooking, there is a thriving commercial industry in designated areas. Chickens and ducks are bred by many rural families and smallholdings, and even in some highly urbanized areas. Many rural families will have a makeshift coop in their backyard where they rear their own chickens, ducks and geese.

In open markets throughout the regions, you can see tricycles and other makeshift modes of transport laden with live birds wending their way through villages and small towns. The dead birds are then brought home, gutted and plunged into boiling water to make the feathers easier to pull off. Small game birds such as quail and squab are also common, often spit-roasted and devoured as a snack. The eggs of all these birds are eaten in a variety of ways.

CHICKEN

Similar to the rest of the world, chickens in major cities of the Philippines and Indonesia are mostly battery reared today, thanks to modern supermarkets and consumer demand. Free-range birds are more expensive and, apart from those bred by rural families, they do not feature much in either Indonesian or Filipino cuisine due to the cost.

DUCK

The rearing of ducks is largely confined to rural communities. Ducks are easy to raise, being foragers needing only table scraps and whatever insects and worms they can find in the soil. In Indonesia, ducks are not only a source of food, but their feathers and down are recycled into bedding and furnishings. Duck is confined to relatively few dishes, such as the Filipino stuffed duck with cabbage (rellenato de pato), Indonesian grilled marinated duck (bebek panggang hijau) and Sumatran duck with chillies (gulai itek), and spicy stews.

GOOSE

Although it is not a common bird in either country, the Chinese, wherever they hang their hats, are past masters at cooking goose. The large bird is braised in a rich broth of soy sauce, sugar, five-spice powder and galangal. It is then sliced and served with a sharp chilli and vinegar sauce and plain rice. Geese are commercially rare and have to be ordered specially from supermarkets.

PIGEON AND QUAIL

Small birds, such as quail and squab, are not very commonly eaten now, but quail's eggs are sold widely in Chinese stores. They usually end up in soups or as an adobo dish such as quail relleno (adobo pugo). They used to be popular

Above: Quail's eggs are a delicacy in the East as much as they are in the West.

as staple Chinese restaurant items, but have become rare. Both birds are excellent when marinated in wine and soy sauce and deep-fried.

EGGS

There is not much one can say about hens' eggs as they are so familiar. Duck eggs, on the other hand, are a delicacy and usually available salted or as century eggs, which are a special treat eaten with pickled ginger. Chinese in origin, salted duck eggs are boiled and eaten with rice congee. They are made by steeping in salted water for a few weeks. Boiled, their whites turn opaque and the yolks a brilliant orange.

Century eggs are made differently, coated with a paste made of mud and rice husks and kept in a dark place for weeks until their whites turn black and their yolks a dull grey. The name century eggs suggests that they are preserved for 100 years. This is a complete myth.

Fertilized duck or hen's eggs that contain the chicken or duck embryo called balut are very much an acquired taste. Filipinos consume them by the thousands as street food, but foreign visitors usually turn their noses up at such fare.

Left: Chicken is usually divided into equal portions on the bone, rather than filleted, before it is cooked in stews or curries. The skin is often left on to keep the meat moist.

MEAT

The consumption of meat varies from region to region, often depending on the dominant faith. In general, meats eaten tend to be related to the restrictions of Islam, Hinduism and Buddhism. Among the Christians and Taoists (ancestor worshippers) there are fewer taboos. Muslims eschew pork, Hindus and devout Buddhists do not eat beef. Pork is therefore more popular in the Philippines, and beef and mutton are the favourite Indonesian meats. The Philippines are predominantly Catholic, with the exception of Western Mindanao, which is mainly Muslim, and share much of their culinary habits with Indonesia and Malaysia.

In Indonesia, most of the people are Muslims, but Hinduism is practised by as many as 93 per cent of the people of Bali, and found in parts of Sumatra, Java, Lombok and Kalimantan.

Above: Oxtail is stewed in one of the most popular Filipino dishes, kare kare.

Officially, only 3 per cent of Indonesians are Hindus, but Indonesian beliefs are too complex to classify as belonging to a single religion. In Java, a substantial number of Muslims follow a non-orthodox, Hindu-influenced form of Islam known as 'Islam Abangan' or 'Islam Kejawèn', while across the archipelago the Hindu legacy, along with the other mystic traditions, influences popular beliefs and cuisine.

LAMB, BEEF AND MUTTON

Beef is enjoyed in both Indonesia and the Philippines, apart from in Hindu Bali and among Buddhists. Much of the beef eaten in Indonesia comes from water buffalo meat, in long-cooked, dry

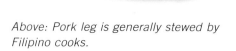

Above: Spare ribs are enjoyed marinated in sticky sauce and barbecued.

curries such as rendang, kormas and smoor dishes, while in the Philippines, a lot of beef is imported from New Zealand and Australia. Filipino beef cooking is generally influenced by Spanish, Mexican and American styles, with beef stew (caldereta), steak (bistek), stuffed beef roll (morcon) and the ubiquitous oxtail stew (kare kare). Beef satay is popular throughout Indonesia and in the Philippines as a staple barbecue item. Lamb and mutton are not widely available in either of the regions and therefore not often consumed; invariably goat meat is more easily available and cheaper.

PORK

Filipino and Balinese chefs have myriad ways to cook pork. Lechon and guleng are classic examples of traditional Filipino and Balinese festive dishes, whole suckling pigs (guleng or guleng celeng) being the offering. This is an iconic Balinese dish, much revered as a festive item. A whole baby pig (suckling) weighing about 8kg/18lb is marinated in a host of spices and roasted on hot charcoal until a rosy red with crisp crackling skin. It is believed to have originated in Polynesia centuries ago when whole pigs were roasted on hot coals at *al fresco* feasts (*luau*).

Types of pork cuts in both countries are quite different from the Western form and lean more towards the Chinese choices. Leg of pork is preferred for stews, and belly for stock and grills, stir-fries and other adobo and curry dishes.

In the Philippines, fillets are generally roasted or stewed in adobos, while in non-Muslim Indonesia, they usually end up in satays and curries. Virtually every part of the pig is eaten and offal is highly popular in sambals and curries.

Pork products

Minced (ground) pork is used to make meatballs and fillings for other recipes; it is also added to porridge for late-night supper dishes.

Indigenous Filipino pork and liver sausages are very popular and eaten as snacks. In non-Muslim Java, they are made into long sausages called celeng, often spiced and fried or steamed. They look much like Western sausages. Pork skin ends up fried as lard chips for garnish, or in the Philippines, processed as crackling for a popular snack.

Filipino lechon (liver sauce) is a classic accompaniment to many dishes, and other offal such as tripe, lungs and kidneys are enjoyed, especially with spicy treatments in Javanese cooking.

Tosino

Probably the most high profile and universally loved pork dish in the Philippines, tosino is roast belly or shoulder of pork seasoned with vinegar, sugar and salt in the Spanish style. Other variations imitate the Cantonese roast pork and include sweet hoisin sauce as a marinade ingredient.

Above: Pork leg is generally stewed by Filipino cooks.

HERBS AND SPICES

Integral to all Asian cooking, ground up in complex blends or used as top notes in curries, soups and stir-fries, herbs and spices play fundamental roles in Indonesian cooking, and to a lesser extent, in Filipino cuisine. Within the plethora of dried whole spices, powders and fresh herbs, the permutations are endless. Subtle, pungent or heady fresh herbs such as basil, lemon grass, coriander (cilantro), mint, chillies, lime leaves, ginger and other esoterics are reputed to have medicinal and restorative properties.

Dried spice powders such as coriander, cumin, fenugreek, aniseed, turmeric and chilli all find a place within the spectrum of spicy cooking. Other flavouring ingredients include tamarind both fresh and dried, in pastes and concentrates, sesame seeds, dried lily buds, sugar cane, palm sugar (jaggery) and limes. The use of herbs in the preparation of curry pastes and sambals is not an exact science. It is learned by experience.

Many of the spices and herbs in the region have been around for centuries, since the Portuguese first came to the seaport of Malacca, bringing with them many unheard-of ingredients from South and Central America. Today they are grown in every home vegetable plot, market farm, hillside and backyard throughout the region. Indeed, many a dish would be a pale shadow of itself but for a herb or two, chopped, torn or added to curries in the last minute to impart their unique, and often elusive, perfumes.

Above: Kaffir lime leaves have a strong and wonderfully zesty fragrance.

Above: The fresh flavour of mint complements many Asian dishes.

FRESH HERBS

Essential for giving a wonderful aroma and explosion of flavour to many dishes.

Laksa leaves

With the botanical name of polygonum, this fragrant leaf has been adopted by Filipinos and Indonesians and is almost *de rigueur* in Indonesian curries, as well as the laksas that gave it its common name. Small, thin leaves jut from slender stalks that have a distinct lemony perfume with hints of coriander, mint and basil. Indeed, a variety grown in Vietnam known as rau rum is also called Vietnamese coriander or mint.

Lime leaves

Also known as kaffir lime leaves, these are native to the Indonesian culinary heritage. Grown widely in all tropical regions, the plant is used mainly for its leaves, which have a distinctive citrus perfume when crushed. Each leaf is shaped like a guitar or figure eight. The fruit is walnut-sized, with a gnarled, bright green skin.

Mint

The most commonly used mint in these two countries is similar to the garden peppermint of the West. It is furry-leaved with a sweet flavour. It is used in salads and as a garnish, often in combination with basil and coriander. There are numerous varieties of mint, including spearmint and peppermint,

Above: Holy basil has a distinct and delicious flavour. It is well worth cultivating a plant on your windowsill.

differing widely in size, shape and flavour. The mint leaves sold in supermarkets work well as a substitute.

Pandan leaf

Popular in both Indonesia and the Philippines, screwpine, commonly known as pandan leaf, grows like a weed in tropical climes. Used as much for its green colouring as for its perfume, pandan leaf imparts a distinctive, vanilla-like scent to puddings. It is also used as a natural wrapper for deep-frying. The long, narrow leaves are knotted or bruised to release their unique flavour before use. The leaves are available fresh or dried in some Asian markets. Some stores also stock pandan extract, but if you can't find either, you could use vanilla pods (beans) instead.

Holy basil

The basil family is large and diverse, encompassing different shapes, sizes, colours and aromatic nuances. The most common varieties found in Asia are Thai sweet basil, holy basil and lemon basil. Thai sweet has the broadest range: aromatically similar to anise, it is mild enough to be eaten as a salad vegetable. In Indonesian cooking, basil is almost always used raw, sprinkled on noodle soups, tossed in salads or added to curries. Asian basil is found in Asian markets, but the sweet Mediterranean basil found in all supermarkets can be substituted.

Above: Chinese chives have a good flavour and make a pretty garnish.

Chives

Across Asia, chives are found in three forms: green chives, with flat stems and slim-bladed leaves; yellow, the same grown under a cloche, which explains its pallor; and Chinese flowering, whose sturdier round leaves are tipped by pointed pale green buds, like little unopened flowers. All have a mild spring onion (scallion) flavour with a hint of garlic.

Coriander (cilantro)

Originally from Central Asia, and ubiquitous in most tropical and temperate countries' cuisines, coriander is the most common culinary herb, especially the seeds, which are ground into powder as a key ingredient in curries. The perfumed leaves are used liberally, especially in soups, pancit dishes, dumpling mixes and garnishes. Bunches of fresh leaves are available in many Asian markets.

Salam leaves (Indonesian bay leaves)

Also known as Indonesian laurel, this herb is not actually a member of the bay family. It can be used fresh or dry and is often added to soups or steamed dishes. Available in Asian stores.

Curry leaves

Very much an Indian herb, curry leaves have diamond-shaped leaves that are tough, bottle-green and hang in even rows from thin stems. They have a warm, peppery scent with citrus notes when crushed. They add a distinct flavour to seafood curries, chutneys, rasams (sour soups) and relishes. They are more often used in Indonesia than in the Philippines because of the former's Hindu heritage.

CHILLIES

Both fresh and dried chillies are used with abandon in Indonesian food and to a lesser extent in Filipino cooking. Most pastes would use dried chillies as they have a more intense red colour, while fresh chillies are the norm for delicate seafood curries, salads and as a dip with soy sauce. There are many types of chillies, their fire ranging from barely-there to flaming inferno! Green ones are often eaten raw like a vegetable.

Thai bird chillies

These tiny pods have a fire that is disproportionate to their size. They come in many colours, ranging from pale yellow to green, orange and bright red, and are best seeded as the seeds are overpoweringly hot. Only two or three Thai bird chillies are sufficient to give incendiary fire to curries and soups. They are available fresh and dried in Asian stores and most supermarkets.

Dried chillies

These are also used to make chilli oil, by infusing them in palm or grape seed oil. Dried chillies can be bought whole, or chopped, in Asian stores and some supermarkets. For complex curry pastes, they are preferred to fresh chilli. If kept in a dry, cool place, dried chillies have a long shelf life.

Chilli powder

This fiery, deep-red powder is made by finely grinding dried red chillies. Any chilli can be used but the hottest powder is made from the dried Thai bird chillies.

Preparing dried chillies

1 Remove the stems and seeds with a knife. Cut into pieces and place in a bowl.

2 Pour over hot water and leave to soak for about 30 minutes. Drain and use according to the recipe.

Left: Green chillies may be fiery hot but are often munched as a vegetable.

Above: Cardamom seeds add a highly distinctive scent to curries.

Above: Bundles of cinnamon can be bought cheaply in Asian markets.

Above: Cloves add warm flavour to many curries, stews and desserts.

Chilli paste

This is made by grinding red chillies, seeded or otherwise, into a fine paste. Whether you add ground garlic, ginger or aromatics depends on what the paste is going to be used for. Oil is added if you want a smooth consistency. Versatile and popular, it is used to season sauces, added to curry pastes, or as a condiment to salads, relishes and dips for fried snacks. Ready-made chilli paste is sold in jars in Asian markets.

DRY SPICES AND HERBS

These store cupboard staples give the essential warmth and depth of flavour.

Agar agar

Not strictly a spice or herb, agar agar, known by the same generic name in both countries, nevertheless plays an important role in Filipino and Indonesian kitchens. Similar to gelatine, agar agar is a gum that is extracted from dried

seaweed and processed into white translucent sticks, or ground to a powder. Once dissolved in boiling water, it turns to jelly and is widely used in jellied desserts. Agar agar is available in stick or powder form in Asian stores.

Cardamom

Grown widely in the Middle East, India and Nepal, cardamoms come in two varieties – large black and small green pods. They play an important role as a peppery note in rice dishes, soups and curries. Black cardamoms are used sparingly as they are hard to come by. Green cardamoms are added whole to a range of curries but must be discarded before serving as they are not edible as such, only used for their spicy aroma.

Cinnamon

A member of the cassia family, the cinnamon tree is grown widely in the Himalayas, Sri Lanka, China and South-

east Asia. The most common type is the bark of the Chinese cinnamon, which is thick, rich in oils and a deep brown colour. A pungent ingredient with constituents of volatile oil, cinnamon is added to soups and rice dishes and some cakes. It is widely available.

Cloves

This spice has been known worldwide since the 5th century and is produced on a large scale in Indonesia. It is used primarily as a culinary herb in soups, cakes and stews. It has a distinctive liquorice flavour and is available in most Indian stores and supermarkets.

Sesame seeds

These tiny white or black seeds are commonly used in many Indonesian, Filipino and Chinese dishes. They have a subtle nutty flavour and are often used to coat meats for deep-frying, or are sprinkled on stir-fries. Ground up and cooked with sugar as a thick gruel, sesame seeds are a favourite snack.

Star anise

Also known as Chinese anise, this is the dried, star-shaped fruit of a slender evergreen tree that grows in China, India and Japan, where the bark is ground to powder and burnt as incense in temples. Not related to aniseed, star anise imparts a strong liquorice flavour and is often used with cloves in aromatic soups and curries. Whole, or crushed, star anise is one of the principal ingredients in five-spice powder. It is available from Asian stores and some supermarkets, sold whole or as a powder.

Left: Star anise imparts good flavour to savoury dishes and looks attractive, but is too tough and woody to be eaten.

AROMATICS AND ROOT HERBS

These are the base ingredients of many spice pastes, marinades and sauces.

Garlic

Highly prized for more than 5000 years, garlic is a member of the onion genus. Each bulb can contain up to 10 cloves, which should be firm with a pungent aroma and flavour. Chopped or crushed, garlic is fried in oil to impart flavour to stir-fries, curries, stews and noodles. It is also used raw to flavour pickles, dips, marinades and sauces. Garlic is thought to be good for the heart. It is available in Asian stores and all supermarkets.

Galangal

Although a member of the ginger family and similar in appearance, galangal is never eaten raw. Its aroma and flavour are best used in tandem with shallots, garlic and chillies in spice pastes and in marinades. The roots can be sliced or bruised and added to soups and curries to impart a more subtle flavour. When young, the rhizomes are creamy pink in colour and have a lemony flavour; the more mature roots are golden and peppery. Fresh galangal will keep for about one week if sealed in a plastic bag and refrigerated. It can also be frozen. Both dried and bottled galangal purée (paste) are available from Asian stores.

Lesser galangal

These little fingers of dark brown ginger are an important herb in Indonesia, often replacing ordinary ginger and

Above: Shallots give a sweet and subtle flavour to wet spice blends.

galangal in spice mixes. Lesser galangal has a faint anise flavour and a strong after taste, and is best used fairly cautiously for this reason.

Ginger

Indigenous to most of South-east Asia, ginger is the oldest and most widely used flavouring across the Asian region, especially in Indian and Indonesian cooking. A herbaceous perennial plant, ginger is knobbly-looking with a smooth, beige skin, and is sold as two types. Young, pale yellow ginger is fresh-looking and tender with a slightly sweet pungency and can be chopped or shredded for stir-fries, stews, rice,

pickles, steamed dishes and puddings. Older ginger is more fibrous and is usually ground into spice blends or pickled as a relish.

Well-documented in traditional Chinese medicine and Indian Ayurvedic practice for its carminative and expectorant action, ginger is believed to be good for alleviating motion sickness and bronchial problems. Fresh ginger is readily available in Asian stores and supermarkets. Choose smooth, plump roots and store in a cool, dry place.

Lemon grass

A woody, fibrous stalk, lemon grass is used throughout all South-east Asian culinary cultures. It imparts a fragrant, citrus flavour to dishes. The pale yellowish-green, paper-like sheath that encases it has to be removed before use. The root end is chopped, pounded or crushed before being added to spice blends, stir-fries, curries and marinades. Lemon grass is one of the principal ingredients in Indonesian cooking but is used sparingly in Filipino cooking. It is available fresh and dried in Asian stores and some supermarkets.

Shallots

These small, marble-sized bulbs form the basis of many spice blends and when deep-fried in oil make a crunchy garnish in many Indonesian and Filipino soups and stews. Green onions, the stems of shallots, appear in many dishes and are often chopped and used as a garnish, added to lumpia and other

Above: Fat bulbs of garlic are a kitchen essential for most cuisines.

Above: Galangal is similar to ginger but has a more specifically 'Asian' flavour.

Above: A piece of fresh root ginger gives heat and flavour to many dishes.

snacks and stir-fries at the last minute. Green onions and spring onions (scallions), which do not mature into shallots, are often confused and have the same culinary uses.

Turmeric

Fresh turmeric root has a subtle, earthy taste and imparts a vivid colour and flavour to spice blends. It may also be dried and ground to a deep-yellow powder that imparts good colour and only a slight hint of flavour. Both fresh and dried are found in Asian markets.

OTHER STORE CUPBOARD ESSENTIALS

These ingredients are useful to keep in supply for the recipes in this book.

Bean sauces

Condiments made from soya beans that have been fermented and puréed come in various guises. Yellow beans are processed into a sauce called taucheo, which is often served on its own or mixed with other ingredients to make a dip. Black beans are made into black bean sauce, a staple in Cantonese cooking. Salty and pungent, bean sauces are used as full-bodied seasonings much like soy sauce, but with more flavour.

Oyster sauce

This thick, brown sauce is known by its common English name in the Philippines. Made from dried oyster extract, sugar, water and salt, strongly flavoured and salty, it is used as a complete seasoning, obviating the need for salt in stir-fries. It is an import into Indonesia and the Philippines, being a resoundingly Cantonese product. It makes a good seasoning for soups and stews and is widely available in Asian stores and good supermarkets.

Palm sugar (jaggery)

Widely used in South-east Asia, palm sugar is extracted from the sap of various palm trees, mostly the coconut. In the Philippines, apart from palm sugar, the favoured sweetener is usually muscovado or sangkaka, a solid brown cake made from molasses. There are several types used in Indonesian cooking. One is dark brown and comes in little can-shaped cylinders, and

Above: A block of palm sugar, which can be shaved or melted as required.

another is in the form of round cakes of a pale peach colour. There's also a thick liquid version in cans that is easier to use. Solid palm sugar has to be scraped, shredded or melted before use. Indian grocers sell another type called jaggery that is basically similar but comes in rough nuggets or cakes. It is indispensable in Indonesian desserts and puddings. Available in Indian, Malaysian and Thai stores.

Sesame oil

Extracted from the seeds, sesame oil is commonly used in stir-fried dishes. Two types are available: plain, pale golden oil, which is mildly nutty and good for frying; and the darker, richer tasting oil made from roasted sesame seeds and usually added in small quantities as a top note just before serving.

Soy sauce

Probably the most commonly used sauce throughout Asia and the Philippines is soy sauce in its various guises. Made from fermented soya beans, wheat and yeast, soy sauce may be light, dark or with mushroom flavouring. Dark soy is used as a marinade for its mahogany colour as well as its saltiness. Light soy sauce is used like salt and has a tantalizing flavour when mixed with lime juice and

chillies as a dip. Naturally fermented soy sauce will not keep forever, but does have a fairly long shelf-life.

Tamarind

A legume tree grown widely in tropical savannas in Africa, India and Malaysia, tamarind bears brittle long brown pods. Each pod may contain 5–10 seeds joined by tough fibres in a mass of sweetish, acid brown pulp. It is this that features widely in Indonesian curries – local vinegar (suka) is the alternative used in Filipino sour dishes. Tamarind comes in various forms: blocks of paste with seeds in it; a dried pod; or processed as a thick concentrate. The fresh pods and dried pulp are available from Asian stores. Easier to find and use are the tubs of tamarind concentrate, which is simply diluted in water to give the sour fruitiness to dishes. Tamarind is available in most Indian greengrocers and some South-east Asian markets.

Preparing tamarind from paste
Many recipes from Indonesia and other areas of South-east Asia will call for tamarind, so it is worth obtaining a tamarind block and having it as a store cupboard staple. You will need warm water and a nylon sieve (strainer) to prepare it.

1 Crumble 300g/11oz of the block and mix with 500ml/17fl oz/ 2 generous cups water. Strain through a fine sieve to obtain a sour, dark brown liquid. Store in a screw-top jar.

2 Add as much tamarind solution as taste dictates to fish and shellfish curries, using a clean spoon to scoop it out each time to avoid contamination.

SOUPS AND
SOUPY STEWS

Many dishes featured here are meals in themselves — satisfying,

warming bowls of meat, seafood and vegetables, bathed in spicy,

fragrant broth. If you are serving one of these dishes as an

appetizer, small portions with colourful garnishes are ideal;

if the soup is the main feature of the meal, then ladle plenty

into each bowl and enjoy it with crusty bread or a side dish of

rice to soak up the flavours.

UNRIPE PAPAYA SOUP

THIS IS A LIGHTLY-SPICED AND HERBY SOUP FROM INDONESIA THAT MAKES GOOD USE OF UNRIPE PAPAYA AND IS AN IDEAL START TO ANY MEAL. IT IS THE KIND OF SOUP MEANT TO PREPARE THE TASTEBUDS FOR WHAT IS YET TO COME — LIGHT AND REFRESHING TO THE PALATE.

SERVES FOUR

INGREDIENTS
  1 unripe papaya, about 800g/1¾lb
  45ml/3 tbsp vegetable oil
  1 litre/1¾ pints/4 cups water
  4 salam leaves (Indonesian bay
    leaves) or sweet basil leaves
  2 lemon grass stalks, 5cm/2in of root
    end bruised
  2.5ml/½ tsp ground black pepper
  5ml/1 tsp salt
  fried shallots or serundeng, to garnish
For the spice paste
  2 lemon grass stalks, 5cm/2in of root
    end finely chopped
  6 shallots, finely chopped
  5 garlic cloves, finely chopped
  10g/¼oz galangal
  15g/½oz terasi (Indonesian
    shrimp paste)
  2.5ml/½ tsp turmeric powder
  4 fresh red chillies, seeded and
    finely chopped
  5ml/1 tsp coriander seeds
  10g/¼oz kencur root (lesser galangal)

1 Grind the spice paste ingredients to a textured paste using a pestle and mortar or an electric food processor or blender.

2 Peel the papaya with a vegetable peeler and slice into two lengthways. Discard any soft pulp and seeds.

3 Slice the papaya into long strips and then crosswise into pieces about 5mm/¼in thick.

COOK'S TIP
It can be difficult to find salam leaves outside of large Asian markets, but fresh bay leaves will work in this recipe and may be used instead.

4 Heat the oil and fry the spice paste over a low heat for 10 minutes, stirring constantly until the fragrances are released and the oil separates.

5 Bring the water to the boil and stir in the fried spice paste. Simmer for 3 minutes.

6 Add the papaya slices, salam leaves, lemon grass, pepper and salt. Cook for 5–8 minutes until the papaya slices are just tender.

7 While the papaya is cooking, prepare your garnishes of fried sliced shallots or serundeng and warm the soup bowls.

8 Take the papaya soup off the heat. Adjust the seasoning if necessary and serve it in individual bowls, garnished as you wish.

Per Portion Energy 189kcal/791kJ; Protein 5.1g; Carbohydrate 21.8g, of which sugars 18.8g; Fat 9.8g, of which saturates 1.1g; Cholesterol 19mg; Calcium 137mg; Fibre 5.2g; Sodium 181mg.

PUMPKIN, BEAN AND BAMBOO SOUP WITH COCONUT

THIS TASTY SOUP IS FROM JAVA, WHERE IT IS SERVED ON ITS OWN WITH RICE OR AS AN ACCOMPANIMENT TO A POACHED OR GRILLED FISH DISH. IN SOME PARTS OF JAVA, THE DISH INCLUDES SMALL PRAWNS BUT, IF IT IS PACKED WITH VEGETABLES ALONE, IT MAKES AN EXTREMELY SATISFYING VEGETARIAN MEAL. GENERALLY, THIS SOUP IS ACCOMPANIED BY A CHILLI SAMBAL, WHICH CAN BE MADE BY POUNDING CHILLIES WITH SHRIMP PASTE AND LIME JUICE, OR WITH GINGER AND GARLIC.

SERVES FOUR TO SIX

INGREDIENTS
    30ml/2 tbsp palm, groundnut
      (peanut) or corn oil
    150g/5oz pumpkin flesh
    115g/4oz yard-long beans, cut in
      pieces
    220g/7¾oz can bamboo shoots,
      drained and rinsed
    900ml/1½ pints/3¾ cups coconut milk
    10ml/2 tsp palm sugar (jaggery)
    130g/4½oz fresh coconut, grated
    salt
For the spice paste
    4 shallots, chopped
    25g/1oz fresh root ginger, chopped
    4 fresh red chillies, seeded
      and chopped
    2 garlic cloves, chopped
    5ml/1 tsp coriander seeds
    4 candlenuts, toasted and chopped
To serve
    cooked rice
    chilli sambal

1 Grind the spice paste ingredients to a textured paste using a pestle and mortar or an electric food processor or blender.

2 Heat the oil in a wok or large, heavy pan, stir in the spice paste and fry until fragrant. Toss the pumpkin, yard-long beans and bamboo shoots in the paste and pour in the coconut milk. Add the sugar and bring to the boil.

3 Reduce the heat and cook gently for 5–10 minutes, until the vegetables are just tender.

4 Season the soup with salt to taste and stir in half the fresh coconut. Place the cooked rice in individual warmed bowls, then ladle the soup over the top, sprinkle with the remaining coconut and serve with a chilli sambal.

COOK'S TIP
Bamboo shoots are available in cans in most Chinese and South-east Asian markets and stores, as well as being sold in large supermarkets.

VARIATION
When pumpkins are not in season, use a different member of the squash family, such as butternut squash or acorn squash, for a change of flavour.

Per Portion Energy 333kcal/1388kJ; Protein 6g; Carbohydrate 26g, of which sugars 23.8g; Fat 23.6g, of which saturates 11.7g; Cholesterol 0mg; Calcium 115mg; Fibre 4.9g; Sodium 258mg.

CORN, TAPIOCA AND PUMPKIN SOUP WITH FRESH BASIL LEAVES

IN RURAL AREAS OF SULAWESI, WHERE FARMING IS THE MAIN INDUSTRY, THE WORKING DAY BEGINS AT THE CRACK OF DAWN. THIS IS AN EASY-TO-COOK DISH FROM THE REGION THAT IS BOTH NOURISHING AND DELICIOUS BECAUSE OF THE TAPIOCA AND PUMPKIN. IT IS A SOUP THAT CAN BE PREPARED THE NIGHT BEFORE AND QUICKLY WARMED UP FOR A CONVENIENT AND SATISFYING SNACK.

1 Steam the tapioca and pumpkin for 15 minutes until soft. Meanwhile, bring the water to the boil, add the rice and cook for 10 minutes.

2 Cut the tapioca into smaller chunks and add to the rice and water with the pumpkin, lemon grass and corn. Cook for 10 minutes, stirring until all the ingredients form a thick consistency.

3 Add the basil leaves, spinach and salt and pepper. Taste and adjust the seasoning if necessary. Serve the soup piping hot.

COOK'S TIPS
• Tapioca is sold at many Asian, Chinese and Caribbean stores. It has a dark brown skin and pale white flesh. Use frozen or processed tapioca for this soup if the fresh version is unavailable.
• After step 2, you can chill or freeze the soup for another time. Just add the final ingredients at serving time.

SERVES FOUR TO SIX

INGREDIENTS
    115g/4oz tapioca flesh, chopped
    115g/4oz pumpkin or butternut
      squash flesh, chopped
    800ml/28fl oz/3¼ cups water
    30ml/2 tbsp rice
    2 lemon grass stalks, 5cm/2in of root
      end bruised
    60ml/4 tbsp corn kernels
    10 sweet basil leaves
    75g/3oz spinach
    5ml/1 tsp salt
    2.5ml/½ tsp ground black pepper

Per Portion Energy 89kcal/379kJ; Protein 0.6g; Carbohydrate 22.6g, of which sugars 0.3g; Fat 0.1g, of which saturates 0g; Cholesterol 0mg; Calcium 8mg; Fibre 0.3g; Sodium 1mg.

SPICY AUBERGINE SOUP
WITH BEEF AND LIME

A DELICIOUS SOUPY STEW FROM NORTH SUMATRA, THIS DISH CAN BE MADE WITH AUBERGINES, GREEN JACKFRUIT OR ANY OF THE SQUASH FAMILY. FOR AN AUTHENTIC MEAL, SERVE THE SOUP WITH A BOWL OF RICE AND A CHILLI SAMBAL, BEARING IN MIND THAT THE QUANTITY OF RICE SHOULD BE GREATER THAN THE SOUPY STEW, AS THE ROLE OF THE SOUP IS TO MOISTEN AND FLAVOUR THE RICE.

SERVES FOUR

INGREDIENTS
    30ml/2 tbsp palm, groundnut
      (peanut) or corn oil
    150g/5oz lean beef, cut into
      thin strips
    500ml/17fl oz/2 cups
      coconut milk
    10ml/2 tsp sugar
    3–4 Thai aubergines (eggplants) or
      1 large Mediterranean aubergine,
      cut into wedges
    3–4 kaffir lime leaves
    juice of 1 lime
    salt
For the spice paste
    4 shallots, chopped
    4 fresh red Thai chillies, seeded
      and chopped
    25g/1oz fresh root
      ginger, chopped
    15g/½oz fresh turmeric, chopped,
      or 2.5ml/½ tsp ground turmeric
    2 garlic cloves, chopped
    5ml/1 tsp coriander seeds
    2.5ml/½ tsp cumin seeds
    2–3 candlenuts
To serve
    cooked rice
    1 lime, quartered (optional)
    chilli sambal (optional)

1 Grind the spice paste ingredients to a coarse paste using a pestle and mortar or an electric food processor or blender.

2 Heat the oil in a wok or heavy pan, stir in the spice paste and fry until fragrant. Add the beef, stirring to coat it well in the spice paste, then add the coconut milk and sugar. Bring the liquid to the boil, then reduce the heat and simmer gently for 10 minutes.

3 Add the aubergine wedges and kaffir lime leaves to the pan and cook gently for a further 5–10 minutes, until tender but not mushy. Stir in the lime juice and season with salt to taste.

4 Ladle the soup into individual warmed bowls and serve with bowls of cooked rice to spoon the soup over, wedges of lime to squeeze on the top and a chilli sambal to eat alongside, if you like.

Per Portion Energy 224kcal/938kJ; Protein 12.1g; Carbohydrate 14.6g, of which sugars 12.6g; Fat 13.6g, of which saturates 3.2g; Cholesterol 22mg; Calcium 79mg; Fibre 3g; Sodium 181mg.

CORN AND CRAB SOUP

THIS DISH IS BELIEVED TO HAVE ORIGINATED IN JAVA, WHERE AT SOME TIME IT WAS COPIED FROM THE CHINESE IMMIGRANTS. IT IS NOW A WELL-LOVED SOUP THROUGHOUT THE ISLANDS, EATEN WHENEVER CORN AND CRAB ARE PLENTIFUL. IT MAKES A DELICIOUS APPETIZER, OR A LIGHT LUNCH WITH RICE OR BREAD.

SERVES FOUR

INGREDIENTS
    750ml/1¼ pints/3 cups water
    1 seafood stock cube
    450g/1lb can creamed corn
    5ml/1 tsp salt
    15ml/1 tbsp sesame oil
    250g/9oz crab meat
    2 eggs
    2 spring onions (scallions),
      trimmed and sliced, to garnish
    black vinegar, to serve

2 Simmer for 5 minutes, then add the crab meat and cook for 3 minutes.

1 Combine all the ingredients except for the crab meat and eggs in a pan and bring to the boil.

3 Lightly beat the eggs and add to the barely simmering soup, stirring quickly to distribute the egg evenly and thicken the soup.

4 Adjust the seasoning and serve garnished with spring onions, with a dish of black vinegar on the side.

COOK'S TIPS
• Nothing quite matches the flavour of fresh crab, but Scandinavian canned crab is an acceptable substitute when the fresh variety is not available.
• Use regular corn and add a dash of cream or coconut cream if you cannot obtain creamed corn.
• Black vinegar is made from fermented rice, millet, wheat, sorghum and barley. Its flavour varies from region to region.

Per Portion Energy 279kcal/1173kJ; Protein 18.6g; Carbohydrate 29.9g, of which sugars 10.8g; Fat 10.3g, of which saturates 1.9g; Cholesterol 140mg; Calcium 19mg; Fibre 1.6g; Sodium 1093mg.

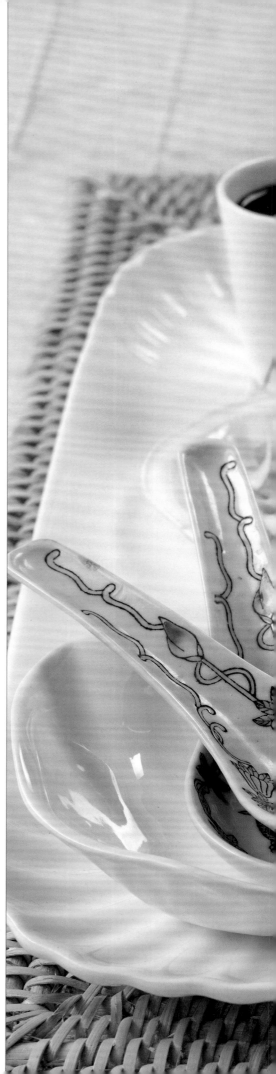

Hot <u>and</u> Sour Filipino Fish Soup

Chunky, filling and satisfying, the Filipino fish soups are meals in themselves. There are many variations on the theme, depending on the region and the local fish, but most are packed with shellfish, flavoured with sour tamarind combined with hot chilli, and served with coconut vinegar flavoured with garlic. Served on its own or with rice, this soup certainly awakens the senses!

SERVES FOUR TO SIX

INGREDIENTS
  2 litres/3½ pints/8 cups fish stock
  250ml/8fl oz/1 cup white wine
  15–30ml/1–2 tbsp tamarind paste
  30–45ml/2–3 tbsp patis (Filipino
    fish sauce)
  30ml/2 tbsp palm sugar (jaggery)
  50g/2oz fresh root ginger, grated
  2–3 fresh red or green chillies,
    seeded and finely sliced
  2 tomatoes, skinned, seeded and cut
    into wedges
  350g/12oz fresh fish, such as trout,
    sea bass, swordfish or cod,
    cut into bitesize chunks
  12–16 fresh prawns (shrimp),
    in their shells
  1 bunch fresh basil leaves,
    roughly chopped
  1 bunch fresh flat leaf parsley,
    roughly chopped
  salt and ground black pepper
To serve
  60–90ml/4–6 tbsp suka (Filipino
    coconut vinegar)
  1–2 garlic cloves, finely chopped
  1–2 limes, cut into wedges
  2 fresh red or green chillies, seeded
    and quartered lengthways

COOK'S TIP
You can shell the prawns (shrimp) if you prefer, as it makes the soup easier to eat, but cooking them in their shells adds depth to the flavour of the broth.

1 In a wok or large pan, bring the stock and wine to the boil. Stir in the tamarind paste, patis, sugar, ginger and chillies. Reduce the heat and simmer for 15–20 minutes.

2 Add the tomatoes to the broth and season with salt and pepper. Add the fish and prawns and simmer for a further 5 minutes, until the fish is cooked.

3 Meanwhile, in a bowl, quickly mix together the suka and garlic for serving and put aside.

4 Stir half the basil and half the parsley into the broth and ladle into bowls.

5 Garnish with the remaining basil and parsley and serve immediately, with the spiked suka to splash on top, the lime wedges to squeeze into the soup, and the chillies to chew on for extra heat.

Per Portion Energy 137kcal/576kJ; Protein 17.7g; Carbohydrate 8.1g, of which sugars 8g; Fat 1g, of which saturates 0.1g; Cholesterol 92mg; Calcium 76mg; Fibre 1.3g; Sodium 644mg.

SPICY TRIPE SOUP <u>WITH</u> LEMON GRASS <u>AND</u> LIME

THIS POPULAR INDONESIAN SOUP IS PACKED WITH SPICES AND THE REFRESHING FLAVOURS OF LEMON GRASS AND LIME. STEAMING BOWLS OF SOTO BABAT ARE SOUGHT-AFTER AT FOOD STALLS AS A GREAT PICK-ME-UP. THE LOCALS PREFER THEIR TRIPE TO BE CHEWY FOR THIS SPICY SOUP, WHICH IS SERVED WITH A PUNGENT CHILLI SAMBAL, BUT IF YOU PREFER, YOU CAN COOK IT FOR LONGER SO THAT THE TRIPE IS TENDER.

SERVES FOUR

INGREDIENTS
- 250ml/8fl oz/1 cup rice wine vinegar
- 900g/2lb beef tripe, cleaned
- 2 litres/3½ pints/8 cups beef stock or water
- 2–3 garlic cloves, crushed
- 2 lemon grass stalks, lightly crushed with a mallet or rolling pin
- 25g/1oz fresh root ginger, grated
- 3–4 kaffir lime leaves
- 225g/8oz mooli (daikon) or turnip, finely sliced
- 15ml/1 tbsp palm, groundnut (peanut) or vegetable oil
- 4 shallots, finely sliced
- salt and ground black pepper

For the sambal
- 15ml/1 tbsp palm, groundnut (peanut) or vegetable oil
- 2 garlic cloves, crushed
- 2–3 fresh hot red chillies, seeded and finely chopped
- 15ml/1 tbsp Chilli and Shrimp Paste (see Essential Recipes)
- 2.5ml/5 tsp tomato purée (paste)

1 Fill a large pan with about 2.5 litres/4½ pints/11¼ cups water and bring it to the boil. Reduce the heat and stir in the vinegar. Add the tripe, season with salt and pepper and simmer on a low heat for about 1 hour.

2 Meanwhile, prepare the sambal. Heat the oil in a small, heavy pan. Stir in the garlic and chillies and fry until fragrant. Stir in the chilli and shrimp paste, then add the tomato purée and mix until thoroughly combined. Tip the paste into a small dish and put aside.

3 When the tripe is cooked, drain and cut into bitesize squares or strips. Pour the stock or water into a large pan and bring it to the boil. Reduce the heat and add the tripe, garlic, lemon grass, ginger, lime leaves and mooli or turnip.

4 Cook gently for 15–20 minutes, until the mooli or turnip is tender. (For tender tripe, omit the mooli or turnip at this stage, simmer the tripe for 4–5 hours and then add the mooli or turnip for the last 15 minutes of cooking.)

5 Meanwhile, heat the oil in a small frying pan. Add the shallots and fry for about 5 minutes until golden brown. Drain on kitchen paper.

6 Ladle the soup into individual warmed bowls and sprinkle the shallots over the top. Serve the soup with the spicy sambal, which can be added in a spoonful and stirred in or served in a bowl on the side, according to individual taste.

Per Portion Energy 160kcal/668kJ; Protein 19.2g; Carbohydrate 5.5g, of which sugars 4.8g; Fat 7g, of which saturates 1.1g; Cholesterol 163mg; Calcium 198mg; Fibre 1.9g; Sodium 299mg.

INDONESIAN CHICKEN BROTH

THIS IS PERHAPS THE MOST POPULAR OF ALL INDONESIAN SOUPS. THROUGHOUT SOUTH-EAST ASIA YOU WILL FIND VARIATIONS OF THIS SOUP; EVEN IN INDONESIA IT VARIES FROM REGION TO REGION, SUCH AS THE BALI VERSION THAT INCLUDES NOODLES INSTEAD OF POTATOES. COLOURFUL AND CRUNCHY, THIS CLASSIC SOUP CAN BE SERVED AS AN APPETIZER OR AS A LIGHT AND REFRESHING DISH ON ITS OWN.

SERVES FOUR TO SIX

INGREDIENTS
  30ml/2 tbsp palm, groundnut
    (peanut) or corn oil
  25g/1oz fresh root ginger,
    finely chopped
  25g/1oz fresh turmeric,
    finely chopped, or 5ml/1 tsp
    ground turmeric
  1 lemon grass stalk, finely chopped
  4–5 kaffir lime leaves, crushed
    with fingers
  4 candlenuts, coarsely crushed
  2 garlic cloves, crushed
  5ml/1 tsp coriander seeds
  5ml/1 tsp terasi (Indonesian
    shrimp paste)
  2 litres/3½ pints/8 cups
    chicken stock

  corn or vegetable oil, for deep-frying
  2 waxy potatoes, finely sliced
  350g/12oz skinless chicken breast
    fillets, thinly sliced widthways
  150g/5oz leafy green cabbage,
    finely sliced
  150g/5oz mung beansprouts
  3 hard-boiled eggs, thinly sliced
  salt and ground black pepper
To serve
  1 bunch fresh coriander (cilantro)
    leaves, roughly chopped
  2–3 spring onions (scallions),
    finely sliced
  2–3 fresh hot red or green chillies,
    seeded and finely sliced diagonally
  2 limes, cut into wedges
  kecap manis (Indonesian sweet
    soy sauce)

1 Prepare the serving ingredients by putting the coriander, spring onions, chillies and lime wedges into a serving bowl.

2 Heat the oil in a heavy pan, stir in the ginger, turmeric, lemon grass, kaffir lime leaves, candlenuts, garlic, coriander seeds and terasi and fry until the mixture begins to darken and become fragrant. Pour in the chicken stock, bring to the boil, then reduce the heat and simmer for about 20 minutes.

3 Meanwhile, heat the oil for deep-frying in a wok. Add the potato slices and fry until crisp and golden brown. Remove from the pan with a slotted spoon, drain on kitchen paper and put aside.

4 Strain the flavoured chicken stock and reserve. Pour back into the pan and season with salt and pepper to taste. Return to the boil, then reduce the heat and add the chicken. Simmer for 2–3 minutes until cooked but still tender.

5 Sprinkle some of the cabbage and beansprouts into the base of each soup bowl. Ladle the broth over the cabbage and beansprouts and divide the chicken between the bowls. Place the boiled eggs and potatoes on top.

6 Serve the hot broth with the serving ingredients, so that each diner can add them to their own bowls as they wish, and pass the kecap manis to drizzle over the top.

Per Portion Energy 296kcal/1238kJ; Protein 21.1g; Carbohydrate 14.8g, of which sugars 3g; Fat 17.5g, of which saturates 2.8g; Cholesterol 136mg; Calcium 63mg; Fibre 2.7g; Sodium 96mg.

CHICKEN SOUP WITH COCONUT

COCONUTS ARE GROWN JUST ABOUT EVERYWHERE IN THE PHILIPPINES BUT IT IS IN THE SOUTHERN PROVINCES, ESPECIALLY MINDANAO, THAT PRODUCTION IS CARRIED OUT ON A LARGE SCALE. COCONUT MILK AS A SOUP BASE HAS ITS EARLY BEGINNINGS IN INDIA CENTURIES AGO, BUT MOVED TO THE INDO-CHINESE COUNTRIES AND THEN TO INDONESIA, THE PHILIPPINES AND MALAYSIA.

SERVES FOUR

INGREDIENTS

30ml/2 tbsp vegetable oil
4 garlic cloves, crushed
6 shallots, chopped
30g/1oz young fresh ginger root, grated
350g/12oz boneless chicken, diced
1 litre/1¾ pints/4 cups water
2 lemon grass stalks, 5cm/2in of
  root end bruised
5ml/1 tsp salt
2.5ml/½ tsp ground black pepper
1 chicken stock cube
1 young coconut, flesh grated and
  coconut water reserved
holy basil or coriander (cilantro)
  leaves, to garnish

1 Heat the oil in a large frying pan or wok and fry the garlic until fragrant and golden brown. Add the shallots and grated ginger and fry for 2 minutes.

2 Add the chicken to the pan and stir-fry for 5 minutes until the pieces are white all over. Transfer to a larger pan if necessary for the next step.

3 Add the water, lemon grass, salt and pepper and crumble in the stock cube.

COOK'S TIP
The water inside a coconut is not coconut milk. This comes from grating and squeezing the meat with a little water.

4 Simmer for 25 minutes until the chicken is very tender. Add the grated coconut flesh and water and simmer for another 5 minutes.

5 Serve garnished with fresh basil or coriander leaves.

Per Portion Energy 87kcal/371kJ; Protein 13.1g; Carbohydrate 6.8g, of which sugars 6.7g; Fat 1.1g, of which saturates 0.4g; Cholesterol 35mg; Calcium 42mg; Fibre 0.3g; Sodium 620mg.

CHICKEN AND GINGER BROTH WITH PAPAYA

In the Philippines, this is a traditional peasant dish that is still cooked every day in rural areas. In the province of Iloilo, located in the Western Visayas, green papaya is added to the broth, as in the version described here. Generally, the chicken and broth are served with steamed rice, but the broth is also sipped during the meal to cleanse and stimulate the palate.

1 Heat the oil in a wok or a large pan that has a lid. Stir in the garlic, onion and ginger and fry until they begin to colour.

2 Stir in the chillies, add the chicken and fry until the skin is lightly browned.

3 Pour in the patis, stock and water, adding more water if necessary so that the chicken is completely covered. Bring to the boil, reduce the heat, cover and simmer gently for about 1½ hours, until the chicken is very tender.

4 Season the stock with salt and pepper and add the papaya. Continue to simmer for a further 10–15 minutes, then stir in the chilli or basil leaves.

5 Ladle the soup over hot rice in warmed serving bowls, and garnish with the leaves.

SERVES FOUR TO SIX

INGREDIENTS
15ml/1 tbsp palm or
 groundnut (peanut) oil
2 garlic cloves, finely chopped
1 large onion, sliced
40g/1½oz fresh root ginger,
 finely grated
2 whole dried chillies
1 chicken, left whole or jointed,
 trimmed of fat
30ml/2 tbsp patis
 (Filipino fish sauce)
600ml/1 pint/2½ cups
 chicken stock
1.2 litres/2 pints/5 cups water
1 small green papaya, cut into
 fine slices or strips
1 bunch fresh young chilli leaves
 or basil leaves, plus extra to garnish
salt and ground black pepper
cooked rice, to serve

Per Portion Energy 290kcal/1219kJ; Protein 46.4g; Carbohydrate 9.8g, of which sugars 8.7g; Fat 7.5g, of which saturates 1.5g; Cholesterol 169mg; Calcium 40mg; Fibre 2.2g; Sodium 150mg.

TAMARIND PORK AND VEGETABLE SOUP

SOUR SOUPS, USUALLY FLAVOURED WITH TAMARIND OR LIME, ARE VERY POPULAR IN SOUTH-EAST ASIA. IN THE PHILIPPINES, THE NATIONAL SOUR SOUP IS SINIGANG, WHICH VARIES FROM REGION TO REGION, SUCH AS THE BICOLANO VERSION MADE WITH COCONUT MILK AND CHILLIES. HOWEVER, IT CAN BE MADE WITH ANY COMBINATION OF MEAT OR FISH AND VEGETABLES AS LONG AS IT IS SOUR. TAMARIND PODS OR KAMIAS, A SOUR FRUIT SIMILAR IN SHAPE TO STAR FRUIT, ARE THE COMMON SOURING AGENTS.

SERVES FOUR TO SIX

INGREDIENTS

2 litres/3½ pints/8 cups pork or
   chicken stock, or a mixture of stock
   and water
15–30ml/1–2 tbsp tamarind paste
30ml/2 tbsp patis (Filipino fish sauce)
25g/1oz fresh root ginger,
   finely grated
1 medium yam or sweet potato, cut
   into bitesize chunks
8–10 yard-long beans
225g/8oz kangkong (water spinach)
   or ordinary spinach, well rinsed
350g/12oz pork tenderloin,
   sliced widthways
2–3 spring onions (scallions), white
   parts only, finely sliced
salt and ground black pepper

1 In a wok or deep pan, bring the stock to the boil. Stir in the tamarind paste, patis and ginger, reduce the heat and simmer for about 20 minutes. Season the mixture with salt and lots of pepper.

2 Add the yam and beans to the pan and cook gently for 3–4 minutes, until the yam is tender. Stir in the spinach and the sliced pork and simmer gently for 2–3 minutes, until the pork is just cooked and turns opaque.

3 Ladle the soup into individual warmed bowls and sprinkle the sliced spring onions over the top. You will need chopsticks and a spoon to eat with.

Per Portion Energy 126kcal/532kJ; Protein 14g; Carbohydrate 12.3g, of which sugars 4.1g; Fat 2.7g, of which saturates 0.9g; Cholesterol 37mg; Calcium 31mg; Fibre 2g; Sodium 417mg.

COLONIAL RICE SOUP <u>WITH</u> PORK

THIS WARMING AND SUSTAINING RICE SOUP COMBINES FILIPINO RICE CULTURE WITH THE SPANISH COLONIAL CULINARY TECHNIQUES OF BROWNING AND SAUTÉING. IT ALSO REFLECTS THE CHINESE HERITAGE OF USING RICE AS AN INGREDIENT, NOT SIMPLY AS A STARCHY ACCOMPANIMENT. THIS BLEND OF MEAT, RICE AND AROMATICS MAKES THE SOUP A MEAL IN ITSELF, IDEAL FOR A HEALTHY AND HEARTY WINTER LUNCH OR LIGHT SUPPER.

SERVES FOUR TO SIX

INGREDIENTS
    15ml/1 tbsp palm or groundnut
      (peanut) oil
    1 large onion, finely chopped
    2 garlic cloves, finely chopped
    25g/1oz fresh root ginger,
      finely chopped
    350g/12oz pork rump or tenderloin,
      cut widthways into bitesize slices
    5–6 black peppercorns
    115g/4oz/scant ⅔ cup short grain rice
    2 litres/3½ pints/8 cups pork
      or chicken stock
    30ml/2 tbsp patis (Filipino fish sauce)
    salt
To serve
    2 garlic cloves, finely chopped
    2 spring onions (scallions), white
      parts only, finely sliced
    2–3 fresh green or red chillies,
      seeded and quartered lengthways

1 Heat the oil in a wok or deep, heavy pan that has a lid. Stir in the onion, garlic and ginger and fry until fragrant and beginning to colour. Add the pork pieces and fry, stirring frequently, for 5–6 minutes, until lightly browned. Stir in the peppercorns.

2 Meanwhile, put the rice in a sieve (strainer), rinse under cold running water until the water runs clear, then drain. Toss the rice into the pan, making sure that it is coated in the mixture. Pour in the stock, add the patis and bring to the boil. Reduce the heat and partially cover with a lid. Simmer for about 40 minutes, stirring occasionally to make sure that the rice doesn't stick to the bottom of the pan. Season with salt to taste.

3 Just before serving, dry-fry the garlic in a small, heavy pan, until golden brown, then stir it into the soup. Ladle the soup into individual warmed bowls and sprinkle the spring onions over the top. Serve the chillies separately, for diners to chew on.

Per Portion Energy 195kcal/813kJ; Protein 14.8g; Carbohydrate 19.9g, of which sugars 3.4g; Fat 6.2g, of which saturates 1.3g; Cholesterol 37mg; Calcium 24mg; Fibre 0.8g; Sodium 399mg.

BEEF AND HEART OF PALM SOUP

FILIPINO BEEF SOUPS CAN RANGE FROM THE VERY SUBTLE AND LIGHT TO HEARTY CONCOCTIONS THAT ARE PRACTICALLY STEWS. THIS ONE, USING HEARTS OF PALM, SITS SOMEWHERE IN-BETWEEN, WITH ITS CLEAR BUT HIGHLY FLAVOURED STOCK. IT TASTES EVEN BETTER IF YOU USE BONES TO MAKE THE STOCK (SEE COOK'S TIP.) TRADITIONALISTS WOULD USE BANANA PLANT HEARTS BUT THESE CAN BE HARD TO FIND. HEARTS OF PALM ARE READILY AVAILABLE IN CANS FROM SUPERMARKETS.

SERVES FOUR

INGREDIENTS
 800g/1¾lb beef brisket or shank
 1.5 litres/2⅔ pints/6 cups water
 1 large onion, finely sliced
 2 hearts of palms (about 225g/8oz)
 30ml/2 tbsp patis (Filipino fish sauce)
 2.5ml/½ tsp ground black pepper
 fried shallots or garlic, to garnish

1 Slice the beef, then cut it into cubes no larger than 2cm/¾in.

2 Put the beef into a pan with the water and onion, bring to the boil, then simmer for 1½ hours uncovered, to reduce the stock by a third.

3 While the stock is simmering, slice the palm hearts.

COOK'S TIP
If you can find beef bones, boil 2kg/4½lb of these in the measured water and strain, discarding the bones. Use this in place of the plain water in step 2.

4 Add the sliced hearts of palm to the hot beef and onion stock and return to simmering point.

5 Add the fish sauce and pepper, and simmer for 30 minutes. Serve the soup hot, garnished with the shallots or garlic.

Per Portion Energy 384kcal/1581kJ; Protein 10g; Carbohydrate 0.7g, of which sugars 0.7g; Fat 37.4g, of which saturates 10.2g; Cholesterol 0mg; Calcium 11mg; Fibre 0g; Sodium 232mg.

STREET SNACKS
AND SATAY

*In the hustle and bustle of urban life, both Indonesians and
Filipinos rely on street snacks for much of their daily
sustenance. Satay is the best-known snack, a spicy, succulent
skewer of grilled meat or fish, often eaten with a peanut or
chilli dip. Snacking is not limited to finger food; lunch for
many workers is a carton of noodles or freshly stir-fried
seafood — nourishing, quick and delicious.*

BOILED AND FRIED EGGS WITH HOT SAMBAL

The two-step method employed here results in the most mouth-watering dish, which usually appears in Indonesian meals with friends. Warungs (street stalls) sell the eggs as an accompaniment to other dishes or simply as a snack. When you are making the sambal, consider doing a large batch, as it is a master sauce that goes with many salads, stir-fries and grilled foods.

SERVES FOUR

INGREDIENTS
    4 hard-boiled eggs, shelled
    15ml/1 tbsp vegetable oil
    sliced cucumber, to serve (optional)
For the sambal
    2 large onions, finely chopped
    6 garlic cloves, finely chopped
    45g/3 tbsp terasi (Indonesian
      shrimp paste)
    10 dried chillies, soaked in warm
      water until soft, then finely chopped
    6 candlenuts
    30g/2 tbsp tomato purée (paste)
    1.5ml/¼ tsp salt
    5ml/1 tsp sugar
    30ml/2 tbsp tamarind concentrate
    45ml/3 tbsp vegetable oil

1 Grind the onions, garlic, terasi, chillies and candlenuts using a mortar and pestle until very fine. Add the remaining sambal ingredients, except for the oil, and continue to pound until a rough paste is formed.

COOK'S TIPS
• If you omit the frying step for the eggs, you still get a lovely spicy egg dish.
• If you cannot find candlenuts, use about eight macadamia nuts instead.

2 Fry the mixture in the oil over a low heat until it is fragrant and separates, so that the oil seeps out.

3 In a clean wok, heat 1 tbsp of oil and fry the eggs all over until a crisp, brown skin forms. Remove and halve.

4 To serve, spoon the sambal over the halved eggs, with sliced cucumber on the side, if you like.

Per Portion Energy 230kcal/956kJ; Protein 14.4g; Carbohydrate 12g, of which sugars 9.1g; Fat 14.3g, of which saturates 2.6g; Cholesterol 247mg; Calcium 198mg; Fibre 2g; Sodium 1070mg.

PEANUT CRACKERS

*DEEP-FRIED IN VAST CAULDRONS, BASKETS OF REMPEYEK ARE
ALWAYS ON THE GO AS A QUICK SNACK IN THE STREETS OR TO
NIBBLE WITH A DRINK AT THE BEACH. ALONG WITH PRAWN
CRACKERS, REMPEYEK COULD BE CONSIDERED INDONESIA'S ANSWER
TO POTATO CRISPS (CHIPS), ALTHOUGH THEY ARE INFINITELY MORE
TASTY. AT MANY RESTAURANTS AND FORMAL DINNER PARTIES,
REMPEYEK ARE OFTEN OFFERED AS A WELCOMING APPETIZER TO TAKE
THE EDGE OFF YOUR HUNGER WHILE YOU WAIT FOR YOUR MEAL.*

SERVES FOUR TO FIVE

INGREDIENTS
  225g/8oz/1¼ cups rice flour
  5ml/1 tsp baking powder
  5ml/1 tsp ground turmeric
  5ml/1 tsp ground coriander
  300ml/½ pint/1¼ cups
    coconut milk
  115g/4oz/¾ cup unsalted peanuts,
    coarsely chopped or crushed
  2–3 candlenuts, crushed
  2–3 garlic cloves, crushed
  corn or groundnut (peanut) oil,
    for shallow frying
  salt and ground black pepper
  chilli sambal, for dipping (optional)
To season
  5ml/1 tsp paprika or fine chilli flakes
  salt

1 Put the rice flour, baking powder,
ground turmeric and ground coriander
into a bowl.

2 Make a well in the centre, pour in the
coconut milk and stir to mix well,
drawing in the flour from the sides. Beat
well to make a smooth batter.

3 Add the peanuts, candlenuts and
garlic and mix well together. Season
with salt and pepper, then put aside for
30 minutes.

4 Meanwhile, in a small bowl, prepare
the seasoning by mixing the paprika or
fine chilli flakes with a little salt.

5 Heat a thin layer of oil in a wok or
large frying pan and drop in a spoonful
of batter for each cracker – the size of
spoon doesn't matter as rempeyak are
supposed to vary in size.

6 Work in batches, flipping the crackers
over when the lacy edges become crispy
and golden brown. Drain on kitchen
paper and toss them into a basket.

7 Sprinkle the paprika and salt over the
crackers and toss them lightly for an
even dusting of seasoning.

8 Serve the peanut crackers
immediately while they are still warm
and crisp. Dip them into some chilli
sambal, if you like.

VARIATION
If you are allergic to peanuts or simply do
not like their flavour, you can adapt the
recipe and use other nuts, such as walnuts
and almonds, or roast some soaked,
drained chickpeas and use them instead.

Per portion Energy 403kcal/1679kJ; Protein 9.7g; Carbohydrate 42.2g, of which sugars 4.6g; Fat 21.3g, of which saturates
3.4g; Cholesterol 0mg; Calcium 44mg; Fibre 2.5g; Sodium 69mg.

SPICY CORN PATTIES

*WHEN IT COMES TO SNACK FOOD, FRIED PATTIES AND FRITTERS
ARE AS POPULAR AS GRILLED FISH AND SATAY AT THE STREET STALLS
IN INDONESIA. EASY TO EAT WITH FINGERS, THESE CORN PATTIES
ARE OFTEN SERVED ON A SQUARE OF BANANA LEAF WITH FRESH LIME
WEDGES. A SMALL DOLLOP OF CHILLI SAMBAL ON THE SIDE GIVES
AN EXTRA FIERY KICK TO THESE ALREADY FAIRLY SPICY SNACKS.*

SERVES FOUR

INGREDIENTS
   2 corn on the cob
   15ml/1 tbsp coconut oil
   3 eggs
   45ml/3 tbsp grated fresh coconut or
     desiccated (dry unsweetened
     shredded) coconut
   2–3 spring onions (scallions),
     white parts only, finely sliced
  corn or groundnut (peanut) oil,
     for shallow frying
   1 small bunch fresh coriander
     (cilantro) leaves, roughly chopped
  salt and ground black pepper
  shredded red chilli, to serve
For the spice paste
   3 shallots, finely chopped
   2 garlic cloves, finely chopped
   25g/1oz fresh galangal or fresh root
     ginger, finely chopped
   1–2 fresh chillies, seeded and
     finely chopped
   2–3 candlenuts, crushed
   5ml/1 tsp ground coriander
   5ml/1 tsp ground cumin
To serve
   1 lime, quartered
   chilli sambal or sweet chilli sauce

1 Put the corn on the cob into a large
pan of water, bring to the boil and boil
for about 8 minutes, until cooked but still
firm. Drain the cobs and refresh under
running cold water. Use a sharp knife to
scrape all the corn off the cob; set aside.

2 For the spice paste, grind the
shallots, garlic, galangal and chillies to
a paste using a pestle and mortar or an
electric food processor or blender. Add
the candlenuts, coriander and cumin
and beat well together.

3 Heat the coconut oil in a small wok or
heavy pan, stir in the spice paste and
stir-fry until the paste becomes fragrant
and begins to colour. Tip the paste on to
a plate and leave to cool.

4 Beat the eggs in a large bowl. Add the
coconut and spring onions and beat in
the corn and the cooled spice paste
until all the ingredients are thoroughly
combined. Season the mixture with salt
and pepper.

5 Heat a thin layer of corn oil or
groundnut oil in a heavy frying pan.
Working in batches, drop spoonfuls of
the corn mixture into the oil and fry the
patties for 2–3 minutes on each side,
until they are golden brown all over.

6 Drain the patties on kitchen paper,
then arrange them on a serving dish on
top of the coriander leaves and garnish
with the shreds of red chilli.

7 Serve the patties hot or at room
temperature with wedges of freshly cut
lime to squeeze over them and a chilli
sambal or sweet chilli sauce for dipping.

Per portion Energy 368kcal/1531kJ; Protein 10.8g; Carbohydrate 18.1g, of which sugars 8.2g; Fat 28.7g, of which saturates
9.7g; Cholesterol 143mg; Calcium 68mg; Fibre 4.1g; Sodium 196mg.

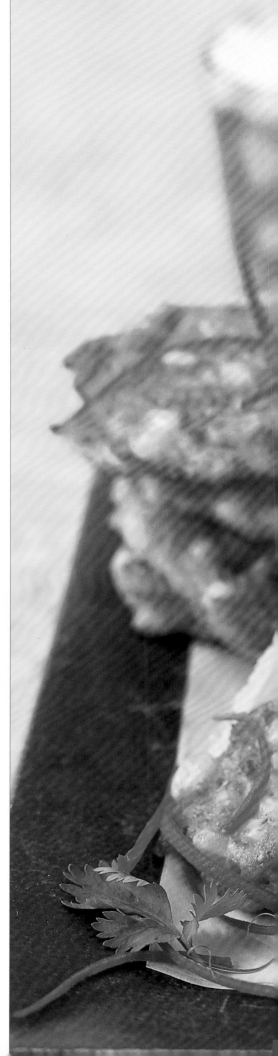

CRISPY FRIED TEMPEH

*OFTEN COOKED AT STREET STALLS, CRISPY FRIED TEMPEH CAN BE SERVED AS A SNACK OR AS PART OF A
SELECTION OF INDONESIAN DISHES. AS A SNACK, THIS FERMENTED TOFU IS OFTEN SERVED WITH STIR-
FRIED NOODLES OR PLAIN RICE AND PICKLED VEGETABLES.*

SERVES THREE TO FOUR

INGREDIENTS
  45ml/3 tbsp coconut
    or groundnut (peanut) oil
  500g/1¼lb tempeh, cut into
    bitesize strips
  4 shallots, finely chopped
  4 garlic cloves, finely chopped
  25g/1oz fresh galangal or
    fresh root ginger, finely chopped
  3–4 fresh red chillies, seeded and
    finely chopped
  150ml/¼ pint/⅔ cup kecap manis
    (Indonesian sweet soy sauce)
  30ml/2 tbsp unsalted
    peanuts, crushed
  1 small bunch fresh coriander
    (cilantro) leaves, roughly chopped
  stir-fried noodles or cooked rice,
    to serve

1 Heat 30ml/2 tbsp of the oil in a wok
or large, heavy frying pan. Add the
tempeh and stir-fry until golden brown.

2 Using a slotted spoon, transfer the
fried tempeh pieces to crumpled
kitchen paper to drain.

3 Wipe the wok or frying pan clean with
kitchen paper.

4 Heat the remaining 15ml/1 tbsp oil in
the wok or pan, stir in the shallots,
garlic, galangal and chillies and fry until
fragrant and beginning to colour.

5 Stir in the kecap manis and toss in
the fried tempeh. Stir-fry until the sauce
has reduced and clings to the tempeh.

6 Tip the tempeh on to a serving dish
and sprinkle with the peanuts and
coriander leaves. Serve hot with stir-
fried noodles or cooked rice.

COOK'S TIP
Tempeh (fermented tofu) can be bought
from Chinese and South-east Asian
supermarkets. If you are unable to buy it,
then tofu can be used as an alternative.

Per Portion Energy 258kcal/1071kJ; Protein 14.8g; Carbohydrate 7.7g, of which sugars 5.5g; Fat 18.9g, of which saturates 2.6g; Cholesterol 0mg; Calcium 682mg; Fibre 1.7g; Sodium 2680mg.

SPANISH-STYLE BITTER MELON OMELETTE

BITTER MELON IS OFTEN COOKED SIMPLY IN A BROTH OR VEGETABLE STEW, BUT IS ALSO COMBINED WITH PORK AND SHRIMPS THROUGHOUT SOUTH-EAST ASIA, AS IN THIS DISH. MADE IN THE STYLE OF A SPANISH OMELETTE, THIS FILIPINO DISH IS OFTEN ENJOYED AS A SNACK, SERVED ON A BANANA LEAF.

SERVES THREE TO FOUR

INGREDIENTS
    450g/1lb bitter melon
    30ml/2 tbsp palm or groundnut
      (peanut) oil
    1 onion, sliced
    2–3 garlic cloves, chopped
    25g/1oz fresh root ginger, chopped
    115g/4oz pork loin, cut into thin,
      bitesize strips
    225g/8oz fresh prawns (shrimp),
      shelled
    2–3 tomatoes, skinned, seeded
      and chopped
    1 small bunch fresh chilli leaves or
      flat leaf parsley, roughly chopped
    3 eggs, beaten
    salt and ground black pepper

1 Fill a bowl with cold water and stir in 10ml/2 tsp salt. Cut the bitter melon in half, remove the spongy core and seeds, then cut the flesh into bitesize chunks. Put the melon into the salted water and leave to soak for 30 minutes. Drain, rinse well under cold water, then pat dry with kitchen paper.

2 Heat the oil in a large frying pan, stir in the onion, garlic and ginger and fry until fragrant and beginning to colour. Add the pork and fry for 2 minutes.

3 Add the prawns and fry until they turn opaque, then add the tomatoes and chilli leaves or parsley.

4 Toss in the bitter melon and fry for 3–4 minutes, until tender. Season the mixture with salt and pepper.

5 Pour the eggs over the ingredients in the pan, drawing in the sides to let the egg spread evenly. Cover the pan and leave to cook very gently until the eggs have set. Do not allow the bottom of the omelette to burn.

6 Serve the omelette hot, straight from the pan, or leave it to cool and serve it at room temperature.

VARIATION
If you have trouble finding bitter melon, use courgettes (zucchini) as a substitute.

Per Portion Energy 255kcal/1064kJ; Protein 24.3g; Carbohydrate 10.5g, of which sugars 10.1g; Fat 13.2g, of which saturates 2.7g; Cholesterol 318mg; Calcium 149mg; Fibre 2.7g; Sodium 247mg.

DRIED SQUID SATAY

ALL SORTS OF DRIED FISH AND SHELLFISH ARE A FEATURE OF SOUTH-EAST ASIAN COOKING AND AT THE LOCAL MARKETS, DRIED SQUID CAN ALWAYS BE SEEN HANGING FROM POLES. IN THE PHILIPPINES, DRIED FISH IS USUALLY DEEP-FRIED AND SERVED WITH GARLIC RICE, AND THE DRIED SQUID IS GRILLED IN THE STREET, LURING PASSERS-BY WITH ITS SWEET AROMA. SIMPLE AND TASTY, THIS DISH IS OFTEN MADE AT THE BEACH AND SERVED WITH ICED FRUIT DRINKS OR CHILLED SERBESA (BEER) TO BALANCE THE SALTINESS. IT IS ALSO GOOD SERVED WITH CHUNKS OF BREAD.

SERVES THREE TO FOUR

INGREDIENTS
    4 whole dried baby squid
    30ml/2 tbsp light soy sauce
    30ml/2 tbsp hoisin sauce
    30ml/2 tbsp smooth peanut butter
    juice of 1 kalamansi or ordinary lime
    wooden or metal skewers
    green mango or papaya salad, to serve

1 Cut each squid into four or five pieces.

2 Put the soy sauce, hoisin sauce, peanut butter and lime juice in a bowl and mix well with a fork to form a thick, well blended marinade.

3 Toss the squid pieces in the peanut marinade, making sure they are completely coated, and leave to marinate at room temperature for about 30 minutes.

4 If using wooden skewers, soak them in water for about 30 minutes to prevent them from charring when you start cooking.

5 Meanwhile, prepare the barbecue or, if you are using the grill (broiler), preheat it on the maximum heat for 5 minutes before you start cooking.

6 Thread the peices of squid on to the skewers.

7 Place the satay on the barbecue or under the grill and cook for 2 minutes on each side, brushing occasionally with any remaining marinade.

8 Serve as an accompaniment to a drink or with chunks of bread and a green mango or papaya salad.

Per Portion Energy 89kcal/374kJ; Protein 9.6g; Carbohydrate 2.2g, of which sugars 1.1g; Fat 4.7g, of which saturates 1.2g; Cholesterol 113mg; Calcium 11mg; Fibre 0.4g; Sodium 615mg.

SPICY PRAWN AND SCALLOP SATAY

ONE OF THE TASTIEST SATAY DISHES, THIS IS SUCCULENT, SPICY AND EXTREMELY MOREISH. THE SPICE PASTE IS VERY FRAGRANT, WITH ITS COMBINATION OF GALANGAL, TURMERIC AND LEMON GRASS, AND THE FLAVOURS ARE GIVEN TIME TO PENETRATE THE POUNDED FISH BEFORE BEING COOKED. SERVE WITH RICE AND A FRUITY SALAD OR PICKLED VEGETABLES AND LIME.

SERVES FOUR

INGREDIENTS
- 250g/9oz shelled prawns (shrimp), deveined and chopped
- 250g/9oz shelled scallops, chopped
- 30ml/2 tbsp potato, tapioca or rice flour
- 5ml/1 tsp baking powder
- 12–16 wooden, metal, lemon grass or sugar cane skewers
- 1 lime, quartered, to serve

For the spice paste
- 2 shallots, chopped
- 2 garlic cloves, chopped
- 2–3 fresh red chillies, seeded and chopped
- 25g/1oz fresh galangal or fresh root ginger, chopped
- 15g/½oz fresh turmeric, chopped, or 2.5ml/½ tsp ground turmeric
- 2–3 lemon grass stalks, chopped
- 15ml/1 tbsp palm or groundnut (peanut) oil
- 5ml/1 tsp terasi (Indonesian shrimp paste)
- 15ml/1 tbsp tamarind paste
- 5ml/1 tsp palm sugar (jaggery)

1 To make the spice paste, pound the shallots, garlic, chillies, galangal, turmeric and lemon grass together.

2 Heat the oil in a wok, stir in the paste and fry until it becomes fragrant and begins to colour. Add the terasi, tamarind and sugar and stir-fry, until the mixture darkens. Leave to cool.

3 In a bowl, pound the prawns and scallops together to form a paste, or blend them together in an electric blender or food processor.

4 Beat in the spice paste, followed by the flour and baking powder, until blended. Chill for about 1 hour.

5 If using wooden skewers, soak in water for about 30 minutes. Prepare the barbecue, or preheat the grill (broiler).

6 Wrap lumps of the shellfish paste and wrap it around the skewers. Barbecue or grill them for 3 minutes on each side, until golden brown. Serve with the lime wedges to squeeze over.

Per Portion Energy 220kcal/922kJ; Protein 27g; Carbohydrate 11.5g, of which sugars 1g; Fat 7.3g, of which saturates 1g; Cholesterol 151mg; Calcium 99mg; Fibre1.5g; Sodium 249mg.

HOT, SWEET AND SOUR SQUID

THE INDONESIANS AND MALAYS LOVE COOKING PRAWNS AND SQUID IN THIS WAY, AND EXPERTLY CRUNCH SHELLS AND SUCK TENTACLES TO SAVOUR ALL THE JUICY CHILLI AND TAMARIND FLAVOURING. SWEETENED WITH THE UBIQUITOUS KECAP MANIS, THE ENTICING AROMA OF THESE DELICIOUS SQUID WILL MAKE YOUR TASTEBUDS TINGLE.

SERVES TWO TO FOUR

INGREDIENTS
  500g/1¼lb fresh baby squid
  30ml/2 tbsp tamarind paste
  30ml/2 tbsp chilli sauce
  45ml/3 tbsp kecap manis
    (Indonesian sweet soy sauce)
  juice of 1 kalamansi or ordinary lime
  25g/1oz fresh root ginger, grated
  2–4 green chillies, seeded and
    quartered lengthways
  ground black pepper
  fresh coriander (cilantro) leaves and
    lime wedges, to serve

1 Clean the squid and remove the head and ink sac. Pull out the backbone and rinse the body sac inside and out. Trim the head above the eyes, keeping the tentacles intact. Pat dry the body sac and tentacles and discard the rest.

2 In a small bowl, mix together the tamarind paste, chilli sauce, kecap manis and lime juice. Beat in the ginger and a little black pepper.

3 Spoon the mixture over the squid and, using your fingers, rub it all over the body sacs and tentacles. Cover and leave to marinate in the refrigerator for 1 hour.

VARIATION
To make hot, sweet and sour prawns (shrimp), devein the prawns and remove the feelers and legs, then rinse, pat dry, and cut along the tail. Marinate and cook in the same way as the squid.

4 Meanwhile, prepare the barbecue or heat a ridged griddle on the hob. Place the squid on the rack or griddle and cook for 3 minutes on each side, brushing them with the marinade as they cook. Serve immediately with the coriander leaves and lime wedges.

Per Portion Energy 110kcal/468kJ; Protein 20g; Carbohydrate 2.8g, of which sugars 1.1g; Fat 2.3g, of which saturates 0.5g; Cholesterol 281mg; Calcium 43mg; Fibre 0.6g; Sodium 943mg.

INDONESIAN DEEP-FRIED SPRING ROLLS

MADE WITH A CRÊPE-STYLE BATTER USING RICE FLOUR, THESE INDONESIAN SPRING ROLLS ARE PACKED WITH VEGETABLES AND STRIPS OF CHICKEN AND THEN DIPPED IN KECAP MANIS, WHICH IS OFTEN SPIKED WITH CHILLIES. EXTRA CHILLIES, SEEDED AND THINLY SLICED, CAN ALSO BE SERVED ON THE SIDE.

SERVES THREE TO FOUR

INGREDIENTS
30ml/2 tbsp palm or corn oil
2–3 garlic cloves, finely chopped
225g/8oz chicken breast fillets,
  cut into fine strips
225g/8oz fresh prawns
  (shrimp), shelled
2 leeks, cut into matchsticks
2 carrots, cut into matchsticks
½ green cabbage, finely shredded
175g/6oz fresh beansprouts
30ml/2 tbsp patis (Filipino fish sauce)
30ml/2 tbsp kecap manis
  (Indonesian sweet soy sauce)
1 egg, lightly beaten
corn or vegetable oil, for deep-frying
4 fresh red or green Thai chillies, or
  a mixture of both, seeded and finely
  sliced, to serve
For the spring roll wrappers
  115g/4oz/⅔ cup rice flour
  30ml/2 tbsp tapioca flour
    or cornflour (cornstarch)
  2 eggs, beaten
  15ml/1 tbsp palm or coconut oil
  about 400ml/14fl oz/1⅔ cups water
  salt
  corn or vegetable oil, for frying
For the dipping sauce
  about 200ml/7fl oz/¾ cup kecap
    manis (Indonesian sweet soy sauce)
  1 fresh red Thai chilli, seeded
    and chopped

1 First make the spring roll wrappers. Sift the rice flour and tapioca flour into a bowl. Make a well in the centre, add the beaten eggs and oil into the well and gradually pour in the water, beating all the time until a smooth batter is formed. Season with salt and leave the batter to rest for 30 minutes.

2 Heat a non-stick frying pan and wipe over a little oil. Using a small cup or ladle, add a little of the batter to the pan, tilting it to spread the batter evenly over the base. There should be enough batter to make 12 wrappers.

3 Reduce the heat and cook gently on one side, until the batter is lightly browned and lifts at the edges. Lift the wrapper on to a plate and keep fresh under a clean, damp dish towel. Repeat with the remaining batter.

4 To prepare the filling, heat 15ml/1 tbsp of the oil in a wok or large, heavy frying pan, stir in the garlic and fry gently until fragrant. Add the chicken and prawns and stir-fry for 2–3 minutes, until just cooked. Tip on to a plate and return the wok to the heat.

5 Add the remaining oil to the wok, then add the leeks, carrots and cabbage and stir-fry for 2–3 minutes. Toss in the beansprouts and stir-fry for a further 1–2 minutes.

6 Add the patis and kecap manis and return the chicken and prawns to the pan, then toss until all the ingredients are thoroughly combined and coated in the sauce. Tip the mixture on to a plate and leave to cool.

7 To fill the spring rolls, place a wrapper on a flat surface and drop a heaped spoonful of the filling on the side nearest to you. Spread the filling to form a log, then roll the edge nearest to you over the mixture, tuck in the sides and continue rolling the wrapper away from you. When you get to the far side, moisten it with a little of the beaten egg to seal the seam. Repeat to make 12 spring rolls.

8 Before frying the spring rolls, quickly prepare the dipping sauce. Pour the kecap manis into a serving bowl, stir in the chopped chilli, and place the bowl next to the serving dish for the spring rolls.

9 In a wok or heavy pan, heat enough oil for deep-frying. Carefully lower one or two spring rolls at a time into the pan and sizzle gently for 3–4 minutes, until golden brown and crisp. Using a slotted spoon, remove from the pan and drain on kitchen paper.

10 Transfer the crisp rolls to the serving dish and serve immediately, with the dipping sauce and sliced chillies on the side for those who appreciate some extra heat.

COOK'S TIP
If you serve fresh chilli as a garnish or on the side, be aware that anyone eating with their fingers should be careful not to rub their eyes afterwards as the juice is an irritant.

Per Portion Energy 585kcal/2446kJ; Protein 35.4g; Carbohydrate 43.5g, of which sugars 7.2g; Fat 43.2g, of which saturates 4.5g; Cholesterol 292mg; Calcium 170mg; Fibre 5.1g; Sodium 744mg.

MEATBALLS <u>WITH</u> TOASTED COCONUT

A GREAT FAVOURITE AT INDONESIAN BUFFET SPREADS AND STREET STALLS, THESE MEATBALLS ARE VERSATILE AND TASTY. THE TASTY, BITESIZE BALLS CAN BE SERVED AS AN APPETIZER WITH A DRINK, AS A SNACK DIPPED IN KECAP MANIS, OR AS A MAIN DISH WITH RICE AND A TANGY SALAD.

SERVES FOUR

INGREDIENTS
  5ml/1 tsp coriander seeds
  5ml/1 tsp cumin seeds
  175g/6oz freshly grated coconut
    or desiccated (dry unsweetened
    shredded) coconut
  15ml/1 tbsp coconut oil
  4 shallots, finely chopped
  2 garlic cloves, finely chopped
  1–2 fresh red chillies, seeded and
    finely chopped
  350g/12oz lean minced (ground) beef
  beaten egg (if necessary)
  rice flour, to coat
  corn oil, for shallow frying
  salt and ground black pepper
To serve
  1 lime, quartered
  kecap manis (Indonesian sweet
    soy sauce)

1 In a small, heavy pan, dry-fry the coriander and cumin seeds until they give off a nutty aroma. Using a mortar and pestle or electric spice grinder, grind the roasted seeds to a powder.

2 In the same pan, dry-fry the coconut until it begins to colour and give off a nutty aroma. Tip the coconut on to a plate and leave to cool.

3 Heat the coconut oil in the same pan, stir in the shallots, garlic and chillies and fry until fragrant and beginning to colour. Tip them on to a plate to cool.

4 Put the beef into a bowl and add the ground spices, all but 2–3 tbsp of the toasted coconut and the shallot mixture. Season the beef mixture with salt and pepper. Mix all the ingredients together, adding a little beaten egg, only if necessary, to bind the mixture together.

5 Knead the mixture and mould it into little balls, not bigger than a fresh apricot. Roll the balls in rice flour to coat them.

6 Heat a thin layer of corn oil in a large frying pan and fry the meatballs for about 5 minutes until they are golden brown all over. Drain on kitchen paper and arrange on a serving dish. Sprinkle the reserved coconut over them and serve with the lime wedges for squeezing and kecap manis for drizzling over them.

Per Portion Energy 559kcal/2312kJ; Protein 20.2g; Carbohydrate 8g, of which sugars 3.7g; Fat 49.6g, of which saturates 30.4g; Cholesterol 53mg; Calcium 23mg; Fibre 6.3g; Sodium 83mg.

Filipino Pork Satay

This is the most popular of all the satay dishes in the Philippines. Pork is the favoured meat and satay is a beautifully simple way of cooking it, so this recipe makes great street food for on-the-go eating as well as good party and picnic food.

1 In a large bowl, mix the oil, soy sauce, patis, lime juice, sugar and garlic well to form a marinade. Stir well to ensure the sugar dissolves thoroughly and season with black pepper.

2 Toss the pork in the marinade, making sure that it is well coated. Cover the bowl with clear film (plastic wrap) and put in the refrigerator for at least 2 hours or overnight. (The longer the pork is marinated, the better the flavour.)

3 Prepare the barbecue, or, if you are using a grill (broiler), preheat 5 minutes before you start cooking. If using wooden skewers, soak them in water for about 30 minutes. Thread the meat, chorizo and onions on to the skewers and place on the barbecue or under the hot grill.

4 Cook the satay for 4–5 minutes on each side, basting the meat with the marinade occasionally.

5 Serve the satay immediately, alongside rice and a salad or some pickled vegetables, and a bowl of Coconut Vinegar Sauce.

SERVES FOUR

INGREDIENTS
  30ml/2 tbsp groundnut (peanut)
    or palm oil
  60–75ml/4–5 tbsp soy sauce
  15ml/1 tbsp patis (Filipino fish sauce)
  juice of 2–3 kalamansi or
    ordinary limes
  15ml/1 tbsp palm sugar (jaggery),
    granulated (white) or muscovado
    (molasses) sugar
  2 garlic cloves, crushed
  500g/1¼lb pork loin, cut into thin
    bitesize squares
  175g/6oz slim chorizo sausage,
    sliced diagonally
  12 baby onions
  ground black pepper
  wooden or metal skewers
To serve
  cooked rice
  salad or pickled vegetables
  Coconut Vinegar Sauce
    (see Essential Recipes)

Per Portion Energy 360kcal/1503kJ; Protein 31.5g; Carbohydrate 11.7g, of which sugars 6.7g; Fat 21.1g, of which saturates 6.8g; Cholesterol 96mg; Calcium 40mg; Fibre 0.6g; Sodium 1048mg.

CRISPY FRIED PORK BELLY

THIS DISH IS A GREAT FILIPINO TREAT. DELICIOUS AND MOREISH, THE CRISPY BELLY PORK CAN BE SLICED AND EATEN AS A SNACK WITH SALAD AND PICKLES, OR IT CAN BE ADDED TO SALADS, SOUPS AND VEGETABLE DISHES, MAKING IT HIGHLY VERSATILE.

SERVES FOUR

INGREDIENTS

3 garlic cloves, chopped
40g/1½oz fresh root ginger, chopped
500g/1¼lb pork belly with the rind,
  cut into thick slabs
3–4 bay leaves
corn, groundnut (peanut) or
  vegetable oil, for deep-frying
salt and ground black pepper

1 Using a mortar and pestle, grind the garlic and ginger with a little salt and pepper, to a fairly smooth paste.

2 Thoroughly rub the paste all over each of the pork slabs. Cover with clear film (plastic wrap) and chill for at least 1 hour or overnight.

3 Fill a large pan with water and bring to the boil. Add the bay leaves, reduce the heat and slip in the marinated pork slabs. Cook gently for about 1 hour, until the meat is tender but still firm.

4 Put the slabs in a colander to drain and leave them there for 30–40 minutes to dry out.

5 Heat enough oil in a wok or pan for deep-frying. Fry the pork pieces for 5 minutes, until they are golden brown. Using a slotted spoon, lift them out and drain on kitchen paper. If eating straight away, slice thinly and serve with rice and pickled vegetables, if you like. Alternatively, store in the refrigerator for up to 5 days to use in soups and stews.

Per Portion Energy 576kcal/2377kJ; Protein 19.2g; Carbohydrate 0.1g, of which sugars 0.1g; Fat 55.4g, of which saturates 17.7g; Cholesterol 90mg; Calcium 14mg; Fibre 0.1g; Sodium 97mg.

FILIPINO BATCHOY

MADE FROM PIG OFFAL, BATCHOY IS SIMILAR TO LIVER SAUSAGE, ALTHOUGH IT IS TRADITIONALLY COOKED TO A SMOOTH MIXTURE IN A PAN RATHER THAN ROLLED INTO A NEAT SAUSAGE. FLAVOURED WITH GARLIC AND GINGER, BATCHOY IS SERVED HOT WITH NOODLES OR RICE AS A POPULAR STREET SNACK AT ANY TIME OF DAY. IN THIS RECIPE, THOUGH, RATHER THAN THE OFFAL BEING BOILED UNTIL IT BECOMES SOFT, THE MEAT IS SAUTÉED SPANISH-STYLE AND SERVED STRAIGHT FROM THE PAN WITH SOME TOASTED BREAD TO ACCOMPANY IT.

SERVES FOUR

INGREDIENTS

- 30ml/2 tbsp groundnut (peanut) or vegetable oil
- 1 onion, finely chopped
- 2 garlic cloves, finely chopped
- 25g/1oz fresh root ginger, finely chopped or grated
- 50g/2oz pig's fat, finely chopped
- 225g/8oz pig's liver, chopped
- 115g/4oz pig's kidney, finely chopped
- 115g/4oz pig's heart, chopped
- 15–30ml/1–2 tbsp patis (Filipino fish sauce)
- a handful of fresh chilli leaves or flat leaf parsley, finely chopped, plus extra to garnish
- about 8 slices French bread or any crusty rustic loaf
- salt and ground black pepper
- 2 fresh red or green chillies, seeded and quartered lengthways, to serve

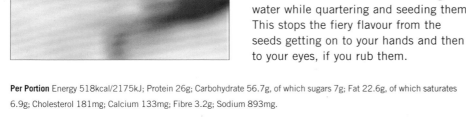

1 Heat the oil in a wok or large, heavy frying pan, stir in the onion, garlic and ginger and fry until fragrant and lightly browned.

2 Add the chopped fat and offal and sauté until lightly browned. Stir in the patis and chilli leaves or parsley and season with salt and lots of black pepper.

3 Lightly toast the slices of bread. Spoon the sautéed offal on top and garnish with chilli leaves. Serve as a snack or a light lunch, with the chillies to chew on.

COOK'S TIP
Hold the chillies under cold running water while quartering and seeding them. This stops the fiery flavour from the seeds getting on to your hands and then to your eyes, if you rub them.

Per Portion Energy 518kcal/2175kJ; Protein 26g; Carbohydrate 56.7g, of which sugars 7g; Fat 22.6g, of which saturates 6.9g; Cholesterol 181mg; Calcium 133mg; Fibre 3.2g; Sodium 893mg.

RICE AND NOODLES

Rice and noodles in their many and varied guises form the
basis of meals throughout Asia and are increasingly respected
throughout the world for their texture and versatility. The
dishes in this chapter include substantial meals and beautiful
side dishes to accompany curries or stir-fries. These are some
of the most popular dishes of Indonesia and the Philippines,
and no feast or family meal would be complete without them.

FESTIVE YELLOW RICE

VIBRANT YELLOW AND RICH IN TASTE, THIS INDONESIAN RICE DISH IS TRADITIONALLY COOKED ONLY ON FESTIVE OCCASIONS, WHEN IT IS OFTEN HEAPED UP HIGH ON A PLATTER TO IMPRESS THE WAITING DINERS. USUALLY MADE WITH MEDIUM GRAIN RICE AND COLOURED YELLOW WITH TURMERIC, THIS IS A STUNNING RICE DISH FOR ANY OCCASION.

SERVES FOUR

INGREDIENTS
- 450g/1lb/2¼ cups long grain rice
- 30ml/2 tbsp vegetable
  or sesame oil
- 2–3 shallots, finely chopped
- 2 garlic cloves, finely chopped
- 400ml/14fl oz/1⅔ cups coconut milk
- 450ml/¾ pint/scant 2 cups water
- 10ml/2 tsp ground turmeric
- 3–4 fresh curry leaves
- salt and ground black pepper
- 2 fresh red chillies, seeded and
  finely sliced, to garnish

1 Put the rice in a sieve (strainer), rinse under cold running water until the water runs clear, then drain. Heat the oil in a heavy pan, stir in the shallots and garlic and fry until just beginning to colour. Stir in the rice until coated in the oil.

2 Add the coconut milk, water, turmeric, curry leaves, 2.5ml/½ tsp salt and pepper to the pan. Bring to the boil, then lower the heat, cover and simmer gently for 15–20 minutes, until all the liquid has been absorbed.

3 Turn off the heat, cover the pan with a lid and leave the rice to steam for a further 10–15 minutes. Fluff up the rice with a fork and serve hot, garnished with red chillies.

COOK'S TIP
Allowing the rice to steam dry once all the liquid has been absorbed produces grains that are light and fluffy.

Per Portion Energy 487kcal/2035kJ; Protein 9.1g; Carbohydrate 96.5g, of which sugars 5.8g; Fat 6.7g, of which saturates 0.9g; Cholesterol 0mg; Calcium 70mg; Fibre 0.8g; Sodium 122mg.

INDONESIAN FRIED RICE

DESPITE ITS DUTCH ORIGINS, THIS DISH OF FRIED RICE (NASI GORENG) IS ONE OF INDONESIA'S NATIONAL FAVOURITES. GENERALLY MADE WITH LEFTOVER COOKED GRAINS, THE FRIED RICE IS SERVED WITH CRISPY SHALLOTS AND CHILLIES, OR ELSE TOSSED WITH PRAWNS (SHRIMP) OR CRAB MEAT AND CHOPPED VEGETABLES. A FRIED EGG ON TOP OF THE DOMED RICE COMPLETES THE DISH.

SERVES FOUR

INGREDIENTS
- ½ cucumber
- 45ml/3 tbsp vegetable or groundnut (peanut) oil
- 4 shallots, finely chopped
- 4 garlic cloves, finely chopped
- 3–4 fresh red chillies, seeded and chopped
- 45ml/3 tbsp kecap manis (Indonesian sweet soy sauce)
- 15ml/1 tbsp tomato purée (paste)
- 350g/12oz/1¾ cups cooked long grain rice
- 4 eggs

1 Cut the cucumber in half lengthways and scoop out the seeds. Cut the flesh into thin sticks. Put aside.

2 In a wok, heat 30ml/2 tbsp of the oil, stir in the shallots, garlic and chillies and fry until they begin to colour. Add the kecap manis and tomato purée and stir for 2 minutes until thick, to form a sauce. Toss in the rice and heat for 5 minutes until well flavoured and hot.

3 Meanwhile, in a large frying pan, heat the remaining oil over a medium heat and crack the eggs into it. Fry for 1–2 minutes until the whites are cooked but the yolks remain runny. Reduce the heat to a minimum while you quickly prepare the servings of rice.

4 Spoon the rice into four deep bowls. Alternatively, use one bowl as a mould to invert each portion of rice on to individual plates, then lift off the bowl to reveal the mound of rice beneath. Place a fried egg on top of each and garnish with the cucumber sticks.

Per Portion Energy 273kcal/1146kJ; Protein 9.9g; Carbohydrate 33g, of which sugars 4.7g; Fat 12.3g, of which saturates 2.5g; Cholesterol 190mg; Calcium 67mg; Fibre 1.1g; Sodium 884mg.

MIXED VEGETABLE RICE

This is a dish that crosses many borders and is a meal featured throughout Indonesia as well as in Malaysia and Singapore. Campur (pronounced 'cham-poor') simply means 'mixed', and the dish can be adapted to include all kinds of savoury ingredients mixed with the hot rice. It is particularly good if served with a spicy relish or sambal.

2 Blanch the beans in boiling water for 2 minutes. Drain, cool and dice finely.

3 Peel the cucumber and remove the seeds. Cut into fine dice.

4 Chop the hard-boiled eggs.

5 Just before serving, toss all the ingredients together and adjust the seasoning. Serve with Cucumber and Pineapple Relish on the side.

SERVES FOUR

INGREDIENTS

- 200g/7oz/1 cup jasmine rice
- 2 yard-long beans or 5 green beans
- ¼ cucumber
- 2 hard-boiled eggs
- 3 fresh red chillies, seeded and chopped
- 4 lime leaves, finely shredded
- 5ml/1 tsp salt
- 1.5ml/¼ tsp ground black pepper
- 30ml/2 tbsp fresh lime juice
- 2 tomatoes, chopped
- 45ml/3 tbsp Cucumber and Pineapple Relish (see Essential Recipes)

1 Put the rice in a sieve (strainer), rinse under cold running water until the water runs clear, then put it in a pan and cover with water up to 4cm/1½in above the rice. Cook for 12–15 minutes until tender.

COOK'S TIP

When you cook the rice, crumble in a vegetarian stock cube. This will give the finished dish a well-rounded flavour.

Per Portion Energy 199kcal/834kJ; Protein 4.6g; Carbohydrate 43.4g, of which sugars 6.6g; Fat 0.7g, of which saturates 0.1g; Cholesterol 105mg; Calcium 23mg; Fibre 1.6g; Sodium 232mg.

JUNGLE RICE

THE NAME OF THIS DISH ALLUDES NOT SO MUCH TO TRIBAL COOKING AS TO THE WILD GREENS AND HERBS FOUND IN TROPICAL FORESTED AREAS. ORIGINALLY, THIS DISH OF INDIGENOUS EDIBLE PLANTS WAS COOKED BY PEOPLE LIVING ON THE FRINGES OF INDONESIAN JUNGLES. TODAY, IT IS LIKELY TO BE PREPARED WITH GARDEN VEGETABLES. THE MAIN FLAVOUR COMES FROM THE SHRIMP PASTE AND CHILLIES.

SERVES FOUR

INGREDIENTS
350g/12oz/1¾ cups jasmine rice
1 whole mackerel or snapper
30ml/2 tbsp vegetable oil
2 eggs
4 shallots, sliced
4 garlic cloves, sliced
2 fresh green chillies, sliced
2 yard-long or 5 green beans, finely diced
2 lime leaves, finely shredded
small sprig fresh sweet basil, chopped
6 fresh mint leaves, shredded
5ml/1 tsp salt

For the sambal
50g/2oz terasi (Indonesian shrimp paste), toasted
5 fresh red chillies, finely chopped
juice of 2 limes

3 Clean the mackerel or snapper, pat dry with kitchen paper, then grill (broil) for about 7 minutes on each side until cooked through.

4 Carefully debone the fish and flake the flesh into a bowl. Discard the skin and bones.

5 Heat the oil and fry the eggs, then remove to a plate.

6 While the rice is still warm, mix in the prepared vegetables, fish, lime leaves and herbs, and mix in the shrimp paste sambal to taste. Place in a large serving bowl, topped with the eggs.

1 Grind all the sambal ingredients with a mortar and pestle until smooth, and set aside.

2 Put the jasmine rice in a sieve (strainer), rinse under cold water until the water runs clear, then put it in a pan and cover with water up to 4cm/1½in above the rice. Bring to the boil and cook for 12–15 minutes until tender.

VARIATION
You can use the equivalent amount of Shallot and Lemon Grass Sambal (see Essential Recipes) in place of this sambal for an even more tangy dish.

Per Portion Energy 487kcal/2032kJ; Protein 16.9g; Carbohydrate 72.7g, of which sugars 0.8g; Fat 14g, of which saturates 2.5g; Cholesterol 112mg; Calcium 46mg; Fibre 1.1g; Sodium 547mg.

NOODLES AND RICE WITH TOFU AND BEANSPROUT BROTH

THE CUSTOM IS TO SERVE THE NOODLES, RICE, TOFU, BROTH AND SAMBAL THAT MAKE UP NASI MI INDIVIDUALLY. EACH PERSON THEN SPOONS RICE INTO A BOWL, FOLLOWED BY THE TOFU AND SAMBAL, THEN A LADLEFUL OF BROTH, WITH THE NOODLES EATEN SEPARATELY.

SERVES FOUR TO SIX

INGREDIENTS
    corn or vegetable oil, for deep-frying
    250g/9oz tofu block, cut into
      4 rectangular pieces
    225g/8oz/1⅛ cup jasmine rice
For the broth
    15ml/1 tbsp palm or corn oil
    2 garlic cloves, finely chopped
    1–2 fresh red or green chillies,
      seeded and finely chopped
    1 lemon grass stalk, finely chopped
    45ml/3 tbsp soy sauce
    2 litres/3½ pints/8 cups
      chicken stock
    450g/1lb fresh mung beansprouts
    ground black pepper
For the noodles
    30ml/2 tbsp palm or corn oil
    4 shallots, finely sliced
    2 garlic cloves, finely chopped
    450g/1lb shelled prawns (shrimp)
    30ml/2 tbsp kecap manis
      (Indonesian sweet soy sauce)
    500g/1¼lb fresh egg noodles or
      225g/8oz dried egg noodles,
      soaked in warm water for 5 minutes
      until softened
To serve
    4–6 spring onions (scallions),
      finely sliced
    chilli sambal

COOK'S TIP
Although the tradition is to serve each ingredient in separate bowls, nasi mi is often served as a self-contained meal in a single dish at many street stalls.

VARIATION
If you don't have or can't find any kecap manis, you can substitute the same quantity of dark soy sauce mixed with a little sugar.

1 Heat enough oil in a wok or heavy pan for deep-frying. Add the tofu pieces and fry for 2–3 minutes, until golden brown on both sides, then drain on kitchen paper.

2 Cut the fried tofu into thin slices and pile them on a serving plate. Set aside.

3 Put the rice in a sieve (strainer), rinse under cold running water until the water runs clear, then drain. Transfer the rice to a pan and add about 600ml/1 pint/2½ cups water to cover the rice. Bring to the boil, then reduce the heat and simmer gently for about 15 minutes, until all the water has been absorbed. Turn off the heat, cover the pan and leave to steam for 10–15 minutes.

4 Meanwhile, make the broth. Heat the oil in a heavy pan, stir in the garlic, chillies and lemon grass and fry until fragrant.

5 Add 15ml/1 tbsp of the soy sauce to the mixture in the pan and pour in the chicken stock. Bring to the boil, then reduce the heat and simmer for 10–15 minutes.

6 Season the broth with the remaining soy sauce and pepper and stir in the beansprouts. Turn off the heat and keep warm in a covered pan over a very low heat or in a casserole in the oven.

7 Finally, prepare the noodles. Heat the oil in a wok, stir in the shallots and garlic and fry until they begin to colour. Toss in the prawns and cook for 2 minutes, then stir in the kecap manis with 15–30ml/1–2 tbsp water. Add the noodles, season and toss well.

8 Tip the rice and noodles into warmed dishes and serve with the tofu, a bowl of spring onions, chilli sambal and a bowl of the steaming hot broth, so that everyone can help themselves.

Per Portion Energy 690kcal/2900kJ; Protein 32.6g; Carbohydrate 97g, of which sugars 5.9g; Fat 20.7g, of which saturates 3.6g; Cholesterol 171mg; Calcium 328mg; Fibre 4.2g; Sodium 833mg.

INDONESIAN STIR-FRIED NOODLES

ORIGINALLY FROM CHINA, STIR-FRIED NOODLES HAVE BECOME AS POPULAR AS STIR-FRIED RICE AT STREET STALLS THROUGHOUT INDONESIA, AND ARE JUST AS VARIED. THIS DISH IS EASY TO PREPARE IN ADVANCE — THE PAR-BOILED NOODLES WILL KEEP FOR HOURS BEFORE THE FINAL PAN-COOKING STAGE, WHICH TAKES ONLY MINUTES. AS IN MANY INDONESIAN AND FILIPINO RECIPES, THE GARNISH IS ESSENTIAL FOR ADDING FLAVOUR AND SHOULD NOT BE REGARDED AS AN OPTIONAL EXTRA.

SERVES FOUR

INGREDIENTS
  450g/1lb fresh egg noodles
  60ml/4 tbsp palm, groundnut
    (peanut) or corn oil, plus extra
    for frying
  2 shallots, finely chopped
  2–3 spring onions (scallions),
    finely chopped
  2–3 garlic cloves, crushed
  3–4 fresh Thai chillies, seeded and
    finely chopped
  15ml/1 tbsp terasi
    (Indonesian shrimp paste)
  15ml/1 tbsp tomato purée (paste)
  15–30ml/1–2 tbsp kecap manis
    (Indonesian sweet soy sauce)
  4 eggs
  salt
To garnish
  15ml/1 tbsp palm or corn oil
  3–4 shallots, thinly sliced

1 First prepare the garnish. Heat the oil in a heavy pan, stir in the shallots and fry until deep golden brown. Drain on kitchen paper and put aside.

2 Fill a deep pan with water and bring it to the boil. Drop in the egg noodles, untangling them with chopsticks, and cook for about 3 minutes until tender but still firm to the bite. Drain and refresh under cold running water.

3 Heat 30ml/2 tbsp of the oil in a wok or large, heavy frying pan and fry the shallots, spring onions, garlic and chillies until fragrant. Add the terasi and cook until the mixture darkens.

4 Toss the noodles into the pan, making sure that they are thoroughly coated in the mixture. Add the tomato purée and kecap manis, toss thoroughly, and cook for 2–3 minutes.

5 Season the noodles with salt to taste. Divide the noodles between four warmed dishes and keep warm.

6 Heat the remaining oil in a large frying pan and crack the eggs into it. Fry for 1–2 minutes until the whites are cooked but the yolks remain runny.

7 Place on the noodles and serve immediately with the fried shallots sprinkled over the top.

Per Portion Energy 549kcal/2317kJ; Protein 20.5g; Carbohydrate 82.9g, of which sugars 3.9g; Fat 17.6g, of which saturates 4.5g; Cholesterol 224mg; Calcium 68mg; Fibre 3.7g; Sodium 549mg.

CANTON-STYLE BRAISED NOODLES

A LARGE NUMBER OF CHINESE IMMIGRANTS HAVE SETTLED IN THE PHILIPPINES, AND BROUGHT CANTONESE COOKING WITH THEM. THEY COOK CANTONESE NOODLES IN MANY DELICIOUS WAYS. THE SPECTRUM IS WIDE, FROM SIMPLE STIR-FRIES TO RICH BLENDS WITH VEGETABLES, MEATS AND SEAFOOD, STIRRED UP WITH RICH SOY SAUCES. THIS RECIPE IS A SUBSTANTIAL AND COLOURFUL BLEND OF PRAWNS, CHICKEN, MUSHROOMS AND MANGETOUTS, COOKED IN A SOY SAUCE-FLAVOURED STOCK.

SERVES FOUR

INGREDIENTS
  150g/5oz dried egg noodles
  30ml/2 tbsp vegetable oil
  3 garlic cloves, crushed
  ½ large onion, sliced
  250g/9oz shelled prawns (shrimp)
  1 chicken breast, sliced
    into matchsticks
  4 dried Chinese mushrooms, soaked
    until soft and sliced thinly
  40g/1½oz mangetouts (snowpeas)
  100g/3½oz pak choy (bok choy), sliced
  350ml/12fl oz/scant 1½ cups water
  1 chicken stock cube
  30ml/2 tbsp dark soy sauce
  sliced fresh red chillies, to garnish

1 Reconstitute the noodles by covering them in plenty of boiling water, then drain and set aside.

2 Heat the oil in a wok and fry the garlic until light brown, stirring constantly to prevent it from burning. Add the onion and stir until soft, but not coloured. Add the prawns, chicken, mushrooms, mangetouts and pak choy and stir for 2 minutes.

3 Add the water to the wok, crumble in the stock cube and add the soy sauce, bringing this stock to a boil. Add the noodles and cook for up to 5 minutes, until tender but not too soft. Serve the noodles garnished with finely sliced red chillies.

Per portion Energy 224kcal/938kJ; Protein 12.1g; Carbohydrate 14.6g, of which sugars 12.6g; Fat 13.6g, of which saturates 3.2g; Cholesterol 22mg; Calcium 79mg; Fibre 3g; Sodium 181mg.

FILIPINO PAELLA

STRIKINGLY SIMILAR TO SPANISH PAELLA, THE FILIPINO VERSION OF THE POPULAR CLASSIC IS PACKED WITH CRABS, CLAMS AND PRAWNS, ALTHOUGH ANY SHELLFISH CAN BE USED. IT IS FLAVOURED WITH GINGER AND BAY LEAVES TO GIVE IT A DISTINCTIVE AND IRRESISTIBLE AROMA THAT SETS IT APART FROM THE MEDITERRANEAN DISH, AND IS SPICED UP WITH A BOWL OF CHILLIES ON THE SIDE.

1 Put the rice in a sieve (strainer), rinse under cold running water until the water runs clear, then drain. Heat the oil in a wok or wide, shallow heavy pan with a lid. Add the chicken drumsticks and wings and fry for about 5 minutes, until browned on both sides. Remove the chicken from the pan and put aside.

2 Add the onions, garlic and ginger to the pan and fry until fragrant and beginning to colour.

3 Add the paprika, tomato purée, bay leaves and drained rice and toss in the chicken. Pour in the stock and bring to the boil. Add the patis and season with salt and lots of black pepper. Cover the pan and simmer gently for 15–20 minutes, until the rice and chicken are almost cooked.

4 Toss in the peas and add the prawns and clams, sitting them on top of the rice. Cover the pan again and cook for a further 10 minutes or until all the liquid has evaporated. Serve warm with the Kalamansi Sauce and a bowl of chillies.

SERVES SIX

NGREDIENTS
- 500g/1¼lb/2½ cups long grain rice
- 45ml/3 tbsp palm or groundnut (peanut) oil
- 12 chicken drumsticks and wings
- 2 onions, finely chopped
- 4 garlic cloves, finely chopped
- 40g/1½ oz fresh root ginger, chopped
- 5ml/1 tsp paprika
- 30–45ml/2–3 tbsp tomato purée (paste)
- 2–3 bay leaves
- 1.2 litres/2 pints/5 cups chicken stock
- 15–30ml/1–2 tbsp patis (Filipino fish sauce)
- 400g/14oz can petits pois (baby peas), drained
- 12 prawns (shrimp) in their shells, cleaned and rinsed
- 12 medium clams, cleaned and rinsed
- salt and ground black pepper

To serve
- Kalamansi Sauce (see Essential Recipes)
- 4 red chillies, seeded and quartered

Per Portion Energy 637kcal/2666kJ; Protein 54.4g; Carbohydrate 78.3g, of which sugars 4.6g; Fat 11.6g, of which saturates 2.1g; Cholesterol 266mg; Calcium 104mg; Fibre 3.8g; Sodium 628mg.

CELEBRATION NOODLES

RESERVED MAINLY FOR SPECIAL OCCASIONS AND CELEBRATIONS, SUCH AS BIRTHDAYS AND WEDDINGS, THIS IS ONE OF THE NATIONAL DISHES OF THE PHILIPPINES. A SUBSTANTIAL AND SATISFYING MEAL, THE INGREDIENTS IN THIS TRADITIONAL STIR-FRIED NOODLE DISH VARY FROM REGION TO REGION BUT THE BASIC RECIPE IS EVERY FILIPINO COOK'S PRIDE AND JOY.

SERVES FOUR

INGREDIENTS

30ml/2 tbsp palm or coconut oil
1 large onion, finely chopped
2–3 garlic cloves, finely chopped
250g/9oz pork loin, cut into
 thin strips
250g/9oz fresh shelled
 prawns (shrimp)
2 carrots, cut into matchsticks
½ small green cabbage,
 finely shredded
about 250ml/8fl oz/1 cup pork
 or chicken stock
50ml/2fl oz/¼ cup soy sauce
15ml/1 tbsp palm sugar (jaggery)
450g/1lb fresh egg noodles
2 hard-boiled eggs, finely chopped
1 lime, quartered

1 Heat 15ml/1 tbsp of the oil in a wok or a large, heavy frying pan over a medium–high heat, stir in the onion and garlic and fry until fragrant and beginning to colour.

2 Toss in the pork and prawns and stir-fry for 2 minutes, then transfer the mixture to a plate and set aside.

COOK'S TIPS
• Fresh egg noodles are available in Chinese and South-east Asian stores.
• If you cannot buy palm sugar, use demerara (raw) sugar instead.
• Cooked prawns will work in this recipe but raw ones are preferable.

3 Return the wok to the heat, add the remaining oil, then stir in the carrots and cabbage and stir-fry for 2–3 minutes. Add the vegetables to the plate with the pork and prawns.

4 Pour the stock, soy sauce and sugar into the wok and stir until the sugar has dissolved. Add the noodles, untangling them with chopsticks, and cook for about 3 minutes, until tender but still firm to the bite.

5 Toss in the pork, prawns, cabbage and carrots, making sure that they are thoroughly mixed.

6 Transfer the noodles on to a warmed serving dish and sprinkle the chopped eggs over the top. Serve the dish while piping hot, with the lime wedges to squeeze over.

Per Portion Energy 728kcal/3069kJ; Protein 43.6g; Carbohydrate 98g, of which sugars 16.9g; Fat 20.8g, of which saturates 5g; Cholesterol 290mg; Calcium 159mg; Fibre 6.3g; Sodium 1303mg.

PADANG CHICKEN RICE <u>WITH</u> LEMON GRASS

THIS DISH IS BELIEVED TO HAIL FROM THE PADANG REGION OF INDONESIA AND IS COOKED FOR FESTIVE OCCASIONS. TRADITIONALLY, A WHOLE CHICKEN IS USED, BUT THIS RECIPE USES JUST CHICKEN FILLETS FOR CONVENIENCE. IT IS A MOST APPETIZING ONE-POT MEAL, AROMATIC WITH LEMON GRASS, NUTMEG, MACE AND GALANGAL.

2 Cook the rice according to the packet instructions but with the nutmeg, pepper and mace. When cooked, remove the mace and keep the rice warm.

3 Place the chicken in small pot with the water, lemon grass, galangal, lime leaves, garlic and salt. Cook for 10 minutes until the liquid has almost entirely been absorbed or has evaporated.

4 Remove the lemon grass and lime leaves (or leave for a rustic presentation).

SERVES FOUR

INGREDIENTS
   60ml/4 tbsp vegetable oil
   8 shallots, peeled and sliced
   400g/14oz/2 cups long grain
     or basmati rice
   pinch of grated nutmeg
   2.5ml/½ tsp ground black pepper
   2 small pieces of mace
   2 chicken breast fillets, thinly sliced
   300ml/½ pint/1¼ cups water
   2 lemon grass stalks, 5cm/2in
     of root end bruised
   5ml/1 tsp ground galangal
   3 lime leaves
   2 garlic cloves
   5ml/1 tsp salt

1 Heat the oil and fry the shallots until crisp and golden brown. Remove and set aside on crumpled kitchen paper.

COOK'S TIP
Fried shallots are required for many Indonesian dishes, so cook a large batch, drain, then store in an airtight container.

5 Mix the chicken with the cooked rice and stir well to incorporate the flavours. Serve garnished with the fried shallots.

Per Portion Energy 557kcal/2328kJ; Protein 26.3g; Carbohydrate 83.1g, of which sugars 1.4g; Fat 12.9g, of which saturates 1.6g; Cholesterol 53mg; Calcium 36mg; Fibre 0.4g; Sodium 538mg.

OIL RICE WITH CHICKEN

THIS IS A FESTIVE TAKE ON THE COCONUT RICE USUALLY EATEN IN INDONESIA AND IS FRAGRANT WITH THE SCENT OF COCONUT OIL. SOME VERSIONS USE GHEE OR CLARIFIED BUTTER, BUT THIS INTENSELY FLAVOURED FAT CAN DISTRACT FROM THE AROMA OF RICE AND CHICKEN, ENDING UP ALMOST LIKE AN INDIAN PILAU RICE. COCONUT OIL IS A SOLID FAT THAT LOOKS LIKE LARD.

SERVES FOUR

INGREDIENTS
    350g/12oz glutinous rice
    45ml/3 tbsp coconut oil
    5ml/1 tsp salt
    1 large banana leaf, about
      30cm/12in square
    2 chicken breasts, cut into
      bitesize pieces
    2 salam leaves (Indonesian bay leaves)
    105ml/7 tbsp coconut milk
    pinch of cinnamon powder
    2.5ml/½ tsp salt
    2 fresh green chillies

1 Soak the glutinous rice for at least 2 hours or overnight in water for a softer consistency, as this is a dense grain.

2 On the day of preparation, drain the rice until it is just moist. Most of the water will have been absorbed.

3 Melt the coconut oil in a small pan, add the salt and and stir to blend well. Pour over the rice and transfer to a bamboo steamer.

4 Blanch the banana leaf in boiling water, then cut it and line the basket. Add the rice and top with more bamboo leaf 'lid' before closing the steamer lid.

5 Steam for 20 minutes, then taste a few grains. If there is no hard edge, the rice is done. If there still is a hard edge, steam for a little longer.

6 While the rice is steaming, combine the chicken with the salam leaves, coconut milk, cinnamon, salt and whole chillies, and simmer in a pan or wok for 10 minutes. During the last 5 minutes of the rice being cooked, remove the bamboo lid and pile the chicken on top. Finish cooking both together, to let the juices mingle. Serve in warmed bowls.

Per Portion Energy 474kcal/1984kJ; Protein 24.7g; Carbohydrate 71.2g, of which sugars 1.3g; Fat 9.6g, of which saturates 7.4g; Cholesterol 53mg; Calcium 29mg; Fibre 0g; Sodium 811mg.

Chicken Vermicelli

The Filipino name for vermicelli, sotanghoon, is taken from the Fujian one for translucent mung bean noodles or tang hoon. These are the only noodles within the realm that are not made from either rice or wheat flour. More often than not, they turn up in soupy dishes, but are also deliciously smooth and succulent when fried.

SERVES FOUR

INGREDIENTS
   30ml/2 tbsp vegetable oil
   ½ large onion, sliced
   2 chicken breast fillets, sliced
      into matchsticks
   15ml/1 tbsp patis (Filipino fish sauce)
   2.5ml/½ tsp ground black pepper
   3 spring onions (scallions), cut into
      5cm/2in lengths
   4 dried Chinese mushrooms, soaked
      until soft, and sliced
   140g/5oz translucent vermicelli,
      soaked until soft
   500ml/17fl oz/2 cups water
   1 chicken stock cube
   chopped spring onions (scallions),
      to garnish (optional)

1 Heat the oil in a wok and stir-fry the onion until soft but not browned. Add the chicken and stir for 3 minutes until the pieces turn opaque.

2 Add the patis, black pepper, spring onions and mushrooms and stir-fry for 2 minutes.

3 Add the vermicelli and water, then the crumbled stock cube, and cook over a low to medium heat for 5 minutes.

4 Serve in warmed soup bowls garnished with chopped spring onions, if liked. Provide chopsticks and spoons to eat the dish with.

Per Portion Energy 263kcal/1099kJ; Protein 21.6g; Carbohydrate 29.2g, of which sugars 1.4g; Fat 6.6g, of which saturates 0.9g; Cholesterol 53mg; Calcium 21mg; Fibre 0.4g; Sodium 227mg.

CUBAN RICE WITH MEAT AND PLANTAINS

THERE IS MORE THAN A LITTLE CREOLE-CARIBBEAN INFLUENCE IN THIS DISH, PLANTAINS BEING A HALLMARK OF THAT CUISINE. THEY MAY LOOK LIKE LARGE BANANAS BUT ARE REGARDED AS A SWEET VEGETABLE RATHER THAN A DESSERT FRUIT. VERY FIRM IN TEXTURE, PLANTAINS RARELY RIPEN TO SOFTNESS AND HAVE TO BE COOKED TO BE REALLY EDIBLE.

SERVES FOUR

INGREDIENTS
  45ml/3 tbsp olive oil
  5 shallots, sliced
  3 garlic cloves, crushed
  2 tomatoes, quartered
  200g/7oz minced (ground) beef
  200g/7oz minced pork
  30ml/2 tbsp soy sauce
  15ml/1 tbsp vinegar
  50g/2oz/⅓ cup sultanas
    (golden raisins)
  2.5ml/½ tsp salt
  2.5ml/½ tsp ground black pepper
  50g/2oz/⅓ cup corn kernels
  400g/14oz/2 cups long grain rice
  60ml/4 tbsp vegetable oil
  200g/7oz plantains, sliced diagonally
    into 2cm/¾in slices
  4 eggs
  fresh mint or coriander (cilantro)
    leaves, to garnish

1 Heat the olive oil in a large wok and fry the shallots until light brown. Add the garlic and fry for 1 minute, then add the tomatoes, beef, pork, soy sauce and vinegar and stir over a medium heat for about 8 minutes, until the meats are cooked through.

2 Add the sultanas, salt, pepper and corn and stir-fry for 1 minute. Remove the wok from the heat and set aside.

3 Meanwhile, boil or steam the rice according to the packet instructions. When it is ready, keep it warm.

4 Heat the vegetable oil in a frying pan and fry the plantain slices until they are slightly caramelized. Remove with a slotted spoon and drain any excess oil on crumpled kitchen paper.

5 Fry the eggs 'sunny side up' in the same oil, then set aside. The yolks should still be runny, and the whites completely set.

6 Press the rice into a small dessert or cereal bowl for each person, then unmould it on to a warmed plate. Top it with a fried egg and serve the cooked meat mixture and the plantains on the side. Garnish with the fresh herbs.

VARIATION
If you are unable to get plantains you could use sweet potato for a colourful and flavoursome alternative. Par-boil slices of sweet potato for 3 minutes, then cook them in the same way as you would the plantains.

Per Portion Energy 929kcal/3878kJ; Protein 35.2g; Carbohydrate 110.7g, of which sugars 16.2g; Fat 38.8g, of which saturates 9.2g; Cholesterol 253mg; Calcium 80mg; Fibre 1.9g; Sodium 721mg.

FRIED RICE WITH CHORIZO AND FRIED EGGS

THIS RICE DISH IS A CLASSIC FILIPINO BREAKFAST. TO MAKE A SUBSTANTIAL MEAL TO START THE DAY, IT IS SERVED AT STREET STALLS AND CAFÉS WITH FRIED DRIED FISH, SUCH AS THE CRISPY DANGGIT FROM CEBU, FRIED EGGS, PORK JERKY OR THE SPICY SAUSAGE LONGANIZA, WHICH CAN BE SUBSTITUTED FOR THE SIMILAR-TASTING SPANISH CHORIZO. THIS DELICIOUS RECIPE IS A GREAT WAY OF USING UP LEFTOVER RICE.

SERVES FOUR

INGREDIENTS
  45ml/3 tbsp palm, groundnut
    (peanut) or vegetable oil
  2–3 garlic cloves, crushed
  450g/1lb cooked long grain rice
  15–30ml/1–2 tbsp patis (Filipino
    fish sauce)
  2 small, thin chorizo sausages, about
    175g/6oz each, sliced diagonally
  4 eggs
  salt and ground black pepper
  suka (Filipino coconut vinegar),
    to serve

1 Heat 15ml/1 tbsp of the oil in a wok or heavy pan, stir in the garlic and fry until fragrant and golden brown. Toss in the rice, breaking up any lumps, and add the patis. Season the rice with salt to taste, if needed, and black pepper. Turn off the heat and cover the wok or pan to keep the rice warm.

2 In another wok or heavy pan, heat 15ml/1 tbsp of the oil, add the sliced chorizo and fry until crispy on both sides. Drain on crumpled kitchen paper.

COOK'S TIP
If you don't have any leftover cooked rice, cook 225g/8oz/generous 1 cup rice, allow to cool and then use.

3 Heat the remaining 15ml/1 tbsp oil in a separate frying pan and fry the eggs for 1–2 minutes.

4 Spoon the rice into individual bowls. Place the fried eggs on top of the rice and arrange the chorizo around the edge. Alternatively, pack the rice into a cup or bowl and invert each portion on to a plate. Serve warm with the suka.

VARIATION
If you prefer, carefully turn the eggs over once cooked on one side, then fry for no more than 30 seconds until a film is set over the yolk without browning.

Per Portion Energy 567kcal/2367kJ; Protein 17.7g; Carbohydrate 45.4g, of which sugars 2g; Fat 36.4g, of which saturates 11.6g; Cholesterol 225mg; Calcium 92mg; Fibre 0.6g; Sodium 1136mg.

FILIPINO RISOTTO WITH STIR-FRIED LIVER

THIS TYPE OF RICE DISH IS USUALLY SERVED AS A SNACK AND MUCH ENJOYED AT CHRISTMAS AND EASTER, WHEN A VAST NUMBER OF PORK-BASED DISHES ARE COOKED AND SHARED WITH NEIGHBOURS. IF YOU CANNOT GET PIG'S LIVER, USE LAMB'S.

SERVES THREE TO FOUR

INGREDIENTS
- 225g/8oz/generous 1 cup sticky or glutinous rice
- 900ml/1½ pints/scant 4 cups pork or chicken stock
- 45ml/3 tbsp groundnut (peanut) or vegetable oil
- 3–4 shallots, finely chopped
- 3 garlic cloves, finely chopped
- 25g/1oz fresh root ginger, finely chopped
- 25g/1oz fresh turmeric, finely chopped
- 175g/6oz/¾ cup small raisins or currants
- 225g/8oz pork fillet, cut into thin bitesize strips
- 450g/1lb pig's liver, cut into bitesize strips
- 30ml/2 tbsp rice flour or plain (all-purpose) white flour
- salt and ground black pepper

To serve
- 45–60ml/3–4 tbsp roasted, unsalted peanuts, crushed
- 2 hard-boiled eggs, quartered
- 2–3 spring onions (scallions), white parts only, sliced
- 2 fresh red or green chillies, seeded and finely shredded
- suka (Filipino coconut vinegar)

1 Put the rice in a sieve (strainer), rinse under cold running water until the water runs clear, then drain. Pour the stock into a pan and bring it to the boil. Make sure it is well seasoned, and then reduce the heat and leave to simmer.

2 Meanwhile, heat 30ml/2 tbsp of the oil in a wok or heavy pan, stir in the shallots, garlic, ginger and turmeric and fry until fragrant and beginning to colour. Add the raisins and toss in the pork. Stir-fry for 2–3 minutes, until the pork is well browned.

3 Toss the rice into the pork mixture, ensuring it is well incorporated.

4 Gradually add ladlefuls of the hot stock to the rice and cook over a medium heat until the liquid has been absorbed, stirring from time to time, before adding another ladleful. When all the stock has been added, cover the pan and leave to cook gently, until almost all the liquid has been absorbed.

5 Meanwhile, toss the liver in the flour. Just before the rice is cooked, heat the remaining oil in a frying pan or wok. Add the liver and stir-fry for 2–3 minutes. Season the liver with salt and pepper.

6 Tip the risotto into warmed individual dishes. Spoon the liver on top and scatter over the crushed peanuts. Arrange the eggs, spring onions and chillies over the dish and serve immediately, with suka as a condiment for diners to add as they wish.

Per Portion Energy 756kcal/3167kJ; Protein 49.2g; Carbohydrate 87.7g, of which sugars 33.3g; Fat 23.3g, of which saturates 4.6g; Cholesterol 423mg; Calcium 74mg; Fibre 2.3g; Sodium 197mg.

FISH AND SHELLFISH

*With the islands' endless miles of idyllic coastline, it is no
surprise that fish and shellfish form an important part of the
Indonesian and Filipino diet. In this chapter you will
encounter special dishes from both regions that make the best of
the local fishermen's catch. Don't miss out on the famous
classic Prawn Adobo, or the fiery Sumatran favourite, Sardines
in Spicy Coconut Milk, for two of the most authentic
flavours of the region.*

SQUID STUFFED
WITH BREADCRUMBS
AND SERRANO HAM

*THIS TRADITIONAL FILIPINO DISH OF BABY SQUID, STUFFED WITH
A TASTY MIXTURE OF BREADCRUMBS AND SPANISH HAM AND THEN
COOKED IN WINE, ONCE AGAIN REFLECTS THE NATION'S COLONIAL
PAST. WHOLE FISH CAN BE STUFFED IN THE SAME MANNER, USING
BREADCRUMBS OR MINCED (GROUND) PORK, SUCH AS RELYENONG
BANGUS. A DISH FOR CELEBRATIONS AND FESTIVAL FEASTS, THESE
STUFFED SQUID ARE DELICIOUS SERVED WITH RICE OR NOODLES
AND A FRESH AND SIMPLE SEAWEED SALAD.*

SERVES FOUR

INGREDIENTS

  16 fresh baby squid
  15ml/1 tbsp palm or groundnut
    (peanut) oil
  2–3 shallots, finely chopped
  2–3 garlic cloves, finely chopped
  115g/4oz Serrano ham,
    finely chopped
  5–10ml/1–2 tsp paprika
  1 small bunch flat leaf parsley,
    finely chopped, reserving a few
    leaves to garnish
  6–8 slices white bread, crusts
    removed, made into breadcrumbs
  300ml/½ pint/1¼ cups dry
    white wine
  300ml/½ pint/1¼ cups chicken stock
  2–3 bay leaves
  salt and ground black pepper
  cooked rice, to serve

1 To prepare the squid, use your fingers
to pull off the head and reach into the
body sac to pull out all the innards and
the flat, thin quill. Rinse the sac inside
and out and peel off the skin. Cut off the
tentacles above the eyes, chop finely and
reserve. Pat the sacs dry before stuffing.

2 Heat the oil in a heavy pan, stir in the
shallots and garlic and fry until fragrant
and beginning to colour. Add the
reserved squid tentacles and Serrano
ham and fry for 2–3 minutes. Stir in the
paprika and chopped parsley and toss
in the breadcrumbs to absorb all the
juices and flavours. Season with salt
and pepper. If the mixture is a little dry,
splash in 15–30ml/1–2 tbsp of the wine.
Leave the stuffing to cool.

3 Fill the squid sacs with the stuffing and
thread a cocktail stick (toothpick) through
the ends to prevent it spilling out.

4 In a wide pan, bring the wine and
stock to the boil. Drop in the bay leaves,
reduce the heat and add the stuffed
squid. Cover the pan and simmer gently
for 5–10 minutes until tender.

5 Pile some cooked rice on to four
warmed plates, place the squid on top
and spoon over some of the cooking
juices. Garnish with the reserved parsley
leaves and serve.

COOK'S TIP

If you are lucky enough to get the squid
ink from the fishmonger, reserve 90ml/
6 tbsp to add to the wine during cooking.

Per Portion Energy 344kcal/1449kJ; Protein 28.9g; Carbohydrate 25.5g, of which sugars 4.2g; Fat 9.6g, of which saturates
1.5g; Cholesterol 298mg; Calcium 104mg; Fibre 1.8g; Sodium 701mg.

FRESH SPRING ROLLS WITH PALM HEART

PREPARED FOR SPECIAL OCCASIONS, LUMPIA UBOD IS QUITE A TREAT AS IT CONTAINS THE TENDER HEART OF A THREE- TO FIVE-YEAR-OLD PALM TREE. COCONUT PALM TREES GROW ALL OVER THE PHILIPPINES AND THERE ARE SOME THAT ARE GROWN SPECIFICALLY FOR THE HEART, ALTHOUGH EVERY PART OF THE PALM TREE IS USED IN SOME WAY.

SERVES THREE TO FOUR

INGREDIENTS

6 spring onions (scallions)
400g/14oz can coconut palm
   hearts, drained
30ml/2 tbsp coconut
   or groundnut (peanut) oil
225g/8oz tofu, rinsed, cut into
   3 rectangular pieces
2 garlic cloves, finely chopped
1–2 carrots, cut into 5cm/2in
   long matchsticks
12 fresh prawns (shrimp), shelled
   and deveined
30–45ml/2–3 tbsp light soy sauce
10ml/2 tsp sugar
soft lettuce leaves
suka (Filipino coconut vinegar),
   to serve
salt and ground black pepper
For the spring roll wrappers
115g/4oz/1 cup plain (all-purpose)
   white flour
15ml/1 tbsp tapioca flour or
   cornflour (cornstarch)
pinch of salt
400ml/14fl oz/1⅔ cups water
corn oil, for frying

1 First make the spring roll wrappers. Sift the flour, tapioca flour and salt into a bowl. Gradually pour in the water and whisk until a smooth batter is formed. Leave to rest for 30 minutes.

2 Heat a non-stick pancake or crêpe pan and, using a piece of kitchen paper, wipe a little oil for frying all over the surface. Ladle a little of the batter into the pan, tilting it to spread the batter evenly over the base. In total there should be enough batter to make 12 wrappers. Cook over a medium-low heat, on one side only, until the batter sets, is pale in colour, begins to bubble up in the middle and loosens at the edges.

3 Carefully transfer the wrapper to a plate. Repeat with the remaining batter. Put the pancakes aside.

4 To prepare the filling, cut off the green stems of the spring onions, halve lengthways and put aside. Cut the white stems into 5cm/2in lengths and then quarter each piece lengthways. Set aside.

5 Blanch the palm hearts in a pan of boiling water for 2–3 minutes, refresh under cold running water, then cut into 5cm/2in strips.

6 Heat the oil in a wok or heavy frying pan, add the tofu pieces and fry until golden brown on both sides. Drain on kitchen paper, then cut each piece into thin strips and set aside.

7 Add the garlic to the wok and fry until fragrant. Toss in the carrots and stir-fry for 2–3 minutes. Add the white parts of the spring onions and the prawns and fry until they turn opaque. Add the palm hearts and tofu strips, followed by the soy sauce and sugar. Season the filling mixture to taste and tip it on to a plate to cool.

8 Place a spring roll wrapper on a flat surface and position a lettuce leaf on it, making sure the frilly edge overlaps the wrapper on the side furthest away from you. Spoon some of the mixture into the middle of the leaf, making sure the strips of carrot, tofu and palm heart overlap the wrapper by the frilly edge of the lettuce. Fold the edge nearest to you over the filling and fold in the sides to form a bundle with the palm heart, carrot, tofu and frill of lettuce poking out of the top.

9 Using the reserved green spring onions, tie the bundle with a green ribbon and place it on a serving dish. Repeat with the remaining wrappers and filling and serve with suka for dipping.

Per Portion Energy 307kcal/1289kJ; Protein 19.5g; Carbohydrate 32.8g, of which sugars 7g; Fat 11.7g, of which saturates 1.4g; Cholesterol 122mg; Calcium 433mg; Fibre 2.8g; Sodium 797mg.

INDONESIAN YELLOW PRAWN CURRY

COLOUR IS AN IMPORTANT PART OF INDONESIAN FOOD AND THE WORD UDANG, MEANING 'YELLOW', IS USED TO DESCRIBE THIS PRAWN DISH AS WELL AS THE POPULAR RICE DISH, NASI KUNING. BIG, JUICY PRAWNS ARE PARTICULARLY FAVOURED FOR THIS DISH IN BALI AND JAVA, BUT YOU CAN EASILY REPLACE THEM WITH SCALLOPS, SQUID OR MUSSELS, OR A COMBINATION OF ALL THREE.

SERVES FOUR

INGREDIENTS
30ml/2 tbsp coconut or palm oil
2 shallots, finely chopped
2 garlic cloves, finely chopped
2 fresh red chillies, seeded and
   sliced lengthways
25g/1oz fresh turmeric,
   finely chopped, or 10ml/2 tsp
   ground turmeric
25g/1oz fresh root ginger,
   finely chopped
2 lemon grass stalks, finely sliced
10ml/2 tsp coriander seeds

10ml/2 tsp terasi (Indonesian
   shrimp paste)
1 red (bell) pepper, seeded and
   finely sliced
4 kaffir lime leaves
about 500g/1¼lb raw prawns
   (shrimp), shelled and deveined
400g/14oz can coconut milk
salt and ground black pepper
cooked rice, to serve

To garnish
4 fried shallots
4 fresh green chillies, seeded and
   sliced diagonally

1 Heat the oil in a wok or heavy pan, stir in the shallots, garlic, chillies, turmeric, ginger, lemon grass and coriander seeds and fry until fragrant.

2 Stir in the terasi and cook the mixture for 2–3 minutes. Add the red pepper and kaffir lime leaves and stir-fry for 1 minute.

3 Toss the prawns into the pan. Pour in the coconut milk and bring to the boil. Season the curry with salt and pepper to taste.

4 Heap some cooked rice on to four warmed plates and spoon the prawn curry over the top.

5 Garnish with fried shallots and sliced green chillies.

COOK'S TIP
For curries and adobo dishes that use a lot of prawns (shrimp), it is often economical to buy frozen raw prawns at an Asian store rather than to obtain them fresh from the supermarket fish counter.

Per Portion Energy 230kcal/965kJ; Protein 26.4g; Carbohydrate 16g, of which sugars 13.5g; Fat 7.2g, of which saturates 1g; Cholesterol 263mg; Calcium 226mg; Fibre 2.7g; Sodium 519mg.

SWEET AND SOUR PRAWNS

INDONESIAN SWEET AND SOUR SAUCE DIFFERS FROM THE TRADITIONAL CHINESE VARIETY IN THAT IT IS A CLASSIC BLEND OF TOMATO KETCHUP, SOY SAUCE AND VINEGAR. THIS IS SIMPLE ENOUGH TO MAKE, AS THIS RECIPE SHOWS, BUT YOU CAN ALSO USE ANY STORE-BOUGHT VARIETY THAT YOU LIKE FOR SPEED AND CONVENIENCE.

SERVES FOUR

INGREDIENTS
  16 raw tiger prawns (jumbo shrimp)
  30ml/2 tbsp cornflour (cornstarch)
  1 egg, lightly beaten
  vegetable oil for deep-frying
For the sweet and sour sauce
  15ml/1 tbsp light soy sauce
  45g/3 tbsp tomato ketchup
  30ml/2 tbsp vinegar
  15ml/1 tbsp sugar
  100ml/3½fl oz/⅓ cup water
  5ml/1 tsp cornflour (cornstarch)

1 Shell the prawns, removing the heads but leaving the tails intact.

2 Dredge the prawns with the cornflour, then dip them in the egg. Heat enough oil for deep-frying, then deep-fry the prawns in batches until crisp and golden brown. Set aside to keep warm.

3 Blend all the sauce ingredients except for the cornflour and bring to the boil in a small pan.

4 Blend the cornflour with a little water and add to the sauce, stirring to prevent any lumps forming.

5 Cook the sauce, stirring, for 1 minute until thickened. Place the prawns in four bowls and pour over the sauce.

Per Portion Energy 224kcal/933kJ; Protein 10.1g; Carbohydrate 16.9g, of which sugars 0.5g; Fat 12.9g, of which saturates 1.7g; Cholesterol 78mg; Calcium 62mg; Fibre 0.3g; Sodium 256mg.

PRAWN ADOBO IN COCONUT MILK

NOTHING IS QUITE AS ICONIC AS ADOBO IN THE PHILIPPINES. THIS IS A BROAD TERM THAT DESCRIBES THE STYLE OF COOKING THAT IS TYPICALLY PRESENT IN A STEW COOKED IN VINEGAR, SOY SAUCE, PEPPER AND GARLIC. THIS RECIPE COMES FROM THE BICOL REGION, WHERE COCONUT MILK IS A MUCH-LOVED BASE FOR MANY DISHES. THE PRAWNS ARE MARINATED FIRST FOR EXTRA FLAVOUR.

1 Blend the marinade ingredients in a shallow container, then marinate the prawns for a few hours or overnight in the refrigerator.

2 Remove the prawns and set aside. Pour the marinade into a heavy pan, add the coconut milk and stir well.

3 Bring the mixture to the boil, then add the crushed garlic, soy sauce and lime juice.

4 Simmer the sauce for 5 minutes, then add the marinated prawns and cook for 5 minutes before serving.

SERVES FOUR

INGREDIENTS
  450g/1lb large raw peeled
    prawns (shrimp)
  300ml/½ pint/1¼ cups coconut milk
  4 garlic cloves, crushed
  30ml/2 tbsp soy sauce
  juice of 3 kalamansi limes
For the marinade
  105ml/7 tbsp suka (Filipino
    coconut vinegar)
  2.5ml/½ tsp ground black pepper
  30ml/2 tbsp garlic purée (paste)
  15ml/1 tbsp patis (Filipino fish sauce)

COOK'S TIPS
• In some regions, Filipino sour fruits called kamias are added, which give a lovely tartness. Kamias are related to star fruit (carambola), which can also be used.
• If you cannot find kalamansi limes, use ordinary limes instead.

Per Portion Energy 121kcal/512kJ; Protein 21.5g; Carbohydrate 7g, of which sugars 4.7g; Fat 1g, of which saturates 0.3g; Cholesterol 219mg; Calcium 115mg; Fibre 0.6g; Sodium 1009mg.

STEAMED SHELLFISH WITH TAMARIND DIP

BOILED, STEAMED, CURRIED OR GRILLED — THERE ARE ABUNDANT WAYS TO EAT THE SEAFOOD HARVEST OF SOUTH-EAST ASIA, AND IN INDONESIA AND THE PHILIPPINES THIS IS ONE OF THE MOST POPULAR SHELLFISH DISHES. WHETHER IT'S A SNACK OR A MAIN DISH, THE LOCALS NEVER SEEM TO TIRE OF IT: CRACKING SHELLS OPEN, SHARING AND DIPPING AND CHATTING ABOUT LIFE AS THEY EAT.

SERVES FOUR TO SIX

INGREDIENTS

2 whole lobsters, each weighing about 450g/1lb
3–4 medium crabs
24 mussels
24 scallops or clams
24 tiger prawns (jumbo shrimp)
6 spring onions (scallions), cut into 2.5cm/1in pieces and then into strips
150ml/¼ pint/⅔ cup suka (Filipino coconut vinegar) or rice vinegar
6 garlic cloves, crushed
about 50g/2oz fresh root ginger, finely sliced
6–8 black peppercorns
lime wedges, to garnish
To serve
Tamarind and Lime Sauce (see Essential Recipes)
cooked rice
green papaya salad

1 Scrub the lobsters, crabs, mussels and scallops or clams under cold running water, removing any beards, barnacles, and discarding any clams, mussels or scallops that are open.

2 Fill the bottom of two large steamers with at least 5cm/2in water, then divide the spring onions, suka, garlic, ginger and peppercorns between them. Cover and bring to the boil. Place the lobster and crab in the basket of one steamer and the small shellfish in the other. (You may need to steam them in batches and top up the water if it gets low.)

3 Cover the pans and steam the lobsters and crabs for 10 minutes and the smaller shellfish for 5 minutes, until they turn opaque and the mussel and clam or scallop shells open.

4 Discard any mussels, clams and scallops that have not opened.

5 Transfer the cooked shellfish to a warmed serving dish, garnish with lime wedges and serve with the Tamarind and Lime Sauce, accompanied by rice and a green papaya salad.

Per Portion Energy 312kcal/1315kJ; Protein 61g; Carbohydrate 3.4g, of which sugars 0.5g; Fat 6.1g, of which saturates 1g; Cholesterol 309mg; Calcium 193mg; Fibre 0.6g; Sodium 769mg.

STUFFED CUCUMBERS WITH CRAB

HERE, THE SIMPLE FRESHNESS OF THE CUCUMBER IS THE PERFECT FOIL TO THE RICH CRAB FILLING. THE DISH MAKES A PRETTY ADDITION TO A BUFFET TABLE BUT WORKS BEST AS A LIGHT AND ELEGANT APPETIZER, WITH HALF A CUCUMBER PER PERSON.

SERVES EIGHT

INGREDIENTS
- 4 whole cucumbers
- 1 small carrot
- 300g/10½oz crab meat
- 2 spring onions (scallions), white parts only, finely chopped
- 30ml/2 tbsp sesame oil
- 15ml/1 tbsp patis (Filipino fish sauce)
- 1 egg, lightly beaten
- 15g/1 tbsp cornflour (cornstarch)

1 Peel the cucumbers and cut each in half lengthways. Remove the seeds.

2 Dice the carrot finely and boil in a little water for 3 minutes, then drain.

3 Combine the crab meat with the spring onions, carrot, sesame oil, patis, egg and cornflour. Mix well.

4 Stuff each cucumber half with the mixture, patting it in well.

5 Place the cucumber halves in steamer baskets and steam over simmering water for 8 minutes until just done. Do not overcook or they will turn mushy. Serve whole or sliced.

COOK'S TIP
Courgettes (zucchini) also make good 'boats' for this dish, and the crab meat can be replaced with prawns (shrimp) or minced (ground) pork.

Per Portion Energy 109kcal/453kJ; Protein 10g; Carbohydrate 3.9g, of which sugars 2g; Fat 6g, of which saturates 0.9g; Cholesterol 55mg; Calcium 22mg; Fibre 0.7g; Sodium 332mg.

SUMATRAN SOUR FISH AND STAR FRUIT STEW

SOMEWHERE BETWEEN A STEW AND A SOUP, THIS REFRESHING DISH IS JUST ONE OF MANY VARIATIONS ON THE THEME OF SOUR FISH STEW FOUND THROUGHOUT SOUTH-EAST ASIA. THE STAR FRUIT ARE ADDED TOWARDS THE END OF COOKING SO THAT THE FRUIT RETAINS SOME BITE.

SERVES FOUR TO SIX

INGREDIENTS
   30ml/2 tbsp coconut or palm oil
   about 900ml/1½ pints/3¾ cups
      water
   2 lemon grass stalks, bruised
   25g/1oz fresh root ginger,
      finely sliced
   about 700g/1lb 9oz freshwater or
      saltwater fish, such as trout or sea
      bream, cut into thin steaks
   2 firm star fruit (carambola), sliced
   juice of 1–2 limes
For the spice paste
   4 shallots, chopped
   4 fresh red chillies, seeded
      and chopped
   2 garlic cloves, chopped
   25g/1oz fresh galangal, chopped
   25g/1oz fresh turmeric, chopped
   3–4 candlenuts, chopped
To serve
   steamed rice
   1 bunch fresh basil leaves (optional)
   1 lime, cut into wedges (optional)

1 Grind the spice paste ingredients to a coarse paste using a pestle and mortar or an electric food processor or blender. Heat the oil in a wok or wide, heavy pan, stir in the spice paste and fry until fragrant. Pour in the water and add the lemon grass and ginger. Bring to the boil, stirring all the time, then reduce the heat and simmer for 10 minutes.

2 Slip the fish into the pan, making sure there is enough liquid to cover the fish and adding more water if necessary.

3 Simmer gently for 3–4 minutes, then add the star fruit and lime juice to taste. Simmer for a further 2–3 minutes, until the fish is cooked.

4 Make heaps of rice in four to six warmed bowls and use spoonfuls of the cooking liquid to moisten the rice.

5 Divide the fish and star fruit between the bowls, spoon more of the cooking liquid over the top and garnish with basil leaves and a wedge of lime to squeeze over, if using.

Per Portion Energy 240kcal/1001kJ; Protein 25.9g; Carbohydrate 7.3g, of which sugars 4.7g; Fat 12.1g, of which saturates 1.2g; Cholesterol 0mg; Calcium 27mg; Fibre 1.7g; Sodium 67mg.

CATFISH WITH A SPICY COCONUT SAUCE

In this popular Indonesian dish, catfish is simply fried and served with a fragrant and spicy sauce. Many Indonesian cooks make up jars of the spice paste base gede, which they keep for flavouring meat, poultry and fish dishes.

SERVES FOUR

INGREDIENTS
 200ml/7fl oz/¾ cup coconut milk
 30ml/2 tbsp coconut cream
 30ml/2 tbsp rice flour, tapioca flour
   or cornflour (cornstarch)
 5ml/1 tsp ground coriander
 8 fresh catfish fillets
 30ml/2 tbsp coconut, palm,
   groundnut (peanut) or corn oil
 salt and ground black pepper
 fresh coriander (cilantro) leaves,
   to garnish
To serve
 boiled rice
 1 lime, quartered
For the spice paste
 2 shallots, chopped
 2 garlic cloves, chopped
 2 fresh red chillies, seeded
   and chopped
 25g/1oz fresh galangal, chopped
 15g/½ oz fresh turmeric, chopped,
   or 2.5ml/½ tsp ground turmeric
 2–3 lemon grass stalks, chopped
 15ml/1 tbsp palm or groundnut
   (peanut) oil
 5ml/1 tsp terasi (Indonesian
   shrimp paste)
 15ml/1 tbsp tamarind paste
 5ml/1 tsp palm sugar (jaggery)

1 Using a mortar and pestle or food processor, pound the shallots, garlic, chillies, galangal, turmeric and lemon grass to a paste.

2 Heat the oil in a wok or heavy pan, stir in the paste and fry until it becomes fragrant and begins to colour. Add the terasi, tamarind paste and sugar and continue to stir until the paste darkens.

3 Stir the coconut milk and cream into the spice paste and boil for about 10 minutes, until the milk and cream separate, leaving behind an oily paste. Season with salt and pepper to taste.

4 Meanwhile, on a large plate, mix the flour with the coriander and season with salt and pepper. Toss the catfish fillets in the flour so that they are lightly coated all over.

5 Heat the oil in a heavy frying pan and quickly fry the fillets for about 2 minutes on each side, until golden.

6 Using a fish slice, transfer the catfish fillets to warmed dishes with helpings of rice in them. Spoon the coconut sauce over the fish and provide lime wedges for squeezing.

COOK'S TIP
Catfish is hugely popular in some areas of the world, but not readily found in many European stores and markets. If you cannot find it, or do not like catfish, use firm, plump fillets of sole or halibut instead.

Per Portion Energy 338kcal/1412kJ; Protein 38.1g; Carbohydrate 11.9g, of which sugars 4.9g; Fat 15.3g, of which saturates 5.7g; Cholesterol 92mg; Calcium 56mg; Fibre 0.9g; Sodium 190mg.

Sardines Cooked in Spicy Coconut Milk with Herbs

A fish dish based on coconut milk, rempah-rempah varies from region to region. In northern Sumatra, where the tolerance for chillies and spice is high, this dish is particularly fiery but is tempered by the inclusion of locally grown herbs. As a substitute for the local herbs, which are not available in the West, this recipe uses fresh mint, basil and flat leaf parsley instead.

<u>SERVES FOUR</u>

INGREDIENTS
    6–8 fresh red chillies, according to
       taste, seeded and chopped
    4 shallots, chopped
    4 garlic cloves, chopped
    1 lemon grass stalk, chopped
    25g/1oz fresh galangal, chopped
    30ml/2 tbsp coconut or palm oil
    10ml/2 tsp coriander seeds
    5ml/1 tsp cumin seeds
    5ml/1 tsp fennel seeds
    1 small bunch fresh mint leaves,
       finely chopped
    1 small bunch fresh flat leaf parsley,
       finely chopped
    15ml/1 tbsp palm sugar (jaggery)
    15ml/1 tbsp tamarind paste
    4 sardines or small mackerel, gutted,
       kept whole
    300ml/½ pint/1¼ cups coconut milk
    salt and ground black pepper
To serve
    steamed rice or sago
    1 large bunch fresh flat leaf parsley
    fresh basil leaves

1 Using a mortar and pestle, pound the chillies, shallots, garlic, lemon grass and galangal to a paste.

2 Heat the oil in a wok or wide, heavy pan, stir in the coriander, cumin and fennel seeds and fry until they give off a nutty aroma. Add the paste and stir until it becomes fragrant and golden in colour. Add the chopped mint and parsley and stir for 1 minute, then add the sugar and tamarind paste.

3 Carefully place the fish in the pan, coating them in the paste, and pour in the coconut milk. Bring to the boil, then reduce the heat and cook gently for 10–15 minutes, until the fish is tender. Season the sauce with salt and pepper to taste.

4 Cover the bottom of a warmed serving dish with parsley and place the fish on top, then spoon the sauce over the top. Serve with a bowl of steamed rice or sago and stalks of fresh parsley and basil leaves.

Per Portion Energy 287kcal/1199kJ; Protein 22.8g; Carbohydrate 11g, of which sugars 10.2g; Fat 17.2g, of which saturates 3.7g; Cholesterol 0mg; Calcium 167mg; Fibre 2.1g; Sodium 213mg.

TWICE-COOKED LAPU LAPU

IT MAY SEEM STRANGE BUT, IN SOUTH-EAST ASIA, IT IS NOT UNUSUAL TO COOK FISH OR MEAT TWICE TO ACHIEVE THE DESIRED TENDER EFFECT. IN THIS FILIPINO DISH FROM CEBU, THE LOCAL FISH, LAPU LAPU, IS FIRST FRIED AND THEN BAKED IN A SAUCE.

SERVES THREE TO FOUR

INGREDIENTS
  1–2 fresh Lapu Lapu, sea bass or red
    snapper, gutted and cleaned, total
    weight 1.2–1.3kg/2½–3lb
  30ml/2 tbsp palm or groundnut
    (peanut) oil
  25g/1oz fresh root ginger, chopped
  4 shallots, finely chopped
  1 large carrot, diced
  1 red (bell) pepper, seeded
    and diced
  30ml/2 tbsp suka (Filipino
    coconut vinegar)
  30ml/2 tbsp light soy sauce
  10ml/2 tsp sugar
  salt and ground black pepper
  4 spring onions (scallions), finely
    shredded, to garnish
  1 lime, cut into wedges,
    to serve

1 Preheat the oven to 180°C/350°F/ Gas 4. Rub the fish with salt. Heat 15ml/1 tbsp of the oil in a large frying pan, add the fish and fry on both sides for 2 minutes. Remove the fish from the pan and put aside.

2 Add the remaining oil to the pan, stir in the ginger, shallots, carrot and pepper and fry for 2–3 minutes until they begin to colour.

3 Stir in the suka, soy sauce and sugar and season well with black pepper.

4 Put the fish in an ovenproof dish, spoon over the sauce and bake in the oven for 25–30 minutes, until tender.

5 Garnish with shredded spring onions and serve with lime wedges to squeeze over the fish.

Per Portion Energy 237kcal/1001kJ; Protein 38.6g; Carbohydrate 10g, of which sugars 9.1g; Fat 5.1g, of which saturates 1g; Cholesterol 69mg; Calcium 100mg; Fibre 1.7g; Sodium 720mg.

CHARGRILLED FISH WITH SAMBAL BADJAK

IN THE COASTAL REGIONS OF INDONESIA, GRILLING FISH OVER CHARCOAL IS A COMMON SIGHT IN THE TOURIST RESORTS, IN THE VILLAGES, ON THE BEACH AND BY THE ROADSIDE. THIS RECIPE IS VERSATILE ENOUGH TO USE WITH MOST FISH, SO JUST CHOOSE WHAT LOOKS BEST AT THE FISHMONGER.

SERVES FOUR

INGREDIENTS
    1 whole large sea fish, such as
      grouper, red snapper, sea bass,
      1 large piece of swordfish,
      or 4 whole smaller fish, such as
      sardines, gutted and cleaned
    30ml/2 tbsp coconut oil
    60ml/4 tbsp dark soy sauce
    2 garlic cloves, crushed
    juice of 1 lime
    cooked rice and fresh coriander
      (cilantro) sprigs, to serve
For the sambal
    50g/2oz tamarind paste
    150ml/¼ pint/⅔ cup boiling water
    4 shallots, chopped
    4 garlic cloves, chopped
    4–6 fresh red chillies, seeded
      and chopped
    25g/1oz fresh galangal, chopped
    2 kaffir lime leaves, crumbled
    10ml/2 tsp terasi (Indonesian
      shrimp paste)
    10ml/2 tsp palm sugar (jaggery)
    30ml/2 tbsp coconut or palm oil

1 Slash the fish at about 2.5cm/1in intervals with a sharp knife. Place in a shallow dish.

2 In a small bowl, mix the coconut oil, soy sauce, garlic and lime juice together. Spoon the marinade over the fish and rub it into the skin and slashes. Leave for about 1 hour.

3 Meanwhile, prepare the sambal. Put the tamarind paste in a bowl, pour over the boiling water and leave to soak for 30 minutes. Strain into a separate bowl, pressing the paste through a sieve (strainer). Discard the solids and put the tamarind juice aside.

4 Using a mortar and pestle, pound the shallots, garlic, chillies, galangal and lime leaves to a coarse paste. Add the terasi and sugar and beat to combine.

5 Heat the oil in a small wok, stir in the paste and fry for 2–3 minutes. Stir in the tamarind juice and boil until it reduces to a thick paste. Turn into a serving bowl.

6 Prepare the barbecue. Place the fish on the rack and cook for 5 minutes on each side, depending on the size of fish, basting it with any leftover marinade. Transfer the fish to a serving plate, garnished with coriander, and serve with the sambal and cooked rice.

Per Portion Energy 359kcal/1507kJ; Protein 42.3g; Carbohydrate 11.8g, of which sugars 9.3g; Fat 16.4g, of which saturates 2.3g; Cholesterol 75mg; Calcium 117mg; Fibre 1.4g; Sodium 1263mg.

MILKFISH STUFFED WITH MINCED PORK AND PEAS

ALTHOUGH MILKFISH IS WIDELY USED THROUGHOUT SOUTH-EAST ASIA, IT IS REGARDED AS THE NATIONAL FISH OF THE PHILIPPINES, WHERE IT IS KNOWN AS BANGUS. IN THIS PARTICULAR DISH, THE BONY FISH IS BASHED GENTLY TO LOOSEN THE SKIN, SO THAT THE FLESH AND BONES CAN BE REMOVED FROM THE FISH WHILE KEEPING IT INTACT. THE FLESH IS THEN COOKED WITH PORK AND STUFFED BACK INTO THE EMPTY FISH SKIN SO THAT IT RESEMBLES A WHOLE FISH ONCE MORE.

SERVES THREE TO FOUR

INGREDIENTS

1–2 fresh milkfish, sea bass or
    mackerel, gutted and cleaned, total
    weight 1.2–1.3kg/2½–3lb
15ml/1 tbsp palm or groundnut
    (peanut) oil
2–3 shallots, finely chopped
2 garlic cloves, finely chopped
115g/4oz minced (ground) pork
30ml/2 tbsp light soy sauce
400g/14oz can petits pois (baby
    peas), drained and rinsed
15ml/1 tbsp groundnut (peanut)
    or vegetable oil, for frying
15g/½oz/1 tbsp butter
salt and ground black pepper

To serve

45–60ml/3–4 tbsp suka (Filipino
    coconut vinegar)
2 red chillies, seeded and
    finely chopped

1 Preheat the oven to 180°C/350°F/ Gas 4. Put the fish on a flat surface and gently bash the body (not the head) with a rolling pin to soften the flesh.

2 Using your fingers, gently massage the skin away from the flesh, being careful not to tear the skin.

3 Using a sharp knife, make an incision on the underside of the fish, just below the gills, and squeeze the flesh from the tail end through this hole, keeping the head and backbone intact. Remove all the small bones from the flesh.

4 Heat the palm or groundnut oil in a heavy frying pan, stir in the shallots and garlic and fry until they turn golden.

5 Add the minced pork and fry for 2–3 minutes, then stir in the fish flesh until mixed well together. Stir in the soy sauce and peas, and season well with salt and pepper.

VARIATIONS

• If you prefer a spicier filling, add finely chopped fresh root ginger and chillies to the pan with the garlic and shallots.
• You can make this dish for non-meat-eaters if you omit the pork, using the same weight of chopped prawns (shrimp) instead, or even a handful of finely chopped, toasted nuts, such as cashews, almonds and pecans.

6 Hold the fish skin in one hand and carefully stuff the fish and pork mixture into the fish with the other.

7 Secure the opening with a cocktail stick (toothpick).

8 Heat the groundnut oil and the butter in a heavy frying pan and fry the stuffed fish on both sides, until well browned.

9 Remove the fish from the pan, wrap it in a sheet of aluminium foil and place it on a baking tray. Bake the fish in the oven for about 35 minutes to allow the flavours to combine.

10 In a bowl, mix the suka and chillies together to make a piquant dressing for the fish.

11 Remove the fish from the oven and cut it into thick, diagonal slices. Neaten the slices with the flat blade of the knife before carefully placing a slice on warmed individual plates. Serve with the spiced suka to spoon over the fish.

COOK'S TIP

Because emptying and stuffing a fish skin may be a new technique to you, it is wise to practise this dish before you cook it for guests. This 'practice run' will also give you the chance to judge how much seasoning you prefer in the filling.

Per Portion Energy 397kcal/1665kJ; Protein 53.3g; Carbohydrate 12.7g, of which sugars 3.4g; Fat 15.4g, of which saturates 4.6g; Cholesterol 102mg; Calcium 116mg; Fibre 4.9g; Sodium 413mg.

FISH COOKED IN BANANA LEAVES

COOKING FISH IN BANANA LEAVES IS A DELIGHTFUL METHOD THAT CAN BE FOUND THROUGHOUT SOUTH-EAST ASIA. THE BANANA LEAVES IMPART THEIR OWN FLAVOUR TO THE FISH, WHICH REMAINS BEAUTIFULLY SUCCULENT AND FRAGRANT WITHIN ITS NATURAL WRAPPING.

SERVES FOUR

INGREDIENTS
  500g/1¼lb fresh fish fillets,
    cut into chunks
  juice of 2 limes
  4–6 shallots, chopped
  2 fresh red chillies, seeded
    and chopped
  25g/1oz fresh root ginger, chopped
  15g/½oz fresh turmeric, chopped
  2 lemon grass stalks, chopped
  3–4 candlenuts, crushed
  10ml/2 tsp palm sugar (jaggery)
  salt
  1–2 banana leaves, cut into
    4 big squares
To serve
  cooked rice
  chilli sambal

1 In a large bowl, toss the fish fillets in the lime juice then leave to marinate at room temperature for 10–15 minutes.

2 Meanwhile, using a mortar and pestle, pound the shallots, chillies, ginger, turmeric and lemon grass to a coarse paste. Add the candlenuts and sugar and season with salt. Turn the paste into the bowl with the fish and toss to coat the fish in it.

3 Place the banana leaves on a flat surface and divide the fish mixture equally among them.

4 Tuck in the sides and fold over the ends to form neat parcels and secure with string.

5 Place the banana leaf parcels in a steamer and cook for 25–30 minutes until tender. Serve hot with rice and a chilli sambal.

COOK'S TIP
Banana leaves are available in South-east Asian, Chinese and African food shops, but if you cannot find them you can use aluminium foil instead, and bake the fish parcels in the oven at 180°C/350°F/Gas 4 instead of steaming them.

Per Portion Energy 225kcal/943kJ; Protein 27.6g; Carbohydrate 14.1g, of which sugars 10.4g; Fat 6.9g, of which saturates 1.2g; Cholesterol 58mg; Calcium 51mg; Fibre 2.5g; Sodium 79mg.

FILIPINO CURED HERRING

GENERALLY SERVED AS AN APPETIZER OR SNACK IN THE PHILIPPINES, KINILAW CAN BE MADE WITH MANY TYPES OF FISH, INCLUDING OCTOPUS, HALIBUT AND SALMON, ALTHOUGH MACKEREL AND HERRING ARE PARTICULARLY SUITABLE. THE FISH MUST BE ABSOLUTELY FRESH.

SERVES FOUR

INGREDIENTS

150ml/¼ pint/⅔ cup suka (Filipino
  coconut vinegar)
juice of 2 kalamansi limes
40g/1½oz fresh root ginger, grated
2 fresh red chillies, seeded and
  finely sliced
8–10 herring fillets, cut into
  bitesize pieces
2 shallots, finely sliced
1 green mango, cut into
  julienne strips
salt and ground black pepper
fresh coriander (cilantro) leaves and
  lime wedges, to serve

1 Put the suka, lime juice, ginger and chillies in a bowl and mix together. Season the mixture with salt and pepper. Put the herring fillets in a shallow dish and scatter the shallots over the top and then the strips of green mango.

2 Pour the suka mixture over the fish. Cover with clear film (plastic wrap) and leave to marinate in the refrigerator for 1–2 hours or overnight, turning the fish several times. Serve with coriander leaves and lime wedges.

Per Portion Energy 408kcal/1699kJ; Protein 36.4g; Carbohydrate 5.9g, of which sugars 5.7g; Fat 26.7g, of which saturates 6.6g; Cholesterol 100mg; Calcium 160mg; Fibre 1.9g; Sodium 260mg.

SOUSED FISH WITH BITTER MELON

WITH THEIR LOVE OF VINEGAR, THIS IS AN EVERYDAY DISH FOR MANY FILIPINOS. SERVED WITH RICE, IT IS NORMALLY EATEN FOR LUNCH OR FOR THE MORNING AND AFTERNOON MERIENDA. THE LOCAL, RATHER BONY, MILKFISH IS OFTEN COOKED IN THIS WAY, BUT TROUT, MACKEREL, HERRING OR SEA BASS ARE JUST AS SUITABLE, AND EASIER TO OBTAIN.

SERVES FOUR

INGREDIENTS
1 small aubergine (eggplant), thickly sliced
1 small bitter melon, cut into thick bitesize slices
4 spring onions (scallions), cut into 2.5cm/1in lengths
2 fresh green chillies, seeded and sliced
25g/1oz fresh root ginger, grated
4–6 black peppercorns
1 whole fish, gutted and cleaned, or fish fillets, total weight 500g/1¼lb
250ml/8fl oz/1 cup suka (Filipino coconut vinegar), rice vinegar or white wine vinegar
200ml/7fl oz/¾ cup water
30ml/2 tbsp light soy sauce
salt and ground black pepper
To serve
cooked rice
soy sauce
fresh chillies, seeded and sliced diagonally

1 Arrange the aubergine and bitter melon slices in the bottom of a wide, heavy pan. Sprinkle the spring onions, chillies, ginger and peppercorns over the top. Place the whole fish, or arrange the fillets, over the vegetables.

2 In a bowl, mix the vinegar, water and soy sauce together, then pour the mixture over the fish and vegetables. Season the dish with a little salt and lots of black pepper. Bring to the boil, then reduce the heat, cover and simmer gently for about 1 hour, until tender.

3 Transfer the fish to a dish, removing the head if you prefer, and spoon the vegetables and cooking liquid over and around it. Leave to cool. Serve the fish with rice, soy sauce and sliced chillies.

COOK'S TIP
Rings of green (bell) pepper may be used instead of bitter melon, and cooked the same way.

Per Portion Energy 151kcal/636kJ; Protein 20.7g; Carbohydrate 8.5g, of which sugars 8.3g; Fat 4g, of which saturates 0.9g; Cholesterol 80mg; Calcium 54mg; Fibre 1.2g; Sodium 647mg.

FRIED ANCHOVIES AND PEANUTS

IN THE REGION OF PADANG, MEALS ARE THOUGHT INCOMPLETE WITHOUT FRIED ANCHOVIES, WHICH ARE OFTEN COMBINED WITH PEANUTS FOR A CRUNCHY KICK. THE PEANUTS USED ARE A SMALL, RED-SKINNED VARIETY AND TRADITIONALLY COOKED WITH THEIR SKINS ON. DRIED ANCHOVIES USUALLY HAVE A FINE COATING OF FLOURY DUST ON THEM. SHAKE THIS OFF BEFORE FRYING.

SERVES FOUR

INGREDIENTS

150g/5oz red-skinned, raw peanuts
75ml/5 tbsp vegetable oil
150g/5oz dried anchovies
100ml/3½fl oz/⅓ cup coconut milk
30g/2 tbsp Shallot and Lemon Grass
   Sambal (see Essential Recipes)
15ml/1 tbsp lime juice
5ml/1 tsp sugar

1 Dry-fry the peanuts in a warm wok for 10–15 minutes, until the skins begin to blister. Remove the peanuts from the wok and set aside.

2 Heat the oil in the wok and fry the dried anchovies until crisp and brown. Drain on kitchen paper.

3 Pour off all but 2 tbsp of the oil and return the nuts and anchovies to the wok.

COOK'S TIP
Small dried anchovies are ideal for this recipe. Larger ones should be used for stock and stews rather than snacking.

4 Fry for 1 minute, then add the coconut milk, sambal, lime juice and sugar. There is no need to add any salt as the sambal is already seasoned.

5 Stir to mix, then serve warm or cold.

Per Portion Energy 419kcal/1738kJ; Protein 19.3g; Carbohydrate 6.4g, of which sugars 3.9g; Fat 35.4g, of which saturates 5.6g; Cholesterol 24mg; Calcium 145mg; Fibre 2.4g; Sodium 1526mg.

FISH CROQUETTES

THIS DISH IS KNOWN IN INDONESIA AS BEGEDEL IKAN. THE WORD BEGEDEL IS OF DUTCH HERITAGE, BUT THE FRENCH WORD 'CROQUETTE' IS A MORE FAMILIAR TERM TO MOST WESTERNERS. POTATOES ARE USUALLY INVOLVED, ALTHOUGH IN SOME REGIONS ONLY FRESH BREADCRUMBS ARE USED. VERSIONS THAT USE SEAFOOD, BEEF OR PORK EXIST, AND EVEN CANNED FISH CAN BE USED.

3 Lightly beat the eggs and mix with the milk. Add the potatoes and fish and mix well. Stir in the flour to make a thick mixture. Add the salt, ground cloves, black pepper and spring onion.

4 Shape the mixture into balls, each the size of a plum, and flatten a little. Dust with flour.

SERVES FOUR

INGREDIENTS
600g/1lb 6oz potatoes
450g/1lb cod or halibut
2 eggs
105ml/7 tbsp milk
40g/1½oz plain (all-purpose) flour, plus extra for dusting
5ml/1 tsp salt
pinch of ground cloves
2.5ml/½ tsp ground black pepper
1 spring onion (scallion), white part only, finely chopped
vegetable oil for deep-frying
chilli sauce, to serve

1 Boil the potatoes until well done, then drain, peel (when cool enough to handle) and mash.

2 Poach the fish in 400ml/14fl oz/ 1⅔ cups water for 10 minutes. Remove the fish using a slotted spoon and place on a plate. Flake or mash the flesh, removing any bones as you go, then discard the poaching water.

VARIATION
Other types of white fish can be used. Canned tuna also works well, and saves cooking time.

5 Heat enough oil for deep-frying and fry the croquettes in batches until golden brown. Drain on crumpled kitchen paper.

6 Serve with a bowl of your favourite chilli sauce, for dipping.

Per Portion Energy 402kcal/1684kJ; Protein 28.1g; Carbohydrate 33.2g, of which sugars 3.3g; Fat 18.3g, of which saturates 3g; Cholesterol 148mg; Calcium 79mg; Fibre 1.8g; Sodium 622mg.

FISH POACHED IN VINEGAR AND GINGER

PAKSIW IN THIS DISH'S NAME (PAKSIW NA ISDA) REFERS TO A SPECIFIC METHOD OF COOKING WITH VINEGAR AND SUGAR, ALMOST A SWEET AND SOUR, AND OFTEN USED TO GIVE NEW ZEST TO LEFTOVER PORK AND BEEF DISHES. ALTHOUGH SIMPLE, IT IS A WELL-REGARDED METHOD. FIRM-FLESHED FISH TURNS OUT PARTICULARLY WELL WHEN PREPARED IN THIS WAY.

SERVES FOUR

INGREDIENTS

30ml/2 tbsp garlic purée (paste)
30ml/2 tbsp grated ginger
5ml/1 tsp black peppercorns, crushed
300ml/½ pint/1¼ cups water
105ml/7 tbsp vinegar
2 whole fish (600g/1lb 6oz total
   weight) such as mullet, cod
   or snapper
15ml/1 tbsp patis (Filipino fish sauce)
15ml/1 tbsp vegetable oil
small bunch fresh coriander (cilantro)
   leaves and15ml/1 tbsp red chilli
   strips, to garnish

3 Turn the fish gently, and with a ladle add the patis and oil. Simmer for another 3 minutes.

4 Serve the fish hot, with the cooking liquid poured over it, garnished with coriander leaves and chilli strips.

COOK'S TIP
Although using a whole fish is the tradition, there is no reason why you cannot use fish fillets. This will remove the chore of having to deal with bones, making the dish easier to serve and eat. You will need to be extra careful when turning the fish if you use fillets, as they will tend to break up, and you may need to reduce the cooking time slightly.

1 Blend the garlic purée, ginger, peppercorns, water and vinegar in a non-metallic dish. Place in a flameproof casserole or baking dish.

2 Clean and gut the fish, trimming off any protruding fins and tail with scissors, and add to the dish. Bring to the boil, then simmer for 5 minutes, covered.

Per Portion Energy 157kcal/658kJ; Protein 28g; Carbohydrate 1.5g, of which sugars 0.4g; Fat 4.3g, of which saturates 0.9g; Cholesterol 78mg; Calcium 40mg; Fibre 0.3g; Sodium 411mg.

POULTRY

After sampling some of the delicious treatments given to chicken, duck and other poultry by Indonesian and Filipino cooks, you may be reluctant to return to traditional Western cooking methods. With fragrant and meltingly tender stews, irresistibly crunchy deep-fried dishes, deliciously different roasts and spicy stuffings, this chapter is full of inspiration for new and experienced cooks alike.

GRILLED CHICKEN STRIPS

THE PHILIPPINE LANGUAGE, TAGALOG, IS VERY SPECIFIC ABOUT TRADITIONAL COOKING TERMS, AND THERE IS A WORD FOR PRACTICALLY EVERY METHOD OF COOKING. WHEN YOU SEE THE WORD INIHAW, AS IN THIS DISH'S NAME, INIHAW MANOC, IT MEANS FOOD — GENERALLY MEAT OR VEGETABLES — COOKED OVER CHARCOAL. FILIPINOS ARE PASSIONATE ABOUT BARBECUING AND DO SO AT EVERY OPPORTUNITY.

1 Put the garlic, suka, soy sauce, pepper and sugar in a bowl and stir well. Add the chicken and leave to marinate for several hours, or overnight.

2 Prepare a barbecue and cook the chicken pieces for 8–10 minutes, until cooked through.

3 Meanwhile, mix the remaining marinade with the lime juice and oil.

4 Brush the marinade over the chicken as it cooks with the lemon grass brush or a pastry brush. Serve hot, garnished with lime slices and coriander, with a chilli sauce dip on the side.

SERVES 4

INGREDIENTS
    30ml/2 tbsp garlic purée (paste)
    105ml/7 tbsp suka (Filipino
        coconut vinegar)
    105ml/7 tbsp soy sauce
    10ml/2 tsp ground black pepper
    5ml/1 tsp sugar
    4 skinless, boneless chicken thighs
        and 2 chicken breasts, cut into
        strips as wide as a finger

juice of 2 kalamansi limes. plus
    some slices of lime to garnish
15ml/1 tbsp vegetabe oil
1 lemon grass stalk, root end cut to
    form a brush
fresh coriander (cilantro), to garnish
chilli sauce dip, to serve

VARIATION
Pork chops are also excellent with this marinade, grilled (broiled) whole instead of in strips.

Per Portion Energy 205kcal/866kJ; Protein 39.9g; Carbohydrate 3.3g, of which sugars 2.1g; Fat 3.7g, of which saturates 1g; Cholesterol 158mg; Calcium 15mg; Fibre 0.3g; Sodium 1025mg.

INDONESIAN FRIED CHICKEN

THIS SPICY DISH PUTS WESTERN FRIED CHICKEN TO SHAME. FIRST OF ALL THE CHICKEN IS COOKED IN SPICE PASTE TO ENSURE A DEPTH OF FLAVOUR AND THEN IT IS SIMPLY DEEP-FRIED TO FORM A CRISP, GOLDEN SKIN. SERVE WITH A SAMBAL OR PICKLE FOR A DELICIOUS SNACK OR, FOR A TASTY MEAL, ACCOMPANY IT WITH YELLOW OR FRAGRANT COCONUT RICE AND A SALAD.

SERVES FOUR

INGREDIENTS
    12 chicken thighs or drumsticks,
       or 12 legs, separated into thighs
       and drumsticks
    30ml/2 tbsp kecap manis (Indonesian
       sweet soy sauce)
    150ml/¼ pint/⅔ cup water
    vegetable oil, for deep-frying
    salt and ground black pepper
    sambal or pickle, to serve
For the spice paste
    2 shallots, chopped
    4 garlic cloves, chopped
    50g/2oz fresh root ginger, chopped
    25g/1oz fresh turmeric, chopped
    2 lemon grass stalks, chopped

1 Grind the spice paste ingredients to a coarse paste using a pestle and mortar or an electric food processor or blender.

2 Put the chicken pieces in a large, flameproof casserole or heavy pan and smear the spice paste over them.

3 Add the kecap manis and the water to the pan and bring to the boil, then reduce the heat and simmer, uncovered, for about 25 minutes.

4 Turn the chicken occasionally, until all the liquid has evaporated. You need the chicken to be dry before you deep-fry it, but the spices should be sticking to it. Season the chicken pieces with salt and pepper.

5 Heat enough oil for deep-frying in a wok. Add the chicken pieces, in batches, and fry for 6–8 minutes until golden brown and crisp. Remove from the wok with a slotted spoon, drain on kitchen paper and serve hot.

COOK'S TIP
Kecap manis is soy sauce sweetened with palm sugar (jaggery). If you cannot find it replace it with the same quantity of dark soy sauce and 15ml/1 tbsp sugar.

Per Portion Energy 410kcal/1719kJ; Protein 60.8g; Carbohydrate 4.6g, of which sugars 3.4g; Fat 16.6g, of which saturates 2.4g; Cholesterol 175mg; Calcium 26mg; Fibre 0.7g; Sodium 686mg.

BALI FRIED POUSSINS

In Bali, siap megoreng is practically a national dish and is offered in reverence to deities during religious festivals. It is usually grilled or barbecued, although it can also be pan-fried, the latter method being easier unless you are using the barbecue anyway. Poussins are best for the dish as they are more tender and cook more quickly than chicken.

SERVES 4

INGREDIENTS

4 poussins
150g/5oz Balinese Spice Paste
  (see Essential Recipes)
450ml/14fl oz/1⅔ cups
  coconut milk
3 lemon grass stalks, 5cm/2in
  of root end bruised
5 salam leaves (Indonesian bay leaves)
5ml/1 tsp salt
5ml/1 tsp black peppercorns, crushed
105ml/7 tbsp vegetable oil
juice of 1 lime
4 limes, halved, to garnish
chilli dipping sauce, to serve

1 Spatchcock each poussin by cutting down the backbone and spreading out the bird so that the breast is one broad piece and the bird lies flat on the work surface. Alternatively, ask your butcher to do this for you.

2 Whisk together the spice paste and coconut milk, and bring to the boil with the lemon grass, salam leaves, salt and peppercorns. Simmer the poussins in this blend for 8 minutes. If your pot is too crowded, cook in two batches.

3 Remove the poussins and drain. Heat the oil in a large wok or frying pan and fry the poussins, two at a time, until the skin is golden brown. Turn once or twice to make sure they cook thoroughly.

4 In the last few minutes, drizzle the lime juice over the poussins and serve warm with a chilli dipping sauce and lime halves to squeeze over.

Per portion Energy 288kcal/1200kJ; Protein 24.3g; Carbohydrate 3.5g, of which sugars 2.9g; Fat 20.6g, of which saturates 4.9g; Cholesterol 123mg; Calcium 47mg; Fibre 0.5g; Sodium 183mg.

SHREDDED CHICKEN

ABON DESCRIBES MEATS THAT HAVE BEEN COOKED AND FLAKED. THIS DISH, AYAM ABON ABON, IS NOT DIFFICULT TO MAKE AT HOME ALTHOUGH IT IS SOLD READY-MADE THROUGHOUT INDONESIA. IT IS OFTEN MADE WITH BEEF AND OCCASIONALLY FISH, WHILE INDONESIAN CHINESE GENERALLY USE PORK, BUT THIS VERSION USES CHICKEN, WHICH IS EASIER TO HANDLE.

SERVES FOUR

INGREDIENTS

   1 chicken, about 600g/1lb 6oz
   5ml/1 tsp ground coriander
   2 slices galangal
   5ml/1 tsp garlic purée (paste)
   2.5ml/½ tsp salt
   60ml/4 tbsp vegetable oil
   shredded cucumber and lettuce

1 Put the chicken in a large pan and just cover it in water. Bring to the boil, then simmer for 35 minutes. Strain and cool, reserving the stock if you wish.

2 Dry-fry the ground coriander over a low–moderate heat until fragrant. Grate the galangal finely.

COOK'S TIPS
• Use skinless chicken breast fillets for a less fatty dish that also saves some time and effort.
• Make your own garlic purée by pulping peeled garlic cloves in a mortar and pestle or rubbing them through a fine grater.

3 Using your hands or a sharp knife, flake the chicken into strips, removing the skin if you prefer.

4 Mix the chicken with the coriander, galangal, garlic and salt. Heat the oil in a large wok and fry the chicken over a high heat until crisp. Serve as a salad on a bed of shredded cucumber and lettuce.

Per portion Energy 324kcal/1342kJ; Protein 19.3g; Carbohydrate 2.1g, of which sugars 0.2g; Fat 26.5g, of which saturates 5.8g; Cholesterol 96mg; Calcium 10mg; Fibre 0.5g; Sodium 76mg.

INDONESIAN CHICKEN AND PRAWN SALAD

SPICY AND REFRESHING CHICKEN AND/OR SHELLFISH SALADS ARE POPULAR AT INDONESIAN FOOD STALLS AND AS PART OF LARGE, CELEBRATORY FEASTS. THIS DISH IS A REAL CLASSIC, WITH TENDER STRIPS OF CHICKEN AND MEATY PRAWNS IRRESISTIBLY FLAVOURED WITH THE SWEET, GINGERY HEAT OF GALANGAL, COLOURED WITH GOLDEN TURMERIC AND TOSSED IN A FRESH, ZESTY TOMATO SAUCE.

1 Cook the chicken pieces by steaming, roasting or boiling. When cooked, if using chicken breast fillets, cut the meat into thin strips; if using thighs, shred the meat with your fingers.

2 Boil or steam the prawns for 2–3 minutes, until opaque. Drain, refresh in cold water and drain again. Put aside.

3 To make the spice paste, using a mortar and pestle, grind the shallots, garlic, chillies, galangal, turmeric, lemon grass and candlenuts together.

4 Heat the oil in a heavy pan, stir in the spice paste and fry until fragrant. Add the terasi and palm sugar and stir for 3–4 minutes, until the paste starts to brown. Add the tomatoes, coriander, mint and lime juice and cook for 5–10 minutes, until the sauce is reduced and thick. Season to taste and leave to cool.

5 Add the chicken and prawns to the sauce and toss together. Turn into a dish and serve with lime wedges to squeeze over, and chillies to chew on.

SERVES FOUR

INGREDIENTS

500g/1¼lb chicken breast fillets
  or thighs
225g/8oz prawns (shrimp), peeled
  and deveined
30ml/2 tbsp groundnut (peanut) oil
5ml/1 tsp terasi (Indonesian
  shrimp paste)
10ml/2 tsp palm sugar (jaggery)
2 tomatoes, skinned, seeded
  and chopped
1 bunch fresh coriander (cilantro)
  leaves, chopped
1 bunch fresh mint leaves, chopped

juice of 1 lime
salt and ground black pepper
For the spice paste
  2 shallots, chopped
  2 garlic cloves, chopped
  2–3 fresh red chillies, seeded
    and chopped
  25g/1oz fresh galangal, chopped
  15g/½ oz fresh turmeric, chopped,
    or 2.5ml/½ tsp ground turmeric
  1 lemon grass stalk, chopped
  2 candlenuts, chopped
To serve
  1 lime, quartered (optional)
  2 green or red chillies, seeded and
    cut into quarters lengthways

Per Portion Energy 274kcal/1154kJ; Protein 41.6g; Carbohydrate 10.4g, of which sugars 8.7g; Fat 7.7g, of which saturates 1.1g; Cholesterol 197mg; Calcium 99mg; Fibre 2.2g; Sodium 193mg.

SPICY CHICKEN PARCELS

TUM AYAM IS POPULAR IN INDONESIA AS AN APPETIZER. TUM MEANS COOKING SPICED FOODS WRAPPED IN BANANA LEAVES. THE METHOD CAN BE APPLIED TO A WHOLE RANGE OF INGREDIENTS SUCH AS FISH CUTLETS, PRAWNS (SHRIMP), PORK, BEEF AND DUCK. MINCED CHICKEN IS PARTICULARLY GOOD AS IT ABSORBS THE SPICE MIX EFFECTIVELY AND COOKS QUICKLY.

SERVES FOUR

INGREDIENTS

- 450g/1lb minced (ground) chicken
- 30ml/2 tbsp Shallot and Lemon Grass Sambal (see Essential Recipes)
- 1 egg, lightly beaten
- 105ml/7 tbsp coconut milk
- 5 salam leaves (Indonesian bay leaves), finely shredded
- 4 lime leaves, finely shredded
- 2.5ml/½ tsp salt
- 2.5ml/½ tsp sugar
- juice of 1 lime
- 10 pieces of banana leaf, each measuring 20cm/8in square

1 Combine all the ingredients except for the banana leaves and mix well.

2 Blanch the banana leaves in boiling water to make them more pliable.

3 Divide the chicken mixture between the banana leaves and wrap up to make 10 parcels.

4 Secure each parcel with cocktail sticks (toothpicks) and place them in a steamer. Cook for 20 minutes and serve warm as an appetizer, either still wrapped in the leaves or unwrapped. Do not eat the banana leaves.

Per portion Energy 148kcal/622kJ; Protein 28.7g; Carbohydrate 1.1g, of which sugars 1g; Fat 3.2g, of which saturates 0.8g; Cholesterol 127mg; Calcium 16mg; Fibre 0.1g; Sodium 109mg.

TANGY CHICKEN STEW

THIS SIMPLE BUT VERY FLAVOURSOME CASSEROLED CHICKEN MAY WELL BECOME ONE OF YOUR FAVOURITE 'EVERYDAY' DISHES. THE TENDER CHICKEN PIECES ARE COATED IN A TANGY, ALMOST SWEET AND SOUR SAUCE THAT IS VERY EASY TO MAKE AND HAS A PLEASANT KICK OF HEAT. THE DISH TASTES WONDERFUL SERVED WITH PLAIN JASMINE RICE AND SOME STEAMED GREEN VEGETABLES.

SERVES FOUR

INGREDIENTS
- 4 whole chicken legs
- 2.5ml/½ tsp salt
- 2.5ml/½ tsp black peppercorns
- 4 garlic cloves, chopped
- 2 bay leaves
- 75ml/2½fl oz/⅓ cup suka (Filipino coconut vinegar)
- 10ml/2 tsp chilli powder
- 200ml/7fl oz/1 cup water
- 6 shallots, sliced
- 2 tomatoes, chopped
- boiled rice, to serve

1 Use a heavy knife to divide each chicken leg into three pieces, removing and discarding any excess skin and fat to leave lean portions.

2 Place the chicken in a pan with the salt, peppercorns, garlic, bay leaves and suka. Bring to the boil, then reduce the heat and simmer very gently for 15 minutes, turning the meat occasionally, until nearly all the liquid has evaporated.

3 Add the chilli powder and continue cooking the chicken for 5 minutes.

4 Add the water, shallots and tomatoes and cook over a high heat until the sauce has reduced by half.

5 Taste and adjust the seasoning as desired, then serve the chicken hot with rice.

Per portion Energy 221kcal/922kJ; Protein 19.8g; Carbohydrate 3.6g, of which sugars 2.4g; Fat 14.3g, of which saturates 3.9g; Cholesterol 116mg; Calcium 19mg; Fibre 0.7g; Sodium 88mg.

CHICKEN WITH GREEN PAPAYA

THIS FILIPINO DISH USES THE GREEN PAPAYA THAT IS PLENTIFUL ON THE ISLANDS. SOME VERSIONS FEATURE COURGETTE (ZUCCHINI) INSTEAD, BUT THIS DOES NOT ACHIEVE QUITE THE AUTHENTIC FLAVOUR AND TEXTURE. THE FILIPINO FISH SAUCE (PATIS) USED HERE IS A STRONG CONDIMENT, SO REPLACE IT WITH LIGHT SOY SAUCE IF YOU PREFER A MILDER TASTE.

SERVES FOUR

INGREDIENTS
1 whole green papaya
30ml/2 tbsp vegetable oil
4 garlic cloves, crushed
1 small onion, sliced
5ml/1 tsp black peppercorns, crushed
4 skinless, boneless chicken
  breasts, cubed
30ml/2 tbsp patis (Filipino fish sauce)
2.5ml/½ tsp sugar
5ml/1 tsp salt
500ml/17fl oz/2 cups water
juice of 1 lime
4 fresh green chillies, seeded
  and sliced
boiled rice, to serve

1 Peel the papaya with a vegetable peeler and remove any seeds or pith. Slice it into thin pieces about 5cm/2in square and 5mm/¼in thick. Wash and drain.

2 Heat the oil in a wok or heavy frying pan and fry the garlic until golden. Add the onion and fry until soft, then add the peppercorns and fry for 1 minute.

3 Add the chicken, patis, sugar and salt to the pan and stir over a high heat until the chicken is sealed and has gone white; about 5 minutes. Add the water.

4 Bring to the boil, then reduce the heat and simmer for 20 minutes. Add the lime juice, chillies and papaya, cook for 5 minutes until soft, then serve with rice.

Per portion Energy 291kcal/1226kJ; Protein 37.6g; Carbohydrate 19.5g, of which sugars 19.2g; Fat 7.5g, of which saturates 1.1g; Cholesterol 105mg; Calcium 61mg; Fibre 4.6g; Sodium 101mg.

CHICKEN IN WHITE COCONUT MILK SAUCE

OPOR DISHES ARE AMONG THE MILDEST OF INDONESIAN RECIPES, OPOR BEING A NAME GIVEN TO NON-CHILLI-BASED CURRIES. THIS MILD, CREAMY STEW MAKES A GOOD INTRODUCTION TO CURRIES FOR THOSE PEOPLE WHO ARE NOT ACCUSTOMED TO CHILLI FIRE. IT IS DELICIOUS SERVED WITH CHUNKS OF CRUSTY BAGUETTE OR WITH PLAIN BOILED RICE.

2 Add the chicken pieces and lemon grass to the pan and continue to fry for 5 minutes, stirring frequently.

3 Transfer to a heavy pan and add the salam leaves, coconut milk and salt. Bring to the boil, then reduce the heat and simmer, covered, for 35 minutes.

4 Serve the dish in warmed bowls, garnished with the reserved fried garlic and shallots, with rice and lime slices.

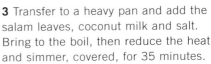

SERVES FOUR

INGREDIENTS
  30ml/2 tbsp vegetable oil
  8 shallots, sliced
  7 garlic cloves, sliced
  15ml/1 tbsp ground coriander
  5ml/1 tsp chopped fresh root ginger
  1 chicken, about 600g/1lb 6oz, cut
    into 5cm/2in pieces on the bone
  2 lemon grass stalks, 5cm/2in of root
    end bruised
  4 salam leaves (Indonesian bay leaves)
  450ml/¾ pint/scant 2 cups
    coconut milk
  5ml/1 tsp salt
  lime slices, to garnish
  boiled rice, to serve

1 Heat the oil in a wok and fry the shallots and garlic until light golden. Remove three-quarters of the shallots and half the garlic from the pan and set aside to use as a garnish. Add the ground coriander and chopped ginger and fry for 2 minutes.

COOK'S TIP
If you want to add a little fire, slit 2 or 3 green chillies lengthways but not all the way through. Seed them and add in the last 10 minutes of cooking.

Per portion Energy 311kcal/1294kJ; Protein 19.8g; Carbohydrate 9.3g, of which sugars 6.9g; Fat 22g, of which saturates 5.5g; Cholesterol 96mg; Calcium 56mg; Fibre 0.4g; Sodium 202mg.

CHICKEN AND GINGER STEW

THE USUAL NAME FOR THIS DISH IN THE PHILIPPINES IS NILAGA. IT IS ALMOST EUROPEAN IN FLAVOUR ASIDE FROM A FILIPINO TOUCH OF GINGER. THE USE OF POTATOES AND CABBAGE HARKS BACK TO THE SPANISH ERA, AND THE WHOLE DISH IS A DELICIOUS MIX OF EAST AND WEST. IT IS A VERY SIMPLE STEW, ALMOST RUSTIC IN TONE.

SERVES FOUR

INGREDIENTS

4 chicken legs, each cut into
  2–3 pieces
1 litre/1¾ pints/4 cups water
30g/1oz fresh root ginger, sliced
½ tsp peppercorns
5ml/1 tsp salt
1 large white onion, sliced
2 potatoes, peeled and quartered
10ml/2 tbsp vegetable oil
½ Chinese cabbage, sliced

3 Add the potatoes to the chicken with the cabbage and simmer for 10 minutes over a medium heat.

4 Serve the stew hot in large, warmed soup bowls.

1 Place the chicken in a heavy pan with the water, ginger, peppercorns, salt and onion and boil over a high heat for 25 minutes.

2 Sauté the potatoes for 5 minutes in the oil until light brown in places.

VARIATION
You could cook this dish in the oven at 180°C/350°F/Gas 4. Reduce the amount of water to 450ml/16fl oz/ scant 2 cups and cook for 45 minutes in a covered casserole dish.

Per portion Energy 363kcal/1518kJ; Protein 22.3g; Carbohydrate 25.1g, of which sugars 6.2g; Fat 19.9g, of which saturates 4.5g; Cholesterol 116mg; Calcium 59mg; Fibre 3.1g; Sodium 107mg.

ADOBO CHICKEN AND PORK COOKED WITH VINEGAR AND GINGER

ORIGINALLY FROM MEXICO, ADOBO HAS BECOME THE NATIONAL DISH OF THE PHILIPPINES. IT CAN BE MADE WITH CHICKEN (ADOBONG MANOK), WITH PORK (ADOBONG BABOY) OR WITH BOTH, AS IN THIS RECIPE. IT CAN ALSO BE PREPARED WITH FISH, SHELLFISH AND VEGETABLES, AS THE NAME ADOBONG REFERS TO THE METHOD — COOKING IN LOTS OF VINEGAR, GINGER AND GARLIC — NOT THE CONTENT.

SERVES FOUR TO SIX

INGREDIENTS
- 30ml/2 tbsp coconut or groundnut (peanut) oil
- 6–8 garlic cloves, crushed whole
- 50g/2oz fresh root ginger, sliced into matchsticks
- 6 spring onions (scallions), cut into 2.5cm/1in pieces
- 5–10ml/1–2 tsp black peppercorns, crushed
- 30ml/2 tbsp palm sugar (jaggery) or muscovado (molasses) sugar
- 8–10 chicken thighs, or a mixture of thighs and drumsticks
- 350g/12oz pork tenderloin, cut into chunks
- 150ml/¼ pint/⅔ cup suka (Filipino coconut vinegar) or white wine vinegar
- 150ml/¼ pint/⅔ cup dark soy sauce
- 300ml/½ pint/1¼ cups chicken stock
- 2–3 bay leaves
- salt

To serve
- stir-fried greens
- cooked rice

1 Heat the oil in a wok with a lid or in a large, heavy pan. Stir in the garlic and ginger and fry until they become fragrant and begin to colour. Add the spring onions and black peppercorns and stir in the sugar.

2 Add the chicken and pork to the wok or pan and fry until they begin to colour. Pour in the vinegar, soy sauce and chicken stock and add the bay leaves. Bring to the boil, then reduce the heat, cover and simmer gently for about 1 hour, until the meat is tender and the liquid has reduced.

3 Season the stew with salt to taste and serve with stir-fried greens and rice, over which the cooking liquid is spooned.

COOK'S TIP
For the best flavour, make this dish the day before eating. Leave the cooked dish to cool, put in the refrigerator overnight, then reheat the next day.

Per Portion Energy 270kcal/1135kJ; Protein 42.2g; Carbohydrate 9g, of which sugars 7.6g; Fat 7.4g, of which saturates 1.6g; Cholesterol 118mg; Calcium 24mg; Fibre 0.6g; Sodium 1892mg.

VISAYAN ROAST CHICKEN <u>WITH</u> LEMON GRASS

THROUGHOUT THE VISAYAN ISLANDS, THE AROMA OF CHICKEN GRILLING WITH LEMON GRASS AND GINGER WILL MAKE YOU FEEL POSITIVELY FAMISHED. SPIT-ROASTED IN THE STREETS OR OVEN-ROASTED IN THE HOME FOR CELEBRATORY FEASTS, INASAL NA MANOK CAN BE FOUND ALL OVER THE PHILIPPINES, BUT ON THE VISAYAN ISLANDS, WHERE LEMON GRASS GROWS WILD IN ABUNDANCE, IT IS PARTICULARLY DELICIOUS.

SERVES FOUR TO SIX

INGREDIENTS
  1 chicken, about 1.25kg/2lb 12oz
  2–3 large sweet potatoes, peeled
    or unpeeled, cut into wedges
  30ml/2 tbsp coconut or groundnut
    (peanut) oil
  40g/1½oz fresh root ginger, cut
    into matchsticks
  6 lemon grass stalks, bruised
  salt and ground black pepper
  green papaya salad, to serve
For the spice paste
  90g/3½oz fresh root ginger, chopped
  2–3 lemon grass stalks, chopped
  3 garlic cloves, chopped
  90ml/6 tbsp light soy sauce
  juice of 1 kalamansi lime or
    1 ordinary lime or lemon
  30ml/2 tbsp palm sugar (jaggery) or
    muscovado (molasses) sugar
  ground black pepper
For the sweet chilli vinegar
  90ml/6 tbsp suka (Filipino coconut
    vinegar)
  15ml/1 tbsp white or soft light brown
    sugar
  1–2 fresh red chillies, seeded
    and chopped

1 Preheat the oven to 180ºC/350ºF/ Gas 4. To make the spice paste, use a mortar and pestle to grind the ginger, lemon grass and garlic to a coarse paste. Beat in the soy sauce, lime juice and sugar and season with pepper.

2 Put the chicken on a flat surface and gently massage the skin to loosen it from the flesh. Make a few incisions in the skin and rub the ginger and lemon grass paste into the slits, pushing it under the skin so that the flesh is infused with flavour and remains moist during cooking.

3 Roast the chicken and sweet potatoes with the oil, ginger, lemon grass and seasoning in the oven for 1–1¼ hours, until the juices run clear. Check after 50 minutes to make sure the sugar in the paste is not burning, and baste the sweet potatoes in the roasting juices. The potatoes should caramelize well during cooking in their own sugars.

4 Make the sweet chilli vinegar. Put the suka and sugar in a small bowl and stir until the sugar has dissolved. Stir in the chillies and put aside.

5 When the chicken and sweet potatoes are cooked, serve immediately with the sweet chilli vinegar to splash over.

Per Portion Energy 434kcal/1812kJ; Protein 26.2g; Carbohydrate 28.6g, of which sugars 12.6g; Fat 24.6g, of which saturates 6.5g; Cholesterol 128mg; Calcium 42mg; Fibre 2.5g; Sodium 1209mg.

SUMATRAN DUCK WITH CHILLIES

THIS UNUSUAL DUCK RECIPE MAKES THE MOST OF THE NATURAL AFFINITY BETWEEN THE RICH DUCK FLESH AND SWEET, SPICY FLAVOURS. THE CHILLIES GIVE A GENTLY PLEASING, BUT NOT OVERPOWERING HEAT, WHILE THE LEMON GRASS AND LIME LEAVES ADD AN IRRESISTIBLE TANGINESS AND AROMA. THE DISH IS BEST ENJOYED WITH STEAMED JASMINE RICE AND TENDER SEASONAL VEGETABLES SUCH AS MANGETOUTS OR PURPLE SPROUTING BROCCOLI.

1 Cut the duck into 8–10 pieces, removing any excess fat and skin.

2 Process or pound the spice paste ingredients in a mortar and pestle to form a fine paste. Heat the oil and fry the paste over a low heat for 5 minutes.

3 Transfer the paste to a large pot and combine with the duck, water, tamarind, salt, sugar and lemon grass. Bring to the boil, then reduce the heat and simmer for 1 hour. The sauce should reduce by half. Slice and add the chillies in the last 5 minutes of cooking. Serve hot with steamed rice and vegetables.

SERVES SIX TO EIGHT

INGREDIENTS
  1 oven-ready duck
  45ml/3 tbsp vegetable oil
  750ml/1¼ pints/3 cups water
  30ml/2 tbsp tamarind concentrate
  1.5ml/¼ tsp salt
  5ml/1 tsp sugar
  2 lemon grass stalks, 5cm/2in of
    root end bruised
  4 fresh green chillies, seeded

For the spice paste
  5 fresh green chillies, seeded
    and chopped
  1 large onion, chopped
  6 candlenuts, chopped
  30ml/2 tbsp ground ginger
  15g/1 tbsp galangal
  2 lemon grass stalks, 5cm/2in of
    root end chopped
  1.5ml/¼ tsp ground turmeric
  4 lime leaves, spines removed
  2.5ml/½ tsp black peppercorns

Per portion Energy 137kcal/573kJ; Protein 14.5g; Carbohydrate 0.2g, of which sugars 0.2g; Fat 8.8g, of which saturates 2g; Cholesterol 75mg; Calcium 15mg; Fibre 0g; Sodium 79mg.

MARINATED DUCK

IN INDONESIA, DUCK IS CALLED DIFFERENT NAMES ACCORDING TO LOCAL DIALECT. IT COULD BE BEBEK, ENTOK OR ITIK, DEPENDING ON WHERE YOU ARE. THIS RECIPE IS IDEAL FOR THE READILY-AVAILABLE BARBARY DUCK BREASTS, WHICH HAVE PLENTY OF FLESH AND LESS FAT THAN AYLESBURY DUCK. ROASTING THEM OVER WATER KEEPS THE FLESH MOIST AND TENDER, AND THE INFUSION OF GINGER AND SPICE IS TRULY HEAVENLY.

SERVES TWO

INGREDIENTS

breasts of one large duck, trimmed of
 fat and excess skin
To serve
 baby spinach leaves and cucumber
 sweet chilli dip
For the spice paste
 3 fresh green chillies, seeded
 and chopped
 4 shallots, chopped
 4 garlic cloves, chopped
 2 candlenuts, chopped
 5ml/1 tsp grated fresh root ginger
 1 lemon grass stalk, 5cm/2in of
 root end chopped
 6 green peppercorns
 juice of 3 limes
 30ml/2 tbsp tamarind concentrate
 1.5ml/¼ tsp salt
 5ml/1 tsp sugar
 120ml/4fl oz/½ cup water

2 Allow to cool, then smear all over the duck breasts and marinate in the refrigerator for a few hours or overnight.

3 Preheat the oven to 200°C/400°F/ Gas 6. Place the duck on a rack in a baking tray and brush with marinade.

4 Half fill the baking tray with water. Roast the duck for 30 minutes, leave to cool, then slice.

5 Serve with baby spinach leaves and sliced cucumber, with a sweet chilli dip on the side.

1 Grind the chillies, shallots, garlic, candlenuts, ginger, lemon grass and peppercorns with a mortar and pestle or blender to a fine paste. Combine with the lime juice, tamarind, salt, sugar and water in a small pan, and cook over a low heat until a thick sauce forms.

COOK'S TIPS
• These duck breasts are also excellent as a barbecue item. Cook on charcoal until the skins just begin to char.
• If you can't buy duck breasts, cut the breasts from a whole duck.

Per portion Energy 249kcal/1045kJ; Protein 32.5g; Carbohydrate 7.3g, of which sugars 4.3g; Fat 12.8g, of which saturates 2.2g; Cholesterol 165mg; Calcium 45mg; Fibre 1.4g; Sodium 660mg.

BALINESE SMOKED DUCK

IN THE VILLAGES OF INDONESIA, THIS DISH OF SLOW-COOKED, TENDER DUCK IS PREPARED FOR FEASTS. SMEARED WITH SPICES AND HERBS AND TIGHTLY WRAPPED IN BANANA OR PANDANUS LEAVES, THE DUCK IS SMOKED IN THE EMBERS OF A FIRE MADE FROM COCONUT HUSKS UNTIL THE AROMATIC MEAT IS SO TENDER THAT IT FALLS OFF THE BONE. THIS VERSION IS COOKED IN THE OVEN.

SERVES FOUR

INGREDIENTS
   1.8kg/4lb oven-ready duck
   1 large banana leaf or aluminium foil
   salt and ground black pepper
For the spice paste
   6–8 shallots, chopped
   4 garlic cloves, chopped
   4 fresh chillies, seeded and chopped
   25g/1oz fresh root ginger, chopped
   50g/2oz fresh turmeric, chopped,
      or 25ml/1½ tbsp ground turmeric
   2 lemon grass stalks, chopped
   4 lime leaves, crumbled
   4 candlenuts, chopped
   10ml/2 tsp coriander seeds
   15ml/1 tbsp terasi (Indonesian
      shrimp paste)
   15–30ml/1–2 tbsp water

1 First make the spice paste. Using a mortar and pestle or a blender, grind all the ingredients except the terasi and water together to form a smooth paste. Add the terasi and water and mix together until the mixture becomes a thick paste.

2 Preheat the oven to 160°C/325°F/ Gas 3. Rub the spice paste all over the duck, inside and out, and sprinkle with salt and pepper. Place the duck in the centre of the banana leaf or a sheet of aluminium foil. If using a banana leaf, secure it with string. If using foil, tuck in the short sides and fold the long sides over the top to form a parcel. Place the parcel in a roasting pan.

3 Roast the duck for 4–5 hours, then open the parcel to reveal the top of the duck and roast for a further 30–45 minutes to brown the skin. Serve immediately.

Per Portion Energy 234kcal/982kJ; Protein 26.9g; Carbohydrate 12.8g, of which sugars 8.4g; Fat 8.8g, of which saturates 2.7g; Cholesterol 135mg; Calcium 75mg; Fibre 3g; Sodium 161mg.

STUFFED DUCK WITH CABBAGE

SIMPLY ROASTING A DUCK IS NOT FOR THE FILIPINOS — THIS RECIPE IS A LITTLE TIME-CONSUMING BECAUSE THERE IS A FRYING STEP FOLLOWED BY A BRAISING STEP, BUT THE RESULTS ARE DEFINITELY WORTH IT. LONG COOKING IS REQUISITE FOR ALL FILIPINO DUCK DISHES. AN OVEN-READY DUCKLING IS BEST FOR THIS RECIPE, AND A LARGE, FLAT-BOTTOMED WOK IS ESSENTIAL.

SERVES SIX

INGREDIENTS

    1 duck, about 2.25kg/5lb
    5ml/1 tsp salt
    1.5ml/¼ tsp ground black pepper
    vegetable oil for deep-frying
    1 chicken stock cube
    2 litres/3½ pints/8 cups water
    4 garlic cloves, crushed
    3 bay leaves
    75ml/5 tbsp orange liqueur such as
      Cointreau, or sweet sherry
    1 whole Chinese cabbage, quartered
For the stuffing
    30ml/2 tbsp vegetable oil
    10 shallots, chopped very finely
    6 Chinese mushrooms, chopped
    250g/9oz minced (ground) pork
      or chicken
    150g/5oz breadcrumbs
    2 eggs, lightly beaten

1 Prepare the stuffing. Heat the oil and fry the shallots gently for 3–4 minutes until softened and turning golden. Transfer to a bowl, allow to cool and add the mushrooms, pork, eggs and breadcrumbs. Mix well with a wooden spoon and set aside.

2 Wash the duck and pat it dry with kitchen towels. Rub the skin with the salt and pepper and pack the cavity with the stuffing. Sew up the opening with strong thread. Make small balls with any leftover stuffing.

3 Heat enough oil for deep-frying in a large, flat-bottomed wok and deep-fry the duck, turning it over carefully until the skin is evenly browned. Remove the duck with slotted spatulas and transfer to a deep roasting pan.

4 Dissolve the stock cube in a little boiling water, then add the measured water, garlic, bay leaves and liqueur or sherry. Pour this all over the duck.

5 Cover with foil and bring to the boil, then reduce the heat and simmer for 45 minutes. Add the cabbage and any stuffing balls to the stock and cook for another 20 minutes.

6 Remove the cabbage and stuffing balls and keep warm. Continue to braise the duck for another 20 minutes, opening the foil a little to let the steam out, until the sauce is thick and glossy.

7 Remove the duck and arrange it on a large plate with the cabbage and extra stuffing. Reduce the stock by fast boiling it in a pan for a couple of minutes, then strain and serve with the duck.

COOK'S TIP
Ideally, ask your butcher to bone the duck. Otherwise, carve it at the table. The duck will be tender and very easy to handle.

Per portion Energy 665kcal/2773kJ; Protein 41.4g; Carbohydrate 29.8g, of which sugars 10.3g; Fat 41.4g, of which saturates 11.5g; Cholesterol 271mg; Calcium 149mg; Fibre 4.6g; Sodium 723mg.

FRIED PIGEON

THE MELLOW, SWEET SPICE MARINADE USED IN THIS RECIPE IMPARTS A WONDERFUL FLAVOUR TO THE BIRDS, WHICH SHOULD BE SERVED WHOLE. WESTERN COOKS ARE ACCUSTOMED TO ROASTING WHOLE BIRDS IN THE OVEN, BUT DEEP-FRYING SMALL FOWL GIVES A GREAT RESULT. HOWEVER, TAKE CARE NOT TO LET THE SWEET COATING BURN IN OVER-HOT OIL. SERVE THE BIRDS WITH A SIMPLE CUCUMBER SALAD AND SPICY DIPPING SAUCE, PERHAPS AS PART OF A MEAL WITH SEVERAL COURSES.

SERVES FOUR

INGREDIENTS
    30ml/2 tbsp honey or maltose
    45ml/3 tbsp soy sauce
    pinch of ground cloves
    30ml/2 tbsp garlic purée (paste)
    2.5ml/½ tsp salt
    4 oven-ready pigeons
    30ml/2 tbsp cornflour (cornstarch)
    vegetable oil for deep-frying
To serve
    chilli sauce
    very thinly sliced cucumber

1 Put the honey or maltose, soy sauce, cloves, garlic purée and salt in a bowl and blend well. Rub the marinade over the pigeons, both inside and outside, then leave to marinate for 20 minutes. Just before frying, dust with the cornflour and shake off any excess.

2 Bring the oil to medium–hot and deep-fry the birds, two at a time, until golden brown. The coating of cornflour will give the skin a nice crisp texture.

3 Serve with a side dip of chilli sauce and some sliced cucumber.

Per portion Energy 442kcal/1842kJ; Protein 29.6g; Carbohydrate 13.3g, of which sugars 6.3g; Fat 30.5g, of which saturates 1.9g; Cholesterol 0mg; Calcium 20mg; Fibre 0g; Sodium 649mg.

QUAIL RELLENO

This is a spectacular dish to serve guests on a special occasion. The discovery of the egg at the centre of the rich stuffing makes the dish a real pleasure to eat. You can detect a Spanish influence in the garlic, chorizo and olive oil, but the addition of water chestnuts to the stuffing gives it the 'Asian twist' so distinctive of Filipino cuisine. It is good served with a salad of peppery leaves, such as rocket or watercress.

SERVES FOUR

INGREDIENTS

  8 quails
  16 quail's eggs, hard-boiled
   and shelled
  2.5ml/½ tsp salt
  2.5ml/½ tsp ground black pepper
  100ml/3½fl oz/⅓ cup melted butter
  2 garlic cloves, sliced
For the stuffing
  15ml/1 tbsp olive oil
  6 shallots, finely chopped
  350g/12oz minced (ground) pork
  1 Spanish chorizo sausage,
   finely diced
  200g/7oz water chestnuts, chopped
  1 egg, beaten
  15ml/1 tbsp cornflour (cornstarch)
  5ml/1 tsp salt
  2.5ml/½ tsp ground black pepper

2 Season each quail with salt and pepper and fill with the stuffing, pushing two eggs into the centre of each. Truss each bird with string so that the stuffing does not fall out.

COOK'S TIP
Tie the birds neatly so that you can serve them with the strings still on.

3 Place the quails in an oiled roasting pan or pans, breast side up. Drizzle the butter all over the birds. Scatter the garlic slices over each quail.

4 Roast for 25–35 minutes, basting the birds often, until they are golden. Allow them to rest for 5 minutes on a warm plate before serving.

1 Preheat the oven to 200°C/400°F/Gas 6. To make the stuffing, fry the shallots gently until soft. In a bowl, mix with the pork, chorizo, water chestnuts, egg, cornflour, salt and pepper.

Per portion Energy 571kcal/2382kJ; Protein 54.9g; Carbohydrate 6.7g, of which sugars 2g; Fat 36.3g, of which saturates 6.8g; Cholesterol 337mg; Calcium 80mg; Fibre 1g; Sodium 978mg.

MEAT

Visitors to the Philippines will most often encounter meat dishes of pork, beef or rabbit, while in Indonesia it is common to eat buffalo and goat. Using their own distinctive local flavourings, such as coconut, spices, tomatoes or vinegar, Filipino and Indonesian cooks like to simmer meat slowly in delicious broths and sauces to make rich stews and curries, which are usually served with mounds of fluffy steamed rice.

SPANISH-STYLE LAMB STEW WITH GREEN OLIVES

PORK IS THE PRINCIPAL MEAT IN THE PHILIPPINES, CLOSELY FOLLOWED BY CHICKEN AND THEN BEEF, BUT LAMB AND GOAT ARE NOT WIDELY EATEN. HOWEVER, IN THE NORTHERN LUZON, THE MOUNTAIN TRIBES EAT LAMB AND GOAT IN HEARTY STEWS. DRAWING FROM SPANISH TRADITION, THE MEAT IS FIRST MARINATED IN A LOCAL ALCOHOL, SUCH AS THE SWEET, PORT-LIKE BASI MADE FROM FERMENTED SUGAR CANE JUICE, TO TENDERIZE AND FLAVOUR IT, AND THEN BROWNED BEFORE BRAISING. THE GREEN OLIVES THAT GROW IN THE LUZON AREA ARE USED IN THIS DISH.

SERVES FOUR

INGREDIENTS
    900g/2lb boneless leg or shoulder
      of lamb, cut into bitesize cubes
    45ml/3 tbsp groundnut (peanut) oil
    15g/½oz/1 tbsp butter
    2 red onions, thickly sliced
    8 garlic cloves, crushed whole
    2–3 fresh red or green chillies,
      seeded and sliced
    2 red or green (bell) peppers,
      seeded and sliced
    5–10ml/1–2 tsp paprika
    15ml/1 tbsp palm sugar (jaggery) or
      cane sugar
    400g/14oz can plum
      tomatoes, drained
    15ml/1 tbsp tomato
      purée (paste)
    2–3 bay leaves
    225g/8oz small green olives,
      with stones (pits)
    300ml/½ pint/1¼ cups water
    salt and ground black pepper
    1 bunch fresh flat leaf parsley,
      roughly chopped, to garnish
    cooked rice, to serve
For the marinade
    250ml/8fl oz/1 cup red wine
    250ml/8fl oz/1 cup port
    120ml/4fl oz/½ cup suka (Filipino
      coconut vinegar) or rice vinegar
    1 onion, roughly sliced
    2 garlic cloves, crushed whole
    8 black peppercorns
    2–3 bay leaves

1 First make the marinade by mixing all the marinade ingredients together in a large bowl.

2 Add the lamb, toss in the marinade, then cover the bowl with clear film (plastic wrap) and leave to marinate in the refrigerator for at least 6 hours or overnight.

3 Using tongs or a slotted spoon, lift the lamb out of the marinade and put it in another large bowl. Put the marinade aside.

4 Heat the oil and butter in a wok with a lid or a large, heavy pan. Add the meat, in batches if necessary, and fry until browned on all sides. Using tongs or a slotted spoon, lift the browned meat out of the pan and put aside. This process seals in the meat's moisture ready for stewing.

5 Add the onions, garlic, chillies and peppers to the remaining oil in the pan and fry for about 5 minutes until they begin to colour. Stir in the paprika and sugar and return the meat to the pan.

COOK'S TIP
Choose olives with stones (pits) in them as they remain intact when cooked and add to the flavour of the stew.

6 Add the tomatoes, tomato purée, bay leaves and olives. Pour in the reserved marinade and the water and bring to the boil. Reduce the heat, cover the pan and simmer gently for about 2 hours, adding a little extra water if the cooking liquid reduces too much.

7 Season the stew with salt and pepper to taste. Sprinkle with the chopped parsley to garnish and serve with rice.

Per Portion Energy 654kcal/2722kJ; Protein 47.4g; Carbohydrate 19.2g, of which sugars 16.7g; Fat 43.6g, of which saturates 15.8g; Cholesterol 179mg; Calcium 93mg; Fibre 5.4g; Sodium 1498mg.

HOT LAMB CURRY

PARSANGA IS AN EXTREMELY AROMATIC AND SPICY DRY CURRY BLENDED WITH FRIED COCONUT, ALMOST LIKE A RENDANG. LAMB IS THE USUAL MEAT, ALTHOUGH THERE IS NO REASON WHY YOU CANNOT CHOOSE PORK OR CHICKEN INSTEAD. IT IS FAIRLY COMPLEX IN PREPARATION BUT THE ACTUAL COOKING IS NOTHING MORE THAN LONG SIMMERING TO ACHIEVE THE DESIRED RESULTS.

SERVES FOUR

INGREDIENTS
150g/5oz desiccated (dry
    unsweetened shredded) coconut
900g/1kg lean lamb
small piece of nutmeg, chopped
3 cloves
2 cardamoms
2 lemon grass stalks, 5cm/2in of
    root end bruised
1 litre/1¾ pints/4 cups coconut milk
1 tsp salt
boiled rice, to serve
To garnish
fresh red chillies, sliced diagonally
coriander (cilantro) leaves
For the spice paste
30ml/2 tbsp ground coriander
10ml/2 tsp black peppercorns
5ml/1 tsp ground cumin
5 fresh red chillies, seeded
    and chopped
4 garlic cloves
30g/2 tbsp grated fresh root ginger
15ml/1 tbsp grated fresh galangal

COOK'S TIP
For a quick dish, you can use curry
powder instead of making the spice
paste, but add a few slices of galangal.

1 Grind the spice paste ingredients to a coarse paste using a pestle and mortar or an electric food processor or blender. Mix with a little water to make a thick paste.

2 Dry-fry the coconut over a low heat for 10 minutes until golden brown, then process in a blender or pestle and mortar until fine.

3 Combine all the ingredients in a pan and bring to the boil. Cook for 20 minutes on high, then turn the heat down to medium to simmer for 1 hour or more, until the liquid is thick and oily.

4 Spoon off any excess oil and discard. Garnish the lamb with chillies and coriander and serve with rice.

Per portion Energy 723kcal/3017kJ; Protein 49.2g; Carbohydrate 19.1g, of which sugars 14.8g; Fat 50.9g, of which saturates 32.5g; Cholesterol 171mg; Calcium 126mg; Fibre 5.2g; Sodium 484mg.

MUTTON KORMA

KORMA IS RESOLUTELY OF INDIAN ORIGIN AND A STAPLE OF THE MUSLIM COMMUNITY IN THE SUB-CONTINENT. IT IS THE GENERAL BELIEF THAT IT CAME FROM THE MUGHAL RULERS, WHO LIKED THEIR SPICED DISHES CREAMY. INDONESIA WAS PART OF THE ANCIENT HINDU KINGDOM OF SRI VIJAYA AND THIS DISH REMAINS A FIRM FAVOURITE OF THE REGION.

SERVES FOUR

INGREDIENTS
   900g/1kg mutton, cut into
   bitesize chunks
   45ml/3 tbsp ghee
   1 large onion, sliced
   4 garlic cloves, chopped
   2 lemon grass stalks, 5cm/2in of
   root end chopped
   1 5cm/2 in cinnamon stick
   4 salam leaves (Indonesian bay leaves)
   600ml/1 pint/2½ cups water
   200ml/7fl oz/¾ cup coconut milk
   105ml/7 tbsp natural (plain) yogurt
   10ml/2 tsp salt
   5ml/1 tsp sugar
   450g/1lb potatoes, cut into
   bitesize chunks
   cooked rice, to serve
For the spice paste
   4 cardamoms
   4 cloves
   12 black peppercorns
   30g/2 tbsp ground coriander
   5ml/1 tsp ground cumin
   5ml/1 tsp ground fennel seeds

1 Grind the cardamoms, cloves and peppercorns with a pestle and mortar until very fine.

2 Mix in the ground coriander, cumin and fennel. Add a little water to make a fairly thick paste.

3 Coat the chunks of mutton well with the spice paste. Leave to marinate for about 20 minutes.

4 Heat the ghee in a large pan or wok and fry the onion and garlic for 2 minutes until soft. Add the mutton and stir-fry for 5 minutes. Add the lemon grass cinnamon, salam leaves and water, bring to the boil, then simmer for 30 minutes.

5 Add the coconut milk, yogurt, salt, sugar and potatoes to the pan, return to the boil, then continue to simmer, covered, for another 30 minutes until the mutton is tender. Serve the mutton curry with rice.

Per portion Energy 679kcal/2838kJ; Protein 50.1g; Carbohydrate 36.1g, of which sugars 13.9g; Fat 38.4g, of which saturates 19.6g; Cholesterol 203mg; Calcium 135mg; Fibre 2.9g; Sodium 1272mg.

BRAISED MUTTON IN KECAP MANIS

SMOOR, OR SEMUR, IS THE NAME FOR DISHES COOKED IN DARK SOY SAUCE AND TOUCHED WITH SUGAR AND TAMARIND. IT IS BELIEVED TO HAVE ORIGINATED IN JAVA, WHERE KECAP MANIS (SWEET SOY SAUCE) IS A PRIMARY INGREDIENT. IT IS A DISH THAT REFLECTS BOTH CHINESE AND INDIGENOUS INDONESIAN ELEMENTS: SOY SAUCE AND THE HEADY SCENT OF NUTMEG, CINNAMON, CLOVES AND STAR ANISE.

2 Heat the oil in a wok or frying pan and fry the onion for 2 minutes until soft. Add the meat and all other ingredients, and stir over a medium heat for 2 minutes.

3 Top up with about 400ml/14fl oz/1⅔ cups of the reserved stock, and cook, uncovered, over a high heat until the sauce is well reduced and thick, lowering the heat if the reduction is too rapid. This will take approximately 30 minutes, depending on your pan: the evaporation rate in a deep pan is less than in a wider wok or frying pan. Adjust the seasoning and serve.

SERVES FOUR

INGREDIENTS
    600g/1lb 6oz lean mutton or lamb
    30ml/2 tbsp vegetable oil
    1 large onion, sliced
    pinch of ground nutmeg
    6 cloves
    1 cinnamon stick, about
        4cm/1½in long
    1 star anise
    2.5ml/½ tsp black peppercorns
    45ml/3 tbsp kecap manis (Indonesian
        sweet soy sauce)
    15ml/1 tbsp tamarind concentrate
    2.5ml/½ tsp salt

1 Boil the mutton or lamb in a large pot of water for 45 minutes or until tender. Strain, reserving the liquid. Cut the meat into thin slices or small chunks, as you prefer.

Per portion Energy 373kcal/1554kJ; Protein 31.7g; Carbohydrate 10.5g, of which sugars 6.3g; Fat 23.2g, of which saturates 8.5g; Cholesterol 114mg; Calcium 48mg; Fibre 1.4g; Sodium 846mg.

BRAISED PORK <u>IN</u> TOMATO SAUCE

ALSO CALLED FRITTATA, THIS IS OF SPANISH ORIGIN AND REFERS TO DISHES COOKED WITH TOMATOES, GARLIC AND OLIVE OIL. FRITTATA MEANS FRIED IN SPANISH AND THE DISTINCTIVE FLAVOUR COMES FROM SAUTÉED MEAT OR CHICKEN SIMMERED WITH TOMATOES AND BULKED UP WITH POTATOES AND ONIONS. IN SOME REGIONS, JALAPEÑO CHILLIES ARE ADDED. THIS TASTES EVEN BETTER THE DAY AFTER COOKING.

SERVES FOUR

INGREDIENTS

    450g/1lb leg of pork, trimmed and
      cut into 2.5cm/1in cubes
    2.5ml/½ tsp salt
    2.5ml/½ tsp ground black pepper
    30ml/2 tbsp olive oil
    105ml/7 tbsp water
    1 large Spanish onion, thinly sliced
    3 garlic cloves, finely chopped
    2 large beef tomatoes, sliced
    105ml/7 tbsp tomato ketchup
    300g/11oz potatoes, diced
    2 jalapeño chillies (optional)
    1 red (bell) pepper, seeded and
      sliced into strips
    15ml/1 tbsp patis (Filipino fish sauce)
    coriander (cilantro) leaves, to garnish

3 Add the water, onion, garlic, tomatoes, tomato ketchup, potatoes and jalapeños, if using, and simmer for 30 minutes.

4 Add the pepper to the pan with the patis. Simmer for another 15 minutes and serve garnished with coriander.

1 Sprinkle the cubed pork with salt and pepper. Set aside at room temperature for 15 minutes.

2 Heat the olive oil in a wok or heavy frying pan and stir-fry the seasoned pork until it is well sizzled and light brown all over.

Per portion Energy 328kcal/1376kJ; Protein 27.8g; Carbohydrate 31.8g, of which sugars 18g; Fat 10.8g, of which saturates 2.4g; Cholesterol 71mg; Calcium 48mg; Fibre 3.6g; Sodium 524mg.

SWEET MARINATED PORK

IN PUERTO RICO THIS IS KNOWN AS TOCINO, A SPANISH SWEET PORK DISH ADOPTED BY FILIPINO COOKS AND USUALLY SERVED WITH FRIED EGGS AND SINIGANG (A SOUR SOUP). THE MARINADE IS SIMPLE BUT IT TAKES AT LEAST ONE DAY'S MARINATING TIME FOR THE PORK TO BE REALLY STEEPED IN THE SEASONINGS. THE ADDITION OF CHINESE HOISIN SAUCE IS A UNIQUE TOUCH THAT OBVIATES THE NEED FOR THE RED FOOD COLOURING THAT IS GENERALLY USED.

SERVES FOUR

INGREDIENTS
900g/1kg belly pork or leg of pork,
   cut into strips
coriander (cilantro) sprigs, to garnish
sambal, to serve

For the marinade
50g/2oz demerara (raw) or soft light
   brown sugar
45ml/3 tbsp suka (Filipino coconut
   vinegar) or cider vinegar
5ml/1 tsp salt
30ml/2 tbsp hoisin sauce
30ml/2 tbsp vegetable oil

1 Mix all the marinade ingredients thoroughly. Add the pork and mix well.

2 Put the pork strips and the marinade into a plastic bag, seal it and give it a good shake. Refrigerate overnight.

3 Thread the pieces of pork on to 12 pre-soaked wooden skewers. Heat the barbecue and grill the skewers for about 3 minutes on each side, until slightly caramelized around the edges.

4 Serve with salads, rice or bread and your favourite sambal.

VARIATION
To cook on the hob, heat a frying pan with a little oil and fry a few pieces of pork at a time until well browned.

COOK'S TIP
This dish keeps well, and reheating in a hot oven (200°C/400°F/Gas 6) for 10 minutes regains the crispness. (Microwaving, by contrast, tends to result in limp meat.)

Per portion Energy 373kcal/1566kJ; Protein 48.2g; Carbohydrate 13.1g, of which sugars 13.1g; Fat 14.5g, of which saturates 3.8g; Cholesterol 142mg; Calcium 23mg; Fibre 0g; Sodium 158mg.

PORK-STUFFED CABBAGE LEAVES

IN SOUTH-EAST ASIA, SPICY PORK OR SHELLFISH MIXTURES ARE OFTEN WRAPPED IN LEAVES AND STEAMED, OR STUFFED INTO BAMBOO STEMS AND SMOKED OVER OPEN FIRES. THIS DISH IS COOKED IN A STEAMER AND THE RESULTANT ROLLS ARE MOIST, DELICIOUS AND VERY HEALTHY — PERFECT FOR A LIGHT LUNCH OR APPETIZER. IF YOU PREFER NOT TO USE LIVER AND HEART, SIMPLY REPLACE THE OFFAL WITH THE SAME AMOUNT OF REGULAR MINCED PORK.

SERVES FOUR TO SIX

INGREDIENTS
1 leafy green cabbage
15ml/1 tbsp palm or groundnut
   (peanut) oil
10ml/2 tsp coriander seeds
2 shallots, finely chopped
2 garlic cloves, finely chopped
2–3 fresh red chillies, seeded and
   finely chopped
25g/1oz fresh galangal, finely chopped
2–3 spring onions (scallions),
   finely chopped
10ml/2 tsp palm sugar (jaggery)
2–3 tomatoes, skinned, seeded and
   finely chopped
30ml/2 tbsp coconut cream
1 small bunch fresh coriander
   (cilantro) leaves, finely chopped
225g/8oz minced (ground) pork
50g/2oz pig's liver, finely chopped
50g/2oz pig's heart, finely chopped
salt and ground black pepper
kecap manis (Indonesian sweet soy
   sauce), for dipping

1 First prepare the cabbage leaves. Carefully pull the cabbage apart so that you have about 20 whole leaves. Steam or blanch the leaves to soften them, then drain and refresh them under cold running water. Cut off any thick stems, stack the leaves and set aside.

2 Heat the oil in a wok or heavy pan, stir in the coriander seeds and fry for 1 minute. Add the shallots, garlic, chillies, galangal, spring onions and sugar and stir-fry until they begin to colour.

3 Stir in the tomatoes, coconut cream and coriander leaves and cook for 5 minutes, allowing the liquid to bubble, until the mixture resembles a thick sauce or paste. Season the mixture with salt and pepper and turn into a bowl. Leave to cool.

4 Add the minced pork and chopped liver and heart. Using your hand or a fork, mix well together.

5 Place a cabbage leaf on a flat surface in front of you and place a spoonful of the mixture in the centre. Fold the sides of the leaf inwards and roll it up into a log, making sure the meat filling is fully enclosed. Repeat with the remaining leaves until the filling is used up.

6 Place the stuffed leaves in a steamer, seam side down, and steam for 25–30 minutes, until the meat is cooked.

7 Serve the cabbage rolls hot with kecap manis for dipping.

Per Portion Energy 183kcal/764kJ; Protein 12.6g; Carbohydrate 7.3g, of which sugars 7g; Fat 11.8g, of which saturates 5g; Cholesterol 56mg; Calcium 55mg; Fibre 2.2g; Sodium 53mg.

CURRIED MEAT PIES

THE EUROPEAN CULINARY HERITAGE IN THE PHILIPPINES IS MOST MANIFEST IN THESE SAVOURY MEAT PIES, OFTEN CALLED SPANISH MEAT PIES. THE FILIPINOS LIKE TO MAKE THE FILLING WITH A RICH MIXTURE OF DIFFERENT MEATS BUT YOU CAN MODIFY AS YOU WISH, AND TO SAVE TIME, USE BOUGHT PASTRY. TRADITIONALLY, A HANDFUL OF SULTANAS AND RELISH ARE ADDED, BUT HERE SWEET BAGOONG AND CURRY POWDER ARE USED INSTEAD.

2 Roll out the pastry to about 5mm/¼in thick and cut out rounds of about 10cm/4in in diameter.

3 Drain off any excess oil from the meat mixture, then place 1 scant tablespoon of filling on each pastry round. Fold the pastry over the filling like a turnover and moisten and press the edges to seal.

MAKES ABOUT 20

INGREDIENTS
    15ml/1 tbsp vegetable oil
    2 garlic cloves, very finely chopped
    ½ large onion, finely chopped
    1 potato, about 150g/5oz, boiled and
      finely diced
    1 carrot, finely chopped
    100g/7oz minced (ground) beef
    100g/7oz minced pork
    15ml/1 tbsp sweet bagoong (Filipino
      shrimp sauce)
    15ml/1 tbsp curry powder
    5ml/1 tsp salt
    2.5ml/½ tsp ground black pepper
    300g/10½oz pack puff pastry
    vegetable oil, for deep-frying

1 Heat the oil in a large wok and fry the garlic and onion for 2 minutes. Add the potato and carrot and fry for 3 minutes. Add the meats, bagoong, curry powder, salt and pepper and cook for 5 minutes. Remove the wok from the heat while you prepare the pastry.

4 Crimp the edges with the prongs of a fork, then deep-fry the parcels in the oil in batches until golden brown. This may be done with care in a deep wok, or using a deep fat fryer. Drain the pies on kitchen towels to absorb any excess oil, then serve them warm.

Per portion Energy 141kcal/588kJ; Protein 3.5g; Carbohydrate 7.5g, of which sugars 0.7g; Fat 11.2g, of which saturates 1.3g; Cholesterol 10mg; Calcium 25mg; Fibre 0.4g; Sodium 190mg.

TAMARIND PICKLED BEEF

IN MANY PARTS OF INDONESIA, BEEF HAS TRADITIONALLY COME FROM WATER BUFFALO. THESE DAYS, HOWEVER, WITH IMPORTED MEAT FROM NEARBY COUNTRIES SUCH AS AUSTRALIA AND NEW ZEALAND, THE INDONESIANS USE THE SAME KIND OF BEEF THAT YOU WOULD FIND IN ANY SUPERMARKET. EVEN WITH CHEAPER BEEF CUTS OR BUFFALO MEAT, WHICH IS ON THE TOUGH SIDE, THE LONG-COOKING STYLES OF INDONESIAN DISHES USUALLY RENDER THE MEAT DELICIOUSLY TENDER.

SERVES FOUR

INGREDIENTS
  450g/1lb stewing steak
  500ml/17fl oz/2 cups water
  25g/1oz galangal
  45ml/3 tbsp oil
  5ml/1 tsp salt
  5ml/1 tsp sugar
  5ml/1 tsp ground black pepper
  30ml/2 tbsp tamarind concentrate
  prawn crackers, to serve

4 Add the tamarind concentrate and continue to fry until nearly dry and the beef is fork tender.

5 Serve as part of a main meal, or as finger food with some prawn crackers.

VARIATION
If you prefer to use sirloin or rump steak, reduce the water by one third.

1 Cut the beef into finger-length pieces, about 1.5cm/½in thick. Put it in a wok or pan with the water and bring to the boil. Cook until almost dry. This should take about 20–25 minutes in a wok.

2 Grind the galangal with a pestle and mortar until fine.

3 Heat the oil in a wok and fry the galangal for 1 minute. Add the boiled beef, salt, sugar and pepper, and stir-fry over a medium heat until the flavours are well incorporated – about 1 minute.

Per portion Energy 279kcal/1158kJ; Protein 25.6g; Carbohydrate 1.9g, of which sugars 1.9g; Fat 18.7g, of which saturates 5.3g; Cholesterol 65mg; Calcium 8mg; Fibre 0g; Sodium 564mg.

SLOW-COOKED BUFFALO IN COCONUT MILK

THIS IS ONE OF INDONESIA'S MOST POPULAR AND BEST-KNOWN MEAT DISHES. TRADITIONALLY MADE WITH THE MEAT OF WATER BUFFALO, ALTHOUGH SOME WELL-HUNG, PRIME BEEF IS EQUALLY DELICIOUS, THE DISH IS COOKED SLOWLY TO ACHIEVE THE REQUIRED TENDERNESS AND TO CREATE A RICH SAUCE.

SERVES SIX

INGREDIENTS

1kg/2¼lb buffalo or beef, such as
   topside (pot roast) or rump (round)
   steak, cut into bitesize cubes
15ml/1 tbsp tamarind paste
90ml/6 tbsp water
115g/4oz fresh coconut, grated,
   or desiccated (dry unsweetened
   shredded) coconut
45ml/3 tbsp coconut, corn or
   groundnut (peanut) oil
2 onions, sliced
3 lemon grass stalks, halved
   and bruised
2 cinnamon sticks
3–4 lime leaves
1.2 litres/2 pints/5 cups
   coconut milk
15ml/1 tbsp sugar
salt and ground black pepper

For the spice paste
   8–10 dried red chillies
   8 shallots, chopped
   4–6 garlic cloves, chopped
   50g/2oz fresh galangal, chopped
   25g/1oz fresh turmeric, chopped
   15ml/1 tbsp coriander seeds
   10ml/2 tsp cumin seeds
   5ml/1 tsp black peppercorns
To serve
   6–8 shallots, sliced
   cooked rice
   a salad (optional)

1 For the spice paste, soak the chillies in warm water for 30 minutes. Drain, remove the seeds, then squeeze dry.

2 With a mortar and pestle or a food processor, grind the chillies, shallots, garlic, galangal and turmeric to a smooth paste.

3 In a heavy pan, dry-fry the coriander, cumin seeds and peppercorns for a few minutes. Grind to a powder, then stir into the spice paste.

4 Put the buffalo or beef in a large bowl, add the spice paste and mix together until coated. Leave to marinate, at room temperature or in the refrigerator, for at least 2 hours if using buffalo or 1 hour if using beef.

5 Meanwhile, put the tamarind paste and water in a bowl and leave to soak for about 30 minutes until soft. Using a heavy frying pan, dry-fry the grated coconut until it is brown and gives off a nutty aroma. Using a mortar and pestle, or a food processor, grind the dry-fried coconut until it resembles brown sugar. Put aside. Squeeze the tamarind to help soften it and then strain to extract the juice. Discard the pulp.

6 Heat the oil in a wok with a lid or large, heavy pan. Add the onions, lemon grass, cinnamon sticks and lime leaves, and fry for 5–10 minutes until the onions begin to colour.

7 Add the beef with all the spice paste and stir-fry until lightly browned. Add the coconut milk and tamarind juice and bring to the boil, stirring all the time. Reduce the heat and simmer gently for 4 hours for buffalo (2–4 hours for beef) until the sauce begins to thicken.

8 Stir in the sugar and ground coconut, cover and simmer very gently for 4 hours for buffalo and 2–4 hours for beef, stirring occasionally, until the meat is tender and the sauce is thick.

9 Meanwhile, fry the sliced shallots in the corn oil until golden, then drain.

10 When the meat is tender, season to taste and spoon it on to a serving dish. Sprinkle the fried shallots over the top and serve with rice and a salad.

Per Portion Energy 494kcal/2064kJ; Protein 40.6g; Carbohydrate 20.9g, of which sugars 18.8g; Fat 28.2g, of which saturates 17g; Cholesterol 97mg; Calcium 95mg; Fibre 3.9g; Sodium 335mg.

OXTAIL BRAISED IN PEANUT SAUCE

IN TRUE SPANISH STYLE, MANY OF THE FILIPINO STEWS ARE RICH AND HEARTY. THE FILIPINOS LOVE OXTAIL AND COOK IT IN MORE WAYS THAN ANY OTHER COUNTRY IN SOUTH-EAST ASIA. THE PEANUTS ENRICH THE SAUCE AND GIVE THIS DISH ITS OWN CHARACTER.

SERVES FOUR

INGREDIENTS

    1.5kg/1lb 5oz oxtail, cut into
    2.5cm/1in pieces
    corn or groundnut (peanut) oil (if
    needed)
    1 onion, sliced
    4–5 garlic cloves, crushed whole
    400g/14oz can plum tomatoes
    30ml/2 tbsp patis (Filipino fish sauce)
    2–3 bay leaves
    1.5 litres/2⅔ pints/6 cups
    beef stock
    40g/1½oz/¼ cup rice flour, dry-fried
    115g/4oz roasted unsalted peanuts,
    finely ground
    1 banana heart (blossom), sliced
    into bitesize pieces
    12 yard-long beans, cut into
    2.5cm/1in pieces
    1 aubergine (eggplant), cut
    into bitesize pieces
    salt and ground black pepper
To serve
    cooked rice
    60–90ml/4–6 tbsp bagoong
    (Filipino shrimp sauce)
    1 firm green mango, finely sliced

1 Heat a large, heavy pan, add the oxtail pieces and cook, stirring and turning, until they have browned on all sides. You may need to add a little oil but usually the oxtail renders sufficient fat. Transfer the meat to a plate.

2 Heat the fat from the oxtail, adding a little more oil if necessary, stir in the onion and garlic and fry until they begin to brown.

3 Add the tomatoes, patis and bay leaves and pour in the stock.

4 Return the oxtail to the pan. Bring to the boil, reduce the heat, cover and simmer gently for 4–5 hours, until tender, adding a little extra water if necessary.

5 Skim the fat off the top and, using a slotted spoon, lift the oxtail out and transfer to a plate.

6 Stir the rice flour and ground peanuts into the stew and whisk until fairly smooth. Add the banana heart, yard-long beans and aubergine and simmer for 5–6 minutes, until tender.

7 Season the stew with salt and pepper to taste. Return the oxtail to the pan and simmer for a further 5 minutes.

8 Serve the braised oxtail and sauce hot, with plain cooked rice, a bowl of bagoong to spoon over the stew, and slices of green mango.

VARIATIONS
• This dish can also be made with meaty beef ribs or shin (shank) of veal.
• Powdered peanuts, available from South-east Asian supermarkets, can be used instead of the ground peanuts.

Per Portion Energy 885kcal/3693kJ; Protein 85.5g; Carbohydrate 19.2g, of which sugars 8.4g; Fat 52g, of which saturates 18.5g; Cholesterol 281mg; Calcium 89mg; Fibre 5.3g; Sodium 958mg.

BEEF AND CHORIZO STEW WITH PLANTAIN

THIS DISH CAN BE MADE WITH BEEF, CHICKEN OR PORK, ALL OF WHICH ARE COOKED IN THE SAME WAY. IN THE PHILIPPINES, IT IS GENERALLY MADE WITH THE SMALL, FIRM SABA BANANAS, WHICH CAN BE USED INSTEAD OF PLANTAINS, IF REQUIRED. THE STEW IS RICH AND VERY FLAVOURSOME, WITH A DISTINCTIVE SPANISH TANG. AS AN AUTUMN OR WINTER WARMER IT IS UNBEATABLE AND CAN MAKE A WELCOME CHANGE FROM TRADITIONAL WESTERN FARE.

1 Heat the oil in a large, heavy pan or wok with a lid, stir in the onion, garlic and ginger and fry until they begin to brown. Add the chorizo and beef and fry until they begin to brown. Add the tomatoes and pour in the stock. Bring to the boil, then reduce the heat, cover and simmer gently for about 45 minutes.

2 Add the plantains and chickpeas to the stew and cook for a further 20–25 minutes, adding a little extra water if the cooking liquid reduces too much.

3 Meanwhile, heat enough corn oil for deep-frying in a wok or large pan. Deep-fry the bananas or plantain, in batches, for about 3 minutes, until crisp and golden brown. Remove from the pan using a slotted spoon, drain on kitchen paper then arrange in a serving dish.

4 Season the stew with salt and pepper to taste and sprinkle with chopped coriander leaves to garnish. Serve with the deep-fried bananas or plantain and stir-fried greens.

SERVES FOUR TO SIX

INGREDIENTS
30ml/2 tbsp groundnut (peanut) or corn oil
1 onion, chopped
2 garlic cloves, chopped
40g/1½oz fresh root ginger, chopped
2 x 175g/6oz chorizo sausages, cut diagonally into bitesize pieces
700g/1lb 9oz lean rump (round) beef, cut into bitesize pieces
4 tomatoes, skinned, seeded and quartered

900ml/1½ pints/3¾ cups beef or chicken stock
2 plantains, sliced diagonally
2 x 400g/14oz cans chickpeas, rinsed and drained
salt and ground black pepper
1 small bunch fresh coriander (cilantro) leaves, roughly chopped, to garnish
To serve
corn oil, for deep-frying
1–2 firm bananas or 1 plantain, sliced diagonally
stir-fried greens

Per Portion Energy 583kcal/2441kJ; Protein 40.5g; Carbohydrate 35.8g, of which sugars 6.2g; Fat 31.9g, of which saturates 11.1g; Cholesterol 91mg; Calcium 104mg; Fibre 6.1g; Sodium 778mg.

STUFFED BEEF ROLL

IN THIS UNUSUAL RECIPE, BEEF IS FILLED WITH CHORIZO, GHERKINS AND HARD-BOILED EGGS BEFORE BEING ROLLED, COOKED AND CUT INTO SLICES. THE VIBRANT, SLIGHTLY SWEET TOMATO SAUCE COMPLEMENTS THE STUFFED BEEF ROLL PERFECTLY AND MAKES THIS A VERY ATTRACTIVE, COLOURFUL DISH THAT WOULD WORK WELL AT LUNCH OR DINNER AS AN APPETIZER OR, WHEN SERVED WITH SAUTÉED POTATOES AND GREEN SALAD, AS A MAIN COURSE.

SERVES FOUR TO SIX

INGREDIENTS

1kg/2¼lb thin skirt (flank) steak, in one piece
2–3 garlic cloves, crushed
juice of 1½ lemons
2 hard-boiled eggs, finely sliced
1 chorizo sausage, about 175g/6oz, finely sliced diagonally
1–2 large sweet gherkins, finely sliced diagonally
2 slices cooked honey-roast ham, cut into strips
30ml/2 tbsp groundnut (peanut) or palm oil
30ml/2 tbsp coconut or white wine vinegar
30–45ml/2–3 tbsp soy sauce
400g/14oz can chopped tomatoes
15ml/1 tbsp palm sugar (jaggery)
about 300ml/½ pint/1¼ cups water
2 bay leaves
salt and ground black pepper

1 Using a sharp knife, cut the steak lengthways through the centre but not all the way to the base, so that it opens out into a wide, flat steak. Rub the garlic and lemon juice all over the steak and season with salt and pepper.

2 Arrange the sliced egg, chorizo, gherkins and ham in rows down the steak, leaving a 1cm/½ in border around the edge. Carefully roll up the steak and secure with a piece of string to make sure that the filling doesn't escape during cooking.

3 Heat the oil in a heavy pan, add the meat and fry until browned on all sides. Remove the meat from the pan and drain on kitchen paper.

4 Add the vinegar, soy sauce, tomatoes, sugar, water and bay leaves to the pan and bring to the boil. Lower the heat. Return the meat to the pan. Cover and simmer for about 1 hour, until the meat is tender. Add more water to the pan if it becomes too dry during cooking.

5 Lift the meat out of the pan and place on a carving dish or board. Boil the liquid in the pan for 3–4 minutes, to thicken slightly, and season with pepper.

6 Meanwhile, remove the string from the meat and carve it into thick slices. Arrange the slices on a serving dish. Serve with the sauce drizzled over them or serve it separately in a bowl.

Per Portion Energy 558kcal/2323kJ; Protein 47.8g; Carbohydrate 12.3g, of which sugars 6.4g; Fat 35.6g, of which saturates 13.3g; Cholesterol 188mg; Calcium 56mg; Fibre 1.1g; Sodium 1065mg.

JAVANESE GOAT CURRY

THROUGHOUT INDONESIA, LEAN GOAT'S MEAT IS MORE COMMONLY USED THAN LAMB OR MUTTON, ALTHOUGH LAMB COULD BE USED AS A SUBSTITUTE IN THIS RECIPE. SLOW-COOKED ON THE HOB WITH LOTS OF PUNGENT SPICES, THE TENDER, TASTY GOAT'S MEAT IS CUSTOMARILY SERVED WITH RICE AND A PICKLE OR SAMBAL. THIS RECIPE IS FROM JAVA, WHERE THE DISH IS ALSO KNOWN AS GULAI KAMBING, BUT THERE ARE MANY LOCAL VARIATIONS THROUGHOUT THE INDONESIAN ARCHIPELAGO.

SERVES FOUR

INGREDIENTS
 30ml/2 tbsp palm, coconut
  or groundnut (peanut) oil
 10ml/2 tsp terasi (Indonesian
  shrimp paste)
 15ml/1 tbsp palm sugar (jaggery)
 5ml/1 tsp coriander seeds
 5ml/1 tsp cumin seeds
 2.5ml/½ tsp grated nutmeg
 2.5ml/½ tsp ground black pepper
 2–3 lemon grass stalks, halved
  and bruised
 700g/1lb 9oz boneless shoulder or
  leg of goat, or lamb, cut into
  bitesize pieces
 400g/14oz can coconut milk
 200ml/7fl oz/¾ cup water (if needed)
 12 yard-long beans
 1 bunch fresh coriander (cilantro)
  leaves, roughly chopped
 salt
For the spice paste
 2–3 shallots, chopped
 2–3 garlic cloves, chopped
 3–4 fresh chillies, seeded
  and chopped
 25g/1oz fresh galangal, chopped
 40g/1½oz fresh turmeric, chopped,
  or 10ml/2 tsp ground turmeric
 1 lemon grass stalk, chopped
 2–3 candlenuts, finely ground
To serve
 cooked rice
 2–3 fresh chillies, seeded and
  finely chopped

COOK'S TIP
Indonesians love strong culinary tastes and odours, but if you find the taste and smell of goat's meat a little too strong, then blanch it in boiling water for 10 minutes and drain it before adding it to the curry pot.

1 Grind the spice paste ingredients to a coarse paste using a mortar and pestle or an electric food processor or blender.

2 Heat 15ml/1 tbsp of the oil in a heavy pan, then stir in the spice paste and fry until it is fragrant and beginning to colour.

3 Add the terasi and palm sugar and continue to stir-fry for 1–2 minutes, until the paste has deepened in colour but is not too dark.

4 Heat the remaining 15ml/1 tbsp oil in a large, flameproof casserole. Stir in the coriander seeds, cumin seeds, nutmeg and black pepper, then add the spice paste and lemon grass. Stir-fry for 2–3 minutes, until the mixture is dark and fragrant.

5 Stir the meat into the pan, making sure that it is well coated in the paste.

6 Pour in the coconut milk, bring to the boil, then reduce the heat, cover and simmer gently for about 3 hours, until the meat is very tender. Check the meat from time to time and add the water a little at a time if the curry becomes too dry.

7 Add the yard-long beans and cook for a further 10–15 minutes until they are just tender and have taken on the flavour of the sauce. Remove the curry from the heat.

8 Toss some of the coriander leaves into the curry, mix well and season with salt to taste.

9 Turn the curry into a warmed serving dish and sprinkle the remaining coriander leaves over the top. Serve with boiled or steamed rice and a bowl of chopped chillies so that diners can add heat as desired.

Per Portion Energy 450kcal/1877kJ; Protein 37.9g; Carbohydrate 10.8g, of which sugars 9.1g; Fat 28.7g, of which saturates 10.3g; Cholesterol 146mg; Calcium 129mg; Fibre 2.4g; Sodium 375mg.

FRIED RABBIT WITH SPICES

THIS WAS ONCE A FAVOURITE DISH IN MINDANAO. AS IN MOST AREAS, RABBIT IS EATEN LESS COMMONLY TODAY, BUT IT IS FAIRLY EASY TO OBTAIN FROM SPECIALIST BUTCHERS AND IS A DELICIOUS MEAT. IF KALAMANSI LIMES ARE NOT AVAILABLE, USE REGULAR LIMES.

SERVES FOUR

INGREDIENTS

1 prepared rabbit, weighing about
   600g/1lb 6oz
15ml/1 tbsp ground coriander
5ml/1 tsp ground black pepper
15ml/1 tbsp garlic purée (paste)
5ml/1 tsp chilli powder
15ml/1 tbsp patis (Filipino fish sauce)
15ml/1 tbsp kalamansi lime juice
45ml/3 tbsp olive oil
30ml/2 tbsp cornflour (cornstarch)
   mixed to a paste with 75ml/5 tbsp
   water or marinade stock
lime wedges, to garnish
cooked rice, to serve

1 Put the rabbit in a pan and add water just to cover it. Bring to the boil, then simmer for 15 minutes. Drain.

2 Blend all the remaining ingredients except the olive oil and cornflour and use to marinate the rabbit for 15 minutes.

3 Lift the rabbit pieces out of the marinade. Heat the olive oil in a pan, and shallow fry the meat, turning frequently until well cooked and aromatic. Set aside on a warm plate.

4 Add the marinade and cornflour paste to the pan, stirring well, and cook until the sauce is thick. Add the rabbit and serve with lime wedges and rice.

COOK'S TIP
You can also boil the rabbit with the marinade and then drain and fry for a slightly more intense flavour. Use the marinade stock instead of water.

Per Portion Energy 270kcal/1135kJ; Protein 42.2g; Carbohydrate 9g, of which sugars 7.6g; Fat 7.4g, of which saturates 1.6g; Cholesterol 118mg; Calcium 24mg; Fibre 0.6g; Sodium 1892mg.

RABBIT CASSEROLE

IN THIS SUPERB FILIPINO STEW, THE RABBIT IS SO TENDER THAT IT SIMPLY FALLS OFF THE BONE AS YOU EAT IT. SOY SAUCE, TOMATOES AND CIDER VINEGAR GIVE THE SAUCE THAT DISTINCTIVE SWEET-SOUR, EAST-WEST FUSION THAT DEFINES SO MANY DISHES OF THE PHILIPPINES.

SERVES FOUR

INGREDIENTS
   2 rabbits, totalling about 900g/2lb
   75ml/5 tbsp cider vinegar
   4 garlic cloves, chopped
   4 bay leaves
   2.5ml/½ tsp ground black pepper
   30ml/2 tbsp soy sauce
   450ml/¾ pint/scant 2 cups water
   5ml/1 tsp salt
   2 tomatoes, quartered
   1 large onion, sliced
   bread or cooked rice, to serve
To garnish
   1 tbsp sliced spring onions (scallions)
   1 tbsp chopped coriander (cilantro)

1 Using a cleaver, divide the rabbits into large chunks and trim off any protruding pieces of bone.

2 Combine all the ingredients in a casserole and marinate for 20 minutes.

3 Preheat the oven to 200°C/400°F/ Gas 6 and cook the casserole, covered, for an hour. Remove the lid for the last 15 minutes to brown the surface a little.

4 Sprinkle the rabbit with the spring onions and coriander and serve with bread or rice.

Per Portion Energy 434kcal/1812kJ; Protein 26.2g; Carbohydrate 28.6g, of which sugars 12.6g; Fat 24.6g, of which saturates 6.5g; Cholesterol 128mg; Calcium 42mg; Fibre 2.5g; Sodium 1209mg.

VEGETABLES
AND SALADS

The beautiful climate of South-east Asia produces fine fruits and vegetables. Blended with local spices and flavourings, they make spectacular side dishes and main courses. This chapter features steamed, curried and stir-fried dishes, as well as pickles and salads to excite and refresh any palate. Don't worry if your local Asian market does not stock all the exotic produce mentioned as you can always substitute ingredients, and experimentation often leads to superb new recipes.

AUBERGINES IN A CHILLI SAUCE

*THIS DISH IS A GREAT INDONESIAN FAVOURITE, BOTH IN THE HOME AND AT THE STREET STALL. YOU
CAN MAKE IT WITH LARGE AUBERGINES, CUT IN HALF AND BAKED, OR WITH SMALL ONES, BUTTERFLIED.
THE SPICY FILLING AND MELTINGLY SOFT AUBERGINE FLESH ARE EXCELLENT WITH RICE OR BREAD.*

SERVES FOUR

INGREDIENTS
    2 large aubergines (eggplants), cut in
      half lengthways, or 4 small
      aubergines, butterflied
    45ml/3 tbsp coconut oil
    400g/14oz can tomatoes, drained
    5ml/1 tsp palm sugar (jaggery)
    juice of 2 limes
    salt
    1 small bunch fresh coriander
      (cilantro), to garnish
For the spice paste
    4 shallots, finely chopped
    4 garlic cloves, finely chopped
    25g/1oz fresh root ginger,
      finely chopped
    3–4 fresh red chillies, seeded and
      finely chopped

1 Preheat the oven to 180°C/350°F/
Gas 4. Put the prepared aubergines on a
baking tray and brush with 30ml/2 tbsp
of the coconut oil. Bake in the oven for
40 minutes, until soft and tender.

2 Grind the spice paste ingredients to a
coarse paste using a pestle and mortar
or an electric food processor or blender.

3 Heat the remaining oil in a wok, stir in
the spice paste and cook for
1–2 minutes.

4 Add the tomatoes and sugar and cook
for 3–4 minutes, then stir in the lime
juice and a little salt to taste.

5 Put the baked aubergines on a
serving dish and press down the flesh
to form a dip, using the back of a
wooden spoon.

6 Spoon the tomato sauce into the dip
and then spoon it over the aubergines.

7 Garnish with the coriander leaves
and serve the aubergines hot or at
room temperature.

Per Portion Energy 100kcal/419kJ; Protein 2.1g; Carbohydrate 9.4g, of which sugars 8.8g; Fat 6.4g, of which saturates 0.9g; Cholesterol 0mg; Calcium 42mg; Fibre 3.7g; Sodium 15mg.

OKRA AND BITTER MELON STEW WITH BAGNET

THIS CLASSIC FILIPINO DISH IS FLAVOURED WITH THE MUCH-LOVED BAGOONG, THE FERMENTED ANCHOVY SAUCE. THE BAGNET LENDS A RICH MEATY FLAVOUR TO THIS STEW, WHICH COMPLEMENTS THE FERMENTED FISH, RESULTING IN A TASTY MAIN COURSE DISH.

SERVES FOUR TO SIX

INGREDIENTS
225g/8oz okra
juice of 1 lime
1 bitter melon
15ml/1 tbsp palm or corn oil
1–3 garlic cloves, crushed
25g/1oz fresh root ginger, grated
4 shallots, thickly sliced
350g/12oz bagnet (crispy fried
   pork belly)
15–30ml/1–2 tbsp bagoong (Filipino
   shrimp paste) or 15ml/1 tbsp of any
   shrimp paste
400g/14oz can plum tomatoes
250ml/8fl oz/1 cup pork or
   chicken stock
1 aubergine (eggplant), cut into
   bitesize wedges, or 2–3 Thai
   aubergines, quartered
salt and ground black pepper
cooked rice, to serve

1 Put the okra in a large bowl, add the lime juice, toss together and leave to marinate for 30 minutes.

2 Cut the melon in half lengthways, remove the core then cut the flesh into bitesize chunks. Put aside.

3 Meanwhile, heat the oil in a wok or a large, heavy pan, stir in the garlic and ginger and fry until fragrant.

COOK'S TIP
If you can't find bagoong, you could replace it with a Filipino, Thai or Indonesian shrimp paste (terasi).

4 Add the shallots and fry for about 5 minutes until golden brown. Stir in the bagnet and fry for 1 minute, then add the bagoong, tomatoes and stock.

5 Bring the stock mixture to the boil, reduce the heat and simmer for about 10 minutes.

6 Drain the okra and add it to the pan with the aubergine and bitter melon.

7 Cook for a further 10–15 minutes until the vegetables are tender but not too soft. Season the stew with salt and pepper to taste and serve with rice.

Per Portion Energy 323kcal/1340kJ; Protein 16.1g; Carbohydrate 9.4g, of which sugars 8.9g; Fat 24.8g, of which saturates 8.2g; Cholesterol 74mg; Calcium 118mg; Fibre 3.3g; Sodium 200mg.

BICOLANO YARD-LONG BEAN STEW

KNOWN AS BICOL, THE SOUTHERN LUZON PENINSULA IN THE PHILIPPINES IS RENOWNED FOR ITS FIERY FOOD, LACED WITH HOT CHILLIES AND COCONUT MILK. IN TYPICAL BICOLANO STYLE, THIS RICH, PUNGENT DISH IS HOT AND, BELIEVE IT OR NOT, DESPITE ALREADY CONTAINING 4–5 CHILLIES, IT IS SERVED WITH EXTRA CHILLIES FOR DINERS TO CHEW ON!

SERVES THREE TO FOUR

INGREDIENTS

30ml/2 tbsp coconut or groundnut
  (peanut) oil
1 onion, finely chopped
2–3 garlic cloves, finely chopped
40g/1½oz fresh root ginger,
  finely chopped
1 lemon grass stalk, finely chopped
4–5 fresh red chillies, seeded and
  finely chopped
15ml/1 tbsp bagoong (Filipino shrimp
  sauce) or 15ml/1 tbsp shrimp paste
15ml/1 tbsp tamarind paste
15ml/1 tbsp palm sugar (jaggery)
2 x 400g/14oz cans coconut milk
4 kaffir lime leaves

500g/1¼lb yard-long beans
salt and ground black pepper
1 bunch fresh coriander (cilantro)
  leaves, to garnish
To serve
  cooked rice
  raw chillies

1 Heat the oil in a wok that has a lid. Stir in the onion, garlic, ginger, lemon grass and chillies and fry until fragrant and just beginning to colour.

2 Add the bagoong or shrimp paste, tamarind paste and sugar and then stir in the coconut milk and lime leaves.

3 Bring the mixture to the boil, then reduce the heat and toss in the beans. Partially cover the pan and cook the beans for 6–8 minutes until tender.

4 Season to taste and coriander to garnish. Serve with rice and chillies.

Per Portion Energy 200kcal/840kJ; Protein 5.5g; Carbohydrate 24.4g, of which sugars 22.9g; Fat 9.7g, of which saturates 1.5g; Cholesterol 19mg; Calcium 158mg; Fibre 3.4g; Sodium 384mg.

YARD-LONG BEANS IN COCONUT SAUCE

HIGHLY VERSATILE YARD-LONG BEANS ARE ALSO KNOWN AS SNAKE BEANS. FRENCH, GREEN OR DWARF BEANS CAN BE USED IF YOU CANNOT FIND YARD-LONG BEANS. THEY CAN BE EATEN RAW BUT ARE BEST LIGHTLY COOKED. KNOWN AS BUAH CACANG IN INDONESIA, THEY ARE USED IN MANY WAYS: FRIED, BOILED AND IN CURRIES. THIS LIGHT SOUPY RECIPE MAKES AN EXCELLENT SIDE DISH.

SERVES FOUR

INGREDIENTS

400g/14oz yard-long beans
2 lemon grass stalks
350ml/12fl oz/scant 1½ cups
  coconut milk
30g/2 tbsp Balinese Spice Paste
  (see Essential Recipes)
5ml/1 tsp salt
3 salam leaves (Indonesian bay leaves)
1.5ml/¼ tsp sugar
fried shallots, to garnish
cooked rice, to serve

3 Combine the coconut milk with the spice paste, salt, salam leaves, lemon grass and sugar in a heavy pan.

4 Add the beans and cook over a high heat until the sauce is creamy. Garnish with fried shallots and serve with rice.

1 Cut the yard-long beans into 5cm/2in lengths, then wash and drain.

2 Bruise the lemon grass stalks by hitting them with a meat tenderizer.

COOK'S TIP

You can make a more complex vegetable dish by combining 120g/5oz each of yard-long beans, spinach and cabbage instead of just beans. Add the spinach in the last two minutes of cooking.

Per portion Energy 50kcal/208kJ; Protein 2.5g; Carbohydrate 7.4g, of which sugars 6.4g; Fat 1.5g, of which saturates 0.3g; Cholesterol 1mg; Calcium 65mg; Fibre 2.3g; Sodium 594mg.

PINEAPPLE AND COCONUT CURRY

THIS SWEET AND SPICY CURRY FROM THE MALUKU SPICE ISLANDS BENEFITS FROM BEING MADE THE DAY BEFORE EATING, ENABLING THE DELIGHTFULLY TROPICAL FLAVOURS TO MINGLE FOR LONGER. IN INDONESIA THE CURRY IS USUALLY EATEN AT ROOM TEMPERATURE, BUT IT IS ALSO DELICIOUS SERVED PIPING HOT, ALONG WITH A BOWL OF FLUFFY WHITE RICE.

SERVES FOUR

INGREDIENTS
  1 small, firm pineapple
  15ml/1 tbsp palm or
    coconut oil
  4–6 shallots, finely chopped
  2 garlic cloves, finely chopped
  1 fresh red chilli, seeded and
    finely chopped
  15ml/1 tbsp palm sugar (jaggery)
  400ml/14fl oz/1⅔ cups coconut milk
  salt and ground black pepper
  1 small bunch fresh coriander
    (cilantro) leaves, to garnish
For the spice paste
  4 cloves
  4 cardamom pods
  1 small cinnamon stick
  5ml/1 tsp coriander seeds
  2.5ml/½ tsp cumin seeds
  5–10ml/1–2 tsp water

1 First make the spice paste. Using a mortar and pestle or electric spice grinder, grind all the spices together to a powder. In a small bowl, mix the spice powder with the water to make a paste. Set aside.

2 Remove the skin and any woody 'eyes' from the pineapple, then cut the flesh lengthways into quarters and remove the core.

3 Cut each quarter widthways into chunky slices and put aside.

4 Heat the oil in a wok or large, heavy frying pan, stir in the shallots, garlic and chilli and stir-fry until fragrant and beginning to colour. Stir in the spice paste and fry for 1 minute. Toss in the pineapple, making sure the slices are coated in the spicy mixture.

5 Stir the sugar into the coconut milk and pour the mixture into the wok. Stir and bring to the boil. Reduce the heat and simmer for 3–4 minutes to thicken the sauce, but do not allow the pineapple to become too soft. Season with salt and pepper to taste.

6 Tip the curry into a warmed serving dish and garnish with the coriander. Serve hot or at room temperature.

COOK'S TIPS
• If you cannot obtain jaggery or palm sugar, use regular sugar or a mild honey to sweeten the coconut milk.
• The dish will be sweet enough for some tastes without any added sugar.

Per Portion Energy 135kcal/573kJ; Protein 1.6g; Carbohydrate 25.4g, of which sugars 23.6g; Fat 3.8g, of which saturates 0.5g; Cholesterol 0mg; Calcium 87mg; Fibre 2.9g; Sodium 131mg.

YOUNG JACKFRUIT CURRY

THIS CREAMY, SWEET CURRY IS A REAL DELIGHT AND FULL OF AUTHENTIC INDONESIAN FLAVOURS.
IT IS PARTICULARLY GOOD TO SERVE AS PART OF A SELECTION OF CURRIES, AS ITS SWEETNESS OFFSETS
THE SPICY AND SAVOURY FLAVOURS OF OTHER DISHES VERY WELL. IF SERVING IT AS A VEGETARIAN
MAIN COURSE IT NEEDS NOTHING BUT PLAIN RICE OR BREAD AS AN ACCOMPANIMENT.

SERVES FOUR

INGREDIENTS
    75ml/5 tbsp vegetable oil
    450g/1lb prepared young jackfruit
    400ml/14fl oz/1⅔ cups coconut milk
    5ml/1 tsp salt
    15ml/1 tbsp lime juice
    1.5ml/¼ tsp demerara (raw) sugar
    cooked rice or bread, to serve
For the spice paste
    1 large onion, chopped
    3 garlic cloves, chopped
    6 fresh red chillies, seeded
      and chopped
    2 lemon grass stalks, chopped
    2.5ml/½ tsp black peppercorns
    10g/¼ oz terasi (Indonesian
      shrimp paste)
    10g/¼oz fresh turmeric, peeled
      and chopped

1 Grind the spice paste ingredients to a fine paste using a mortar and pestle or an electric food processor.

2 Heat the oil in a wok or heavy frying pan and fry the spice paste over a low heat until it releases its fragrances. This should take about 4 minutes.

VARIATIONS
• Some variations to this dish feature bamboo shoots and tapioca leaves, which you would add at step 4.
• For a more substantial main dish you can also add a few chunks of sweet potato, but par-boil this for 5 minutes before adding it to the coconut milk.

3 Quarter, wash and drain the prepared jackfruit, then cut it into bitesize chunks using a sharp knife. Discard any of the fibrous pith and stones (pits). Place the jackfruit pieces into a heavy pan.

4 Add the coconut milk with the spice paste, salt, lime juice and demerara sugar to the jackfruit and stir.

5 Bring to the boil, then simmer for 10 minutes. Serve hot with rice or bread.

Per portion Energy 173kcal/719kJ; Protein 3.9g; Carbohydrate 7.3g, of which sugars 6.9g; Fat 14.5g, of which saturates 1.8g; Cholesterol 19mg; Calcium 132mg; Fibre 1.5g; Sodium 833mg.

CABBAGE CURRY

CALLED KOBIS LEMAK (LEMAK APPLIES TO ALL DISHES COOKED WITH COCONUT MILK, AND IMPLIES AN INTRINSIC RICHNESS THAT ONLY THIS INGREDIENT CAN GIVE), THIS IS A SIMPLE DISH WITH PEASANT ORIGINS. IT IS COOKED WITH VARYING BLENDS OF SPICES DEPENDING ON THE REGION: IN SUMATRA IT IS SUBTLE, WHILE IN BALI IT CAN BE VERY FIERY. YOU CAN USE THE BALINESE SPICE PASTE BESE GADE, OR SHALLOT AND LEMON GRASS SAMBAL (SAMBAL MATAH) DEPENDING ON YOUR TASTE.

SERVES FOUR

INGREDIENTS
1 whole cabbage
45ml/3 tbsp Shallot and Lemon Grass
  Sambal (see Essential Recipes)
350ml/12fl oz/scant 1½ cups
  coconut milk

5ml/1 tsp salt
2.5ml/½ tsp sugar
3 salam leaves (Indonesian
  bay leaves)

1 Cut the cabbage into small pieces, removing the tough core, then blanch in boiling water for 2 minutes.

2 Combine the remaining ingredients in a wok and bring to the boil. Add the cabbage and simmer for 15 minutes.

COOK'S TIP
For added bulk, take a square of firm tofu cut into triangles and add the pieces in the last 5 minutes of cooking.

Per portion Energy 97kcal/406kJ; Protein 3.9g; Carbohydrate 17.9g, of which sugars 17.5g; Fat 1.3g, of which saturates 0.3g; Cholesterol 1mg; Calcium 151mg; Fibre 5.3g; Sodium 629mg.

SPICY VEGETABLES IN COCONUT MILK

LODEH REFERS TO ANY VEGETABLE COMBINATION COOKED IN COCONUT MILK AND SPICES, AND USUALLY ACCOMPANIES THE INDONESIAN STAPLE OF COMPRESSED RICE (LONTONG). IT SERVES WELL AS A FLAVOURSOME MAIN DISH AS THE SAUCE ENRICHES PLAIN RICE BEAUTIFULLY. THE CLASSIC VEGETABLES TO USE ARE AUBERGINE, CABBAGE, CAULIFLOWER AND LONG BEANS. SPICE BLENDS VARY FROM REGION TO REGION, THIS ONE BEING EXCEPTIONALLY FRAGRANT WITH A MIX OF EIGHT HERBS.

SERVES FOUR

INGREDIENTS

   200g/7oz cauliflower
   1 purple aubergine or 2 brinjals
   5 yard-long beans
   200g/7oz cabbage
   30ml/2 tbsp vegetable oil
   450ml/16fl oz/scant 2 cups
     coconut milk
   2.5ml/½ tsp salt
   2.5ml/½ tsp sugar
For the spice paste
   4 dried chillies, soaked in warm
     water until soft
   5 shallots chopped
   3 garlic cloves, chopped
   4 candlenuts
   5g/⅛oz fresh turmeric, peeled
   3 thin slices fresh galangal
   10g/⅓oz terasi (Indonesian
     shrimp paste)
   2 lemon grass stalks, 5cm/2in of root
     end chopped

2 Grind the spice paste ingredients to a fine paste using a pestle and mortar or a food processor or blender. Heat the oil in a wok or frying pan and fry the paste for 4 minutes until the oil separates.

3 Transfer the fried spices to a pan and add the coconut milk, salt and sugar. Bring to the boil and add the vegetables. Cook for 15 minutes until all the vegetables are soft.

1 Slice the cauliflower, aubergine, yard-long beans and cabbage into bitesize pieces. Wash and drain.

Per portion Energy 59kcal/248kJ; Protein 2.2g; Carbohydrate 11.3g, of which sugars 10.9g; Fat 0.9g, of which saturates 0.3g; Cholesterol 0mg; Calcium 105mg; Fibre 4.8g; Sodium 175mg.

SQUASH WITH COCONUT MILK

MANY DIFFERENT TYPES OF SQUASH AND TUBERS ARE FILIPINO STAPLES IN CASSEROLES SUCH AS THIS CREAMY COCONUT DISH. PUMPKIN, SWEET POTATOES, TAPIOCA, BUTTERNUT SQUASH AND JAPANESE SQUASH (KALABASA) ARE THE MOST POPULAR, BEING WIDELY AVAILABLE WHEN IN SEASON. ALL SQUASH HAVE A SWEETNESS THAT IS MELLOW AND RICH, NEVER OVERPOWERING.

SERVES FOUR

INGREDIENTS
   450g/1lb Japanese or
      other squash
   30ml/2 tbsp vegetable oil
   4 shallots, sliced
   3 garlic cloves, crushed
   100ml/3½fl oz/⅓ cup water
   1 meat stock cube
   15ml/1 tbsp patis (Filipino fish sauce)
   2.5ml/½ tsp ground black pepper
   350ml/12fl oz/scant 1½ cups
      coconut milk

1 Peel off the outer rind of the squash and remove the core and seeds. Cut into bitesize chunks, wash and drain.

2 Heat the oil in a pan and fry the shallots until golden brown, then add the garlic. Fry for 1 minute.

3 Add the water, stock cube, patis, black pepper and coconut milk.

4 Bring to the boil, then add the squash and simmer the mixture for about 15 minutes. Do not overcook as the squash will become mushy and spoil the dish.

COOK'S TIP
To temper the sweetness of the coconut milk, add a quartered potato at the same time as adding the squash.

Per portion Energy 90kcal/378kJ; Protein 1.4g; Carbohydrate 8.3g, of which sugars 7.3g; Fat 6g, of which saturates 0.9g; Cholesterol 0mg; Calcium 63mg; Fibre 1.3g; Sodium 364mg.

SALTED MUSTARD GREENS

WHILE SALTED MUSTARD GREENS ARE WIDELY AVAILABLE, IT IS REWARDING TO MAKE YOUR OWN. THE PICKLE CAN BE EATEN AFTER FOUR DAYS, BUT A WEEK WILL ALLOW A RICHER FLAVOUR. THE USE OF RICE COOKING WATER GIVES THE PICKLE A DISTINCTIVELY HUSKY TASTE. IT IS A VERSATILE PICKLE THAT CAN BE SERVED AS A RELISH, SIDE DISH, OMELETTE STUFFING OR IN SOUPS IF CHOPPED FINELY.

SERVES FOUR TO SIX

INGREDIENTS
 115g/4oz/scant ⅔ cup white jasmine
  or basmati rice
 1.2 litres/2 pints/5 cups water
 500g/1½lb mustard greens
 35g/1oz salt

1 Wash the rice in a colander, then bring to the boil in a large pan with the water. Cover and simmer for 12 minutes. Drain the rice, saving the liquid. Either save the rice for another dish or serve it with this one. There should be about 600ml/1 pint/2½ cups of liquid left.

2 Wash the mustard greens in plenty of water and dry thoroughly, using a kitchen towel to pat each leaf and stalk. It is important that they are fully dry.

3 Cut the thick stalks of large greens into thin slices. Cut smaller stalks into 3 lengths and mix with the salt in a non-metallic bowl. Leave for 30 minutes, then squeeze out as much moisture as possible. Salt will cling to the leaves.

4 When the rice water is completely cold, pour it over the leaves in a jar and seal tightly. Place in a cool spot for 4 days, or up to a week.

5 To serve, pick up the pieces with chopsticks, drain and chop up into smaller pieces as a side dish.

Per portion Energy 123kcal/514kJ; Protein 4.2g; Carbohydrate 25.3g, of which sugars 9.8g; Fat 0.5g, of which saturates 0g; Cholesterol 0mg; Calcium 102mg; Fibre 4.2g; Sodium 1324mg.

SPICED STEAMED CAULIFLOWER

THIS INDONESIAN RECIPE IS A GREAT WAY TO SERVE CAULIFLOWER, GIVING IT SOME MUCH-NEEDED PUNCHY FLAVOUR AND A WARM COLOUR. THE BEAUTIFUL CRUNCHINESS OF THE VEGETABLE IS RETAINED, AS ARE THE NUTRIENTS, BY COOKING IT IN A STEAMER.

2 Toss the florets in a large mixing bowl with the ground cloves and cinnamon, then mix in the garlic purée, sesame oil and salt.

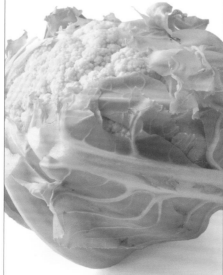

3 Place the cauliflower in a steaming tray and steam for 20 minutes. It can be served warm or cold as an accompaniment to a curry.

SERVES FOUR

INGREDIENTS
    600g/1lb 6oz cauliflower
    pinch of ground cloves
    pinch of ground cinnamon
    30g/2 tbsp garlic purée (paste)
    30ml/2 tbsp sesame oil
    2.5ml/½ tsp salt

1 Break the cauliflower into small florets, then wash and drain the pieces.

Per portion Energy 108kcal/447kJ; Protein 6g; Carbohydrate 5.7g, of which sugars 3.9g; Fat 6.9g, of which saturates 1.1g; Cholesterol 0mg; Calcium 34mg; Fibre 3g; Sodium 260mg.

SPANISH POTATO SALAD

THIS POPULAR FILIPINO SALAD IS OBVIOUSLY FROM IBERIAN STOCK. IT IS A SUBSTANTIAL DISH AND VERY EASY TO PREPARE. IT MAKES A GOOD BUFFET SALAD SERVED COLD BUT IS WARMING AND HEARTY WHEN EATEN HOT. USE ANCHOVY- OR PIMIENTO-STUFFED OLIVES FOR EXTRA PUNCH.

SERVES FOUR

INGREDIENTS
- 4 hard-boiled eggs
- 600g/1lb 6oz potatoes
- 1 green (bell) pepper
- 1 red (bell) pepper
- 1 large beef tomato
- 150g/5oz green olives
- 50ml/2fl oz extra virgin olive oil
- 1.5ml/¼ tsp salt
- 15ml/1 tbsp suka (Filipino coconut vinegar)

To garnish
- 2 fried sliced shallots
- 3 spring onions (scallions), chopped

3 Remove the stalk, pith and seeds from the peppers and chop them into chunks of about 1.5cm/½in. Chop the tomato into similar-sized chunks. Toss all the vegetables into a bowl.

4 Blend the olive oil, salt and suka with a whisk, then pour over the salad.

5 Place in a serving dish and garnish with the shallots and spring onions.

1 Peel and quarter the boiled eggs.

2 Peel the potatoes and cut each into quarters. Bring to the boil in a pan of water and cook for 20 minutes until they are tender. Drain and, when cool enough to handle, slice into small cubes.

VARIATION
A store-bought French vinaigrette or a creamy mayonnaise will also complement this potato dish.

Per portion Energy 324kcal/1352kJ; Protein 10.2g; Carbohydrate 30.5g, of which sugars 8.1g; Fat 18.8g, of which saturates 3.6g; Cholesterol 190mg; Calcium 69mg; Fibre 4.2g; Sodium 936mg.

PICKLED VEGETABLES

WHILE THIS IS CALLED A PICKLE, IT IS ACTUALLY STIR-FRIED IN THE PICKLING SOLUTION, WHICH IS MORE OF A SEASONING MIX. THERE IS NO LONG STEEPING PROCESS APART FROM THE SALTING OF THE VEGETABLES. THIS MEDLEY OF DIFFERENT VEGETABLES MAKES A COLOURFUL SALAD OR APPETIZER AS WELL AS A BEAUTIFUL CONDIMENT THAT CAN BE SERVED WARM OR COLD.

SERVES FOUR

INGREDIENTS

2 celery stalks, sliced diagonally into 1.5cm/½in wide pieces

½ cucumber, peeled, cored and cut into 1.5cm/½in wide pieces

1 carrot, cut into matchsticks

1 bitter melon, halved lengthways, soft core and seeds removed and sliced into 1.5cm/½in wide pieces

1 onion, thickly sliced

1 green (bell) pepper, seeded and cut into 1.5cm/½in wide strips

15ml/1 tbsp salt

30ml/2 tbsp vegetable oil

For the pickling liquid

30ml/2 tbsp suka (Filipino coconut vinegar)

15ml/1 tbsp garlic purée (paste)

15ml/1 tbsp ginger purée

15ml/1 tbsp bagoong (Filipino shrimp sauce)

2.5ml/½ tsp sugar

1 Place all the vegetables in a large bowl and sprinkle salt over them. Leave for 20 minutes, then squeeze out the moisture from the vegetables by hand.

2 Blend the ingredients for the pickling liquid in a bowl, stirring vigorously.

3 Heat the oil and fry the vegetables for 2 minutes over a high heat, then add the pickling liquid. Continue to stir for 5 minutes, tossing well.

VARIATION

If you omit the salting step, you still end up with a good vegetable dish with a subtle pickled texture and sharp flavours.

Per portion Energy 88kcal/366kJ; Protein 2.1g; Carbohydrate 6.9g, of which sugars 4.6g; Fat 6g, of which saturates 0.7g; Cholesterol 0mg; Calcium 51mg; Fibre 2.5g; Sodium 1537mg.

CHINESE LEAVES WITH SHRIMP SAUCE

TENDER CABBAGE COOKED WITH GARLIC AND THE FAMOUS FILIPINO CONDIMENT, BAGOONG, IS A WONDERFUL, HEALTHY DISH TO SERVE ALONGSIDE MANY OF THE MEAT AND FISH RECIPES FEATURED IN THIS BOOK. USE CHINESE LEAVES FOR THEIR DISTINCTIVE CRUNCH OR TRY SPRING GREENS OR GREEN CABBAGE INSTEAD, IF THEY ARE IN SEASON.

SERVES FOUR

INGREDIENTS
    600g/1lb 6oz Chinese leaves
    30ml/2 tbsp vegetable oil
    4 garlic cloves, crushed
    30ml/2 tbsp bagoong (Filipino
      shrimp sauce)
    ¼ tsp salt
    200ml/7 fl oz/1 cup water

1 Separate the cabbage into individual leaves and trim off about an inch from the root end of the stalk.

2 Cut the leaves into 2.5cm/1in strips, wash and drain.

3 Heat the oil and fry the garlic very gently for 2 minutes. Add the bagoong and salt and stir for 1 minute.

COOK'S TIP
Chinese leaves exude a lot of water when cooked, so you do not need to add much to the braising pan. They are best braised in a wok, where the evaporation rate is higher than that of a regular pan.

4 Add the cabbage, stirring vigorously to coat it in the flavourings, then stir-fry for 2 minutes. Add the water, cover loosely and braise over a medium heat until half of the liquid has evaporated and the cabbage is tender. Serve.

Per portion Energy 109kcal/453kJ; Protein 5g; Carbohydrate 9.1g, of which sugars 7.5g; Fat 6g, of which saturates 0.7g; Cholesterol 19mg; Calcium 121mg; Fibre 3.6g; Sodium 173mg.

PICKLED WATER SPINACH

KANGKUNG OR WATER SPINACH IS GENERALLY STIR-FRIED BUT TAKES TO PICKLING VERY WELL. THIS RECIPE CALLS FOR ONLY THE STALKS, WHICH REMAIN FAIRLY WHOLE, FIRM AND STILL CRUNCHY. IT IS A ROBUST SIDE DISH THAT COMPLEMENTS FRIED OR GRILLED SEAFOODS.

2 Split each stalk and cut into small pieces about 5cm/2in long. Wash and drain and dry handfuls on kitchen paper.

3 Sprinkle the stalks with salt and leave for 20 minutes. Squeeze out the moisture with your hands.

4 Combine the pickling solution ingredients in a large, heavy pan or earthenware pot and simmer until the sugar is completely dissolved. Remove from the heat to cool completely.

SERVES FOUR

INGREDIENTS
    675g/1½lb water spinach (kangkung)
    10ml/2 tsp salt
For the pickling solution
    4 garlic cloves, crushed
    50g/2oz sugar
    200ml/7fl oz/¾ cup suka (Filipino coconut vinegar)
    5ml/1 tsp salt

COOK'S TIP
Use the pickled water spinach within 3 days of making it.

1 Wash and drain the water spinach stalks after trimming away the leaves. The yield will be about 600g/1¼lb.

5 Pour the solution over the kangkung, toss well to coat, and store in a preserving jar for a day or two before serving with grilled (broiled) poultry or seafood.

Per portion Energy 96kcal/405kJ; Protein 5.2g; Carbohydrate 16.6g, of which sugars 15.7g; Fat 1.4g, of which saturates 0.2g; Cholesterol 0mg; Calcium 295mg; Fibre 3.8g; Sodium 729mg.

WATER SPINACH IN TANGY SAUCE

THERE ARE FEW ASIAN VEGETABLES THAT CAN MATCH WATER SPINACH (KANGKUNG) FOR FLAVOUR, TEXTURE AND VERSATILITY. IT GROWS IN SWAMPY LAND LIKE A WEED AFTER A SUMMER SHOWER. THIS DISH, THEREFORE, IS HIGHLY ECONOMICAL FOR INDONESIAN COOKS — AND VERY DELICIOUS.

SERVES FOUR

INGREDIENTS
600g/1lb 6oz water
    spinach (kangkung)
30ml/2 tbsp oil
4 garlic cloves, crushed
200g/7oz minced (ground) pork
200g/7oz small fresh prawns
    (shrimp), peeled
200ml/7fl oz/¾ cup water
100ml/3½fl oz/⅓ cup suka (Filipino
    coconut vinegar)
5ml/1 tsp salt

3 Add the prawns, spinach stems, water, suka and salt. Braise over a high heat, stirring to incorporate all the ingredients, for 3–4 minutes, then fold in the water spinach leaves. Serve hot.

1 Wash the water spinach well. Pinch off the leaves and slice the stalks thinly.

2 Heat the oil and fry the garlic until light brown, then add the pork. Fry for 4 minutes until cooked through.

COOK'S TIPS
• Water spinach grows in brackish or swampy water, so slice the hollow stems through to see if there is any mud inside.
• Water spinach contains a lot of water, so if you prefer a dry dish, reduce the amount of water by half.

Per portion Energy 207kcal/861kJ; Protein 22.6g; Carbohydrate 2.4g, of which sugars 2.3g; Fat 11.9g, of which saturates 2.7g; Cholesterol 131mg; Calcium 298mg; Fibre 3.2g; Sodium 829mg.

STIR-FRIED MIXED VEGETABLES

CAP CAI CA IS A SINO-INDONESIAN STIR-FRY; THE NAME IS A PHONETIC SPELLING FROM THE FUJIAN DIALECT, WHICH LITERALLY MEANS 'TEN VEGETABLES FRY' BUT ACTUALLY ALLUDES TO ANY MULTIPLE VEGETABLE DISH. THIS CHINESE DISH HAS BEEN ABSORBED INTO THE INDONESIAN CULINARY LEXICON AND IS FEATURED ON MANY LOCAL RESTAURANT MENUS.

SERVES FOUR

INGREDIENTS
- 200g/7oz pak choi (bok choy)
- 16 mangetouts (snow peas)
- 200g/7oz canned bamboo shoot slices
- 30ml/2 tbsp vegetable oil
- 3 garlic cloves, crushed
- 16 water chestnuts
- 8 Chinese mushrooms, soaked until soft and sliced
- 15ml/1 tbsp light soy sauce
- 15ml/1 tbsp oyster sauce
- 15ml/1 tbsp sesame oil
- 2.5ml/½ tsp ground black pepper
- 105ml/7 tbsp water
- 10ml/2 tsp cornflour (cornstarch)

1 Cut the pak choi leaves into short lengths. Trim the tops and tails of the mangetouts.

2 Wash and drain the bamboo shoots to remove some of the canning liquid scent, which can be overpowering.

3 Heat the oil and fry the garlic over a low heat until golden brown, then add the pak choi, mangetouts, bamboo shoots, water chestnuts and mushrooms. Stir-fry over a high heat for 3 minutes.

4 Add the soy sauce, oyster sauce, sesame oil and black pepper to the pan and continue to stir well, coating all the vegetables in each flavouring.

5 Mix the water with the cornflour to form a smooth, thin blend and pour into the pan. Stir over a medium-high heat until the sauce is fairly thick, then serve the dish immediately with noodles or rice or as a vegetable side dish.

Per portion Energy 84kcal/352kJ; Protein 5.4g; Carbohydrate 7.9g, of which sugars 4.2g; Fat 3.6g, of which saturates 0.5g; Cholesterol 0mg; Calcium 121mg; Fibre 3.2g; Sodium 610mg.

MIXED SALAD <u>WITH</u> COCONUT

URABS ARE TRADITIONAL INDONESIAN SALAD OR VEGETABLE DISHES, WHICH MAY USE A RANGE OF COOKED OR RAW INGREDIENTS. MANY CALL FOR DIFFERENT VEGETABLES BUT YOU CAN ALSO USE JUST ONE IF TIME DOES NOT PERMIT THE PREPARATION OF A MORE COMPLEX DISH. THE DRESSING IS GOOD WITH MANY VEGETABLE DISHES, SO CONSIDER MAKING A BATCH FOR USE ANOTHER DAY.

SERVES FOUR

INGREDIENTS
115g/4oz cabbage
100g/3½oz spinach
100g/3½oz beansprouts
15ml/1 tbsp desiccated (dry
  unsweetened shredded) coconut
30g/2 tbsp shallots, to garnish
2 fresh red chillies, seeded and sliced
For the dressing
30ml/2 tbsp garlic purée (paste)
1 fresh red chilli, finely chopped
juice of 3 limes
1 lemon grass stalk, 5cm/2in of root
  end, finely sliced
4cm/1.5in piece kencur root (lesser
  galangal), finely chopped
1.5ml/¼ tsp salt
2.5ml/½ tsp ground black pepper
2.5ml/½ tsp sugar
15ml/1 tbsp olive oil

1 Cut the cabbage into thin strips and blanch in a pan of boiling water for 2 minutes. Drain.

2 Blanch the spinach as in step 1. Wash and drain the beansprouts.

3 Dry-fry the desiccated coconut for 3 minutes over a low–medium heat until golden brown. Set aside.

VARIATION
Introduce a fruity flavour by reducing the amount of each vegetable slightly and adding some sliced green mango strips at step 4.

4 Fry the shallots until crisp and golden, for the garnish. Drain off any excess oil on kitchen paper and set aside.

5 Use your hands to gently mix the cabbage, spinach, beansprouts and chillies in a salad bowl.

6 Add the dressing ingredients to a jar and shake well to blend. Pour the dressing over the vegetables and toss for an even coating. Garnish the salad with fried shallots and the dry-fried coconut before serving.

Per portion Energy 141kcal/585kJ; Protein 4.5g; Carbohydrate 6.4g, of which sugars 5.1g; Fat 11g, of which saturates 9.1g; Cholesterol 8mg; Calcium 54mg; Fibre 4.6g; Sodium 86mg.

PICKLED CUCUMBER AND ONION

THERE IS A DELICIOUS EAST-WEST FLAVOUR TO THIS FILIPINO SALAD KNOWN AS ACHARANG PIPINO. ACHARANG DERIVES FROM THE INDIAN-INDONESIAN WORD ACAR (PRONOUNCED ACHAR) FOR SPICY PICKLES. PIPINO IS THE LOCAL NAME FOR CUCUMBERS. THIS IS A FAIRLY SIMPLE PICKLE AND VERY VERSATILE, SO IT IS WORTH MAKING A LARGE BATCH AND KEEPING SOME IN YOUR REFRIGERATOR.

SERVES SIX

INGREDIENTS
  2 whole cucumbers
  16 white pickling onions
  60ml/4 tsp salt
For the pickling solution
  15ml/1 tbsp grated fresh root ginger
  4 garlic cloves, crushed
  150g/5oz/¾ cup sugar
  200ml/7fl oz/¾ cup suka (Filipino coconut vinegar)
  5ml/1 tsp salt
  6 native Filipino chillies or Spanish jalapeño chillies

1 Wash and drain the cucumbers. Cut each into four pieces lengthways and remove the soft cores. Slice into diamond shapes, each 2cm/¾in wide.

2 Slice each pickling onion into two (or leave whole if small). Place a layer of cucumber in a ceramic bowl (never metal) and sprinkle with salt. Repeat with the onions and remaining cucumber, sprinkling salt all over each layer until the vegetables are used up.

3 Cover the dish and set it aside overnight to sweat. On the following day, squeeze out as much moisture as possible, a handful at a time, and drain the vegetables in a colander.

4 Combine the ingredients for the pickling solution in a non-metallic flameproof dish and simmer until the sugar is completely dissolved. Remove from the heat and cool completely.

5 Pour the pickling solution over the vegetables and store the pickle in a preserving jar or other non-metallic lidded container.

6 Keep the pickle for a few days in the refrigerator to mature, before serving with grilled (broiled) meats and poultry.

Per portion Energy 109kcal/461kJ; Protein 1.1g; Carbohydrate 27.2g, of which sugars 27.2g; Fat 0.2g, of which saturates 0g; Cholesterol 0mg; Calcium 30mg; Fibre 0.4g; Sodium 332mg.

SEAWEED SALAD WITH GREEN MANGO

IN JAPAN, SEAWEED IS CONSUMED WIDELY IN ITS VARIOUS FORMS BUT THIS TRADITION HAS NOT FILTERED THROUGH THE REST OF SOUTH-EAST ASIA TO THE SAME DEGREE. IN THE PHILIPPINES THOUGH, VARIOUS TYPES OF SEAWEED ARE ENJOYED IN SALADS AND THE OCCASIONAL STIR-FRY. SERVE THIS SALAD AS AN APPETIZER OR AS AN ACCOMPANIMENT TO MEATS AND FISH.

SERVES FOUR

INGREDIENTS

50g/2oz fine thread seaweed, reconstituted in water, or 225g/8oz fresh seaweed, cut into strips
1 green mango, flesh grated
2–3 ripe tomatoes, skinned, seeded and chopped
4–6 spring onions (scallions), white parts only, sliced
25g/1oz fresh root ginger, grated
45ml/3 tbsp suka (Filipino coconut vinegar) or cane vinegar
10ml/2 tsp chilli oil
15ml/1 tbsp sugar
salt and ground black pepper

1 Bring a large pan of water to the boil and drop in the seaweed, then remove from the heat and leave to soak for 15 minutes.

2 Drain and refresh the seaweed under cold running water. Using your hands, squeeze the seaweed dry.

3 Put the seaweed, mango, tomatoes, spring onions and ginger in a large bowl.

4 In a separate bowl, mix together the suka, chilli oil and sugar until the sugar has dissolved. Pour the dressing over the salad, toss well together and season with salt and pepper to taste.

Per Portion Energy 75kcal/315kJ; Protein 2.4g; Carbohydrate 12g, of which sugars 11.8g; Fat 2.2g, of which saturates 0.3g; Cholesterol 0mg; Calcium 110mg; Fibre 2.8g; Sodium 85mg.

RED MUSTARD LEAF SALAD

LEAFY GREENS, SUCH AS WATER SPINACH AND CHINESE LEAVES ARE RARELY SERVED AS A SALAD IN SOUTH-EAST ASIA; INSTEAD THEY ARE STIR-FRIED AND SERVED WITH RICE TO BALANCE A MEAL. HOWEVER, THE FILIPINOS ENJOY RED MUSTARD LEAVES AND THE LEAVES OF THE SWEET POTATO PLANT IN COLD APPETIZERS SUCH AS THIS ONE, WHICH MAKES AN IDEAL ACCOMPANIMENT TO FRIED FISH, OR ROASTED OR GRILLED MEAT.

1 Rinse the mustard leaves very well in cold water, then drain thoroughly. Put the leaves in a large bowl and sprinkle with salt. Rub the salt into the leaves, crunching and squeezing them with your fingers, to soften them and begin to draw out their juices.

2 Leave the salty leaves to stand for 30 minutes to draw out the bitter juices.

3 Lift up the leaves in your hands and squeeze them tightly to drain off the juice. Rinse the leaves again in cold water and drain well.

4 Put the leaves in a salad bowl and add the prepared tomatoes and spring onions.

SERVES FOUR

INGREDIENTS
    700g/1lb 9oz mustard leaves
    3 ripe tomatoes, skinned,
      seeded and chopped
    4–6 spring onions
      (scallions), chopped
    30–45ml/2–3 tbsp suka (Filipino
      coconut vinegar) or cane vinegar
    salt and ground back pepper

5 Add the suka and season with a little salt, if required, and pepper, then toss well together.

COOK'S TIP
Red mustard leaves are available in Chinese and South-east Asian stores.

Per Portion Energy 58kcal/242kJ; Protein 5.6g; Carbohydrate 5.4g, of which sugars 5.2g; Fat 1.7g, of which saturates 0.3g; Cholesterol 0mg; Calcium 306mg; Fibre 4.5g; Sodium 252mg.

PEPPERED YARD-LONG BEANS

THROUGHOUT INDONESIA AND THE PHILIPPINES, THE SERVING OF VEGETABLES IS REGARDED AS ESSENTIAL NUTRITIONAL BALANCE AT EVERY MEAL. INDONESIAN COOKS ARE ADEPT AT ENHANCING THE FAIRLY NEUTRAL FLAVOUR OF BASIC VEGETABLES BY COOKING THEM WITH DIFFERENT BLENDS OF SPICES AND AROMATICS. THIS IS A GREAT WAY TO PREPARE SIMPLE GREEN BEANS; THE FRESH, SPICY FLAVOURS MAKE THIS HUMBLE VEGETABLE INTO A REAL TREAT.

SERVES FOUR

INGREDIENTS
- 400g/14oz yard-long beans
- 15ml/1 tbsp vegetable oil
- 4 shallots
- 1.5ml/¼ tsp ground turmeric
- 1.5ml/¼ tsp ground black pepper
- 1 lemon grass stalk, 5cm/2in of root end finely sliced
- 5ml/1 tsp palm sugar (jaggery)
- 2 fresh red chillies
- 5ml/1 tsp salt
- 10g/⅓oz terasi (Indonesian shrimp paste)
- 75ml/5 tbsp coconut milk

1 Wash, top and tail the beans and cut each into 2–3 pieces. Peel and finely chop the shallots. Slice the chillies finely (do not seed them unless you want a mild dish).

2 Heat the oil and fry the shallots for 2 minutes. Add the turmeric, black pepper, lemon grass, sugar, chillies and salt and stir for 2 minutes.

3 Add the beans and stir for 1 minute.

4 Add the terasi and coconut milk and simmer for 8 minutes, stirring well. Serve warm, as coconut milk congeals when it gets cold.

COOK'S TIP
This dish keeps well, so you can prepare it ahead and warm it through for serving the next day.

Per portion Energy 68kcal/284kJ; Protein 3.5g; Carbohydrate 6.4g, of which sugars 5.1g; Fat 3.4g, of which saturates 0.5g; Cholesterol 13mg; Calcium 76mg; Fibre 2.4g; Sodium 130mg.

KAMIA AND CUCUMBER RELISH

THIS IS A WONDERFULLY DIFFERENT RELISH TO INTRODUCE TO YOUR REPERTOIRE, AND IDEAL WITH BARBECUED MEAT OR FISH OR SPICY CURRIES. IT IS COOLING, SWEET AND SALTY ALL AT ONCE, AND THE TEXTURES OF THE KAMIA AND CUCUMBER COMPLEMENT EACH OTHER BEAUTIFULLY.

SERVES FOUR

INGREDIENTS

    12–15 kamias or star fruit (carambola)
    1 whole cucumber
    5ml/1 tsp salt
    15ml/1 tbsp sweet bagoong (Filipino
        shrimp sauce)
    30ml/2 tbsp rice vinegar
    10ml/2 tsp sugar

1 Slice each kamia into two lengthways and remove any flat seeds. Slice each halved fruit into two again.

2 Peel the cucumber and remove the soft core. Slice into 4 lengthways and then slice into diamond-shaped pieces.

3 Mix the cucumber and kamias and sprinkle salt all over them. Toss well and leave them to sweat for 30 minutes.

COOK'S TIP

Kamia fruits are the size of a fat thumb, and pale green or yellow in colour. They are similar to star fruit (carambola), and are usually pickled or cooked in curries to impart a pleasantly sour flavour.

4 Gently squeeze out the juice from the cucumber and kamias and pat them dry with kitchen paper. Discard the juice.

5 Blend the bagoong with the vinegar and sugar and cook in a small pan for 1 minute to warm and melt the sugar.

6 Cool the bagoong mixture and then toss it into the kamia and cucumber mix. Eat the relish within 2 days.

Per portion Energy 87kcal/372kJ; Protein 3.4g; Carbohydrate 17.8g, of which sugars 17.8g; Fat 0.9g, of which saturates 0.3g; Cholesterol 19mg; Calcium 63mg; Fibre 0.3g; Sodium 659mg.

BELIMBING LEAF SALAD

BELIMBING LEAVES ARE CRUNCHY WITH A FAINTLY BITTER EDGE. THANKS TO THE SUBTLE BLEND OF SPICES AND THE RICHNESS OF COCONUT MILK, THIS SALAD HAS A WELL-ROUNDED FLAVOUR WITH AN ALMOST CURRY-LIKE TASTE. IT MAKES A PERFECT COMPLEMENT TO MEAT AND SEAFOOD DISHES.

SERVES FOUR

INGREDIENTS

350g/12oz belimbing (sour star fruit) leaves
30ml/2 tbsp Balinese Spice Paste (see Essential Recipes)
3 salam leaves (Indonesian bay leaves)
400ml/14fl oz/1⅔ cups coconut milk
200g/7oz minced (ground) beef
2.5ml/½ tsp black peppercorns, crushed
2.5ml/½ tsp salt
2.5ml/½ tsp sugar
15ml/1 tbsp lime juice

3 Add the beef, peppercorns, salt, sugar and lime juice and simmer for 10 minutes until the sauce is thick.

4 Add the blanched belimbing leaves and toss together. Adjust the seasoning before serving.

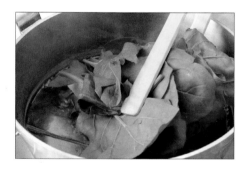

1 Bring a small pan of water to the boil and blanch the belimbing leaves for 4 minutes. Drain and allow to cool completely.

2 Combine the spice paste, salam leaves and coconut milk in a pan and bring to the boil, then simmer for 5 minutes.

VARIATION
If you cannot find belimbing, use young spinach leaves instead.

Per portion Energy 166kcal/690kJ; Protein 13g; Carbohydrate 6.8g, of which sugars 6.7g; Fat 9.9g, of which saturates 3.8g; Cholesterol 31mg; Calcium 190mg; Fibre 1.9g; Sodium 539mg.

STEAMED VEGETABLES AND FRUIT WITH PEANUT SAUCE

THIS CLASSIC INDONESIAN DISH OF VEGETABLES IN A PEANUT SAUCE, KNOWN AS GADO GADO, IS ENJOYED THROUGHOUT THE ISLANDS, WHICH MEANS THERE ARE MANY VARIATIONS AS EACH REGION WILL INCORPORATE THEIR LOCAL VEGETABLES AND FRUIT. SERVED AT ROOM TEMPERATURE WITH A BOWL OF RICE, THIS DISH COULD BE AN APPETIZER OR A MEAL ON ITS OWN.

SERVES FOUR TO SIX

INGREDIENTS
 corn oil, for deep-frying
 500g/1¼lb tofu block, cut into 4
  rectangular pieces
 4 shallots, finely sliced
 3 carrots, sliced diagonally
 12 yard-long beans, cut into
  bitesize pieces
 225g/8oz water spinach (kangkung),
  washed and thinly sliced
 1 firm mango, pitted and cut into
  bitesize chunks
 ½ pineapple, cored and cut into
  bitesize chunks
 225g/8oz mung beansprouts
 2 hard-boiled eggs, quartered
 salt
For the peanut sauce
 30ml/2 tbsp coconut or groundnut
  (peanut) oil
 3 shallots, finely chopped
 3 garlic cloves, finely chopped
 3–4 fresh red chillies, seeded and
  finely chopped
 175g/6oz/1 cup unsalted roasted
  peanuts, finely ground
 15g/½oz fresh galangal or root
  ginger, finely chopped
 5–10ml/1–2 tsp terasi (Indonesian
  shrimp paste)
 15ml/1 tbsp palm sugar (jaggery)
 600ml/1 pint/2½ cups coconut milk
 juice of 1 lime
 30ml/2 tbsp kecap manis (Indonesian
  sweet soy sauce)

COOK'S TIP
Other ingredients commonly used for gado gado include shredded cabbage, sweet potato, turnip, papaya and star fruit (carambola).

1 First make the peanut sauce. Heat the oil in a wok or heavy pan, stir in the shallots, garlic and chillies and fry until fragrant and beginning to colour.

2 Add the peanuts, galangal, terasi and palm sugar and fry for about 4 minutes, until the peanuts begin to darken and ooze a little oil.

3 Pour the coconut milk, lime juice and kecap manis into the pan and bring to the boil. Reduce the heat and simmer gently for 15–20 minutes, until the sauce has reduced a little and thickened. Leave to cool.

4 Heat enough oil in a wok or large pan for deep-frying, add the tofu pieces and fry until golden brown.

5 Using a slotted spoon, remove the tofu from the pan and drain on kitchen paper. Cut the tofu into slices and put aside.

6 Heat 15ml/1 tbsp of the oil from the deep-frying in a small, heavy pan, add the shallots and fry until deep golden in colour. Drain on crumpled kitchen paper and put aside.

7 Fill a large pan a third of the way up with water and place a steamer basket over it. Bring the water to the boil and put the carrots and yard-long beans in the basket. Put the lid on, reduce the heat and steam for 3–4 minutes.

8 Add the water spinach to the steamer for a minute, then drain the vegetables and refresh under cold running water.

9 Put the vegetables in a large bowl. Add the mango, pineapple and beansprouts and pour in half the peanut sauce. Toss well and tip on to a serving dish. Arrange the egg quarters and tofu slices and drizzle the remaining peanut sauce over the top. Sprinkle with the reserved fried shallots to garnish.

Per Portion Energy 449kcal/1873kJ; Protein 22.2g; Carbohydrate 24.5g, of which sugars 20.7g; Fat 30g, of which saturates 5.1g; Cholesterol 108mg; Calcium 611mg; Fibre 5.1g; Sodium 675mg.

RAW VEGETABLE AND COCONUT SALAD

THIS INDONESIAN SALAD IS TYPICAL OF THE TYPE OF DISH THAT IS SERVED AS A SNACK WITH RICE ON A BANANA LEAF OR WITH FISH AND MEAT. STREET STALLS OFTEN PREPARE A SIMPLE SALAD OF THIS KIND TO ACCOMPANY THE MAIN DISH. THE INGREDIENTS OF THE SALAD VARY WITH THE SEASONS.

SERVES FOUR TO SIX

INGREDIENTS
  225g/8oz yard-long beans,
    cut into bitesize pieces
  3–4 tomatoes, skinned, seeded and
    cut into bitesize chunks
  4–6 spring onions (scallions), sliced
  225g/8oz beansprouts
  ½ fresh coconut, grated
For the dressing
  1–2 fresh red or green chillies,
    seeded and chopped
  2 garlic cloves, chopped
  25g/1oz galangal or fresh root
    ginger, grated
  5–10ml/1–2 tsp terasi (Indonesian
    shrimp paste)
  juice of 2–3 limes
  salt and ground black pepper

1 To make the dressing, using a mortar and pestle, grind the chillies, garlic and galangal or ginger to a paste. Add the terasi and juice of 2 limes. If the limes are not juicy, then squeeze the juice of the extra lime and add to the dressing, or add a little water, so that it is of pouring consistency. Season the dressing with salt and pepper to taste.

2 Put the yard-long beans, tomatoes, spring onions, beansprouts and grated coconut into a large bowl. Using your fingers or two spoons, mix the ingredients together thoroughly.

3 Toss the dressing into the salad with clean hands, transfer to a yard-long bowl and serve immediately.

Per Portion Energy 141kcal/584kJ; Protein 4.5g; Carbohydrate 6.4g, of which sugars 5.1g; Fat 11g, of which saturates 9.1g; Cholesterol 8mg; Calcium 54mg; Fibre 4.6g; Sodium 86mg.

GREEN PAPAYA SALAD

THROUGHOUT SOUTH-EAST ASIA, GREEN PAPAYAS HAVE EARNED HUGE POPULARITY FOR THE UNIQUE TEXTURE AND FLAVOUR THEY LEND TO SALADS. THIS IS NOT A SALAD TO BE REGARDED AS A MERE SIDE SHOW, BUT AS A FEATURE DISH THAT IS SATISFYING YET LIGHT.

SERVES FOUR

INGREDIENTS

2 green papayas, seeded
  and grated
4 shallots, finely sliced
1–2 fresh red chillies, seeded, halved
  lengthways and finely sliced
150g/5oz/1 cup plump sultanas
  (golden raisins) or raisins
2 garlic cloves, crushed
25g/1oz fresh root ginger, grated
45–60ml/3–4 tbsp suka (Filipino
  coconut vinegar) or cane vinegar
50g/2oz palm sugar (jaggery)
coriander (cilantro) leaves, to garnish

1 Put the papaya, shallots, chillies, sultanas, garlic and ginger into a bowl. In a separate small bowl, mix together the suka and palm sugar until the sugar has dissolved.

2 Pour the sweet vinegar mixture over the salad and toss well together. Leave the salad to marinate for at least 1 hour or, for the best flavour, in the refrigerator overnight to allow the flavours to mingle. Serve garnished with coriander leaves.

Per Portion Energy 232kcal/988kJ; Protein 2.5g; Carbohydrate 58.3g, of which sugars 57.6g; Fat 0.4g, of which saturates 0g; Cholesterol 0mg; Calcium 81mg; Fibre 5.5g; Sodium 19mg.

REFRESHING FRUIT SALAD IN A TANGY DRESSING

Entrenched in the Indonesian culinary culture, rujak appears in many guises — as a snack, as a salad to accompany fried and grilled dishes, or as a festive dish. In Java, it is traditionally served before the birth of the first child. In the 19th century, Javanese settlers introduced it to Malaysia, where it has been adapted by the Chinese, Indians and Malays to suit their tastes. Designed to be flexible, this refreshing salad, tossed in a pungent and tangy dressing, can include any choice of fruit and vegetables that you like.

SERVES FOUR TO SIX

INGREDIENTS
1 green mango, finely sliced
1 ripe, firm papaya, finely sliced
1–2 star fruit (carambola),
    finely sliced
½ pineapple, finely sliced and cut
    into bitesize pieces
½ pomelo, segmented
1 small cucumber, roughly peeled,
    seeded and finely sliced
1 yam bean, finely sliced
a handful of beansprouts
For the sauce
10ml/2 tsp terasi (Indonesian
    shrimp paste)
225g/8oz/1½ cups roasted peanuts
4 garlic cloves, chopped
2–4 fresh red chillies, seeded
    and chopped
15ml/1 tbsp tamarind paste
30ml/2 tbsp palm sugar (jaggery)
salt

1 To make the sauce, dry-fry the terasi in a small, heavy frying pan until it is golden and emits a toasted aroma.

2 Using a mortar and pestle or an electric blender, pound the peanuts, garlic and chillies to a coarse paste. Beat in the dry-fried terasi, tamarind paste and sugar. Add enough water to make a thick pouring sauce, then stir until the sugar has dissolved. Season the sauce with salt to taste.

3 Put all the fruit and vegetables, except the beansprouts, into a large bowl. Pour in some of the sauce and toss gently together. Leave the salad to stand for 30 minutes.

4 Turn the salad into a serving dish. Scatter the beansprouts over the top and serve with the remaining sauce drizzled on top.

Per Portion Energy 321kcal/1344kJ; Protein 12.3g; Carbohydrate 30g, of which sugars 27.2g; Fat 17.7g, of which saturates 3.3g; Cholesterol 8mg; Calcium 91mg; Fibre 6.2g; Sodium 81mg.

SWEET SNACKS AND DRINKS

Swaying sugar palms all over the islands give a clue to the

Filipinos' sweet tooth. Native dishes made from rice, cassava,

bananas and coconuts, and sweetened with palm sugar, are

enjoyed at all times of day. The islanders also enjoy many

puddings with an obvious Spanish influence.

In Indonesia, it is typical to have a piece of fruit, if anything,

at the end of a meal, rather than a sweet dessert. However,

sugary snacks are enjoyed in the daytime, as are syrupy drinks.

STICKY COCONUT CREPES

A GREAT FAVOURITE AT STREET STALLS, THIS IS ONE OF THE INDONESIAN SWEET SNACKS THAT TOURISTS IN BALI AND JAVA RAVE ABOUT. INDONESIANS LOVE THEM TOO, DEVOURING THEM IN GREAT QUANTITIES, AS THEY ARE SO SIMPLE AND TASTY. MADE WITH THE SAME BATTER USED FOR SAVOURY SPRING ROLLS, THE CRÊPES ARE FILLED WITH A STICKY COCONUT MIXTURE AND SERVED EITHER AT ROOM TEMPERATURE OR HOT.

SERVES THREE TO FOUR

INGREDIENTS
   15ml/1 tbsp palm or coconut oil
   30ml/2 tbsp corn oil
   5ml/1 tsp cardamom seeds
   225g/8oz/1½ cups fresh coconut,
      finely grated or shredded
   60ml/4 tbsp palm sugar (jaggery)
   pinch of salt
   sugar, to sprinkle (optional)
For the crêpes
   115g/4oz/⅔ cup rice flour
   30ml/2 tbsp tapioca flour or
      cornflour (cornstarch)
   2 eggs, beaten
   about 400ml/14fl oz/1⅔ cups water
   corn or vegetable oil, for frying
   salt

1 To make the crêpes, sift the rice flour and tapioca into a bowl and make a well in the centre. Add the beaten eggs and palm oil into the well and gradually pour in the water, whisking all the time, until it forms a smooth batter. Season with salt and leave to rest for 30 minutes.

2 Heat a heavy, non-stick pancake or crêpe pan and, using a piece of kitchen paper, wipe a little of the corn oil all over the surface. Using a small cup or ladle, add a little batter to the pan, tilting it at the same time to spread the batter evenly over the base.

3 Reduce the heat and cook the crêpe gently until the batter sets and lifts at the edges, then flip the crêpe over and cook on the other side until just lightly browned.

4 Carefully lift the crêpe on to a plate and repeat with the remaining batter. In total there should be enough batter to make 12 crêpes.

5 In a heavy, non-stick pan, heat the palm (coconut) oil and stir in the cardamom seeds. Toss in the coconut, and then add the sugar and salt.

6 Over a low heat, toss the coconut continuously for 3–5 minutes, until it caramelizes. Remove from the heat and leave to cool.

7 Place a crêpe on a flat surface in front of you and heap 15–30ml/1–2 tbsp of caramelized coconut just off centre. Fold the edge nearest to you over the filling, tuck in the sides, and roll over to form a log.

8 Repeat with the remaining crêpes and filling.

9 Serve the crêpes at room temperature, or heat in a lightly oiled, heavy frying pan with an extra sprinkling of sugar to make them sticky, and serve hot.

Per Portion Energy 475kcal/1972kJ; Protein 7g; Carbohydrate 38.6g, of which sugars 1.6g; Fat 32.4g, of which saturates 17.8g; Cholesterol 95mg; Calcium 30mg; Fibre 4.2g; Sodium 48mg.

PANDANUS CUSTARD WITH GLUTINOUS RICE

THE RICH EGG AND COCONUT MILK CUSTARD USED HERE IS TRADITIONALLY MADE AS A TOPPING FOR STEAMED GLUTINOUS RICE AND IS CALLED SRI MUKA IN INDONESIA. AS A BREAKFAST SPREAD FOR TOAST IT'S KNOWN AS KAYA. THE PANDANUS LEAVES GIVE THE GLUTINOUS RICE BASE A DELICIOUSLY SUBTLE SCENT, AND COLOUR THE CUSTARD A DELICATE GREEN.

SERVES SIX TO EIGHT

INGREDIENTS
    200g/7oz/scant 1 cup glutinous rice,
        soaked over night in water to cover
    200ml/7fl oz/¾ cup coconut milk
    2.5ml/½ tsp salt
    2 pandanus (screwpine) leaves
For the topping
    2 pandanus (screwpine) leaves
    6 eggs
    115g/4oz/½ cup sugar
    300ml/½ pint/1¼ cups thick
        coconut milk
    15ml/1 tbsp rice flour
    5ml/1 tsp cornflour (cornstarch)

1 Place the soaked glutinous rice, which should have absorbed all of the water, in a steamer.

2 Sprinkle over the coconut milk and salt. Cut up the pandanus leaves into pieces and press them all over the rice.

3 Steam the rice until it is set but not cooked through. Remove the pandanus leaves and discard.

4 For the topping, cut the pandanus leaves into small pieces and grind using a mortar and pestle.

5 Squeeze out the green juice through a fine sieve (strainer) into a small bowl.

6 Beat the eggs with the sugar for 2–3 minutes, or until the sugar is completely dissolved. Sieve (strain) the mixture into a bowl.

7 Whisk together the coconut milk, rice flour and cornflour, then pour on to the egg and sugar mixture and whisk thoroughly to make a smooth, thin custard.

8 Stir in the pandanus juice. The mixture will have a delicate green tint.

9 Pour the mixture into a non-stick pan and cook over a low heat for about 5 minutes until it becomes thick, beating hard with a wooden spoon to prevent lumps forming,

10 Press the rice down to compact it. Pour the custard topping mixture on to the rice, cover and steam for 20 minutes or until the custard is set firm.

11 Allow the dessert to cool fully before cutting it into diamond shapes to chill and serve as a snack.

Per Portion Energy 172kcal/721kJ; Protein 6.9g; Carbohydrate 26.2g, of which sugars 3.1g; Fat 4.5g, of which saturates 1.3g; Cholesterol 143mg; Calcium 45mg; Fibre 0g; Sodium 122mg.

SWEET SPRING ROLLS
WITH BANANA AND JACKFRUIT

'TURON TURON' SHOUT THE FILIPINO STREET VENDORS AS YOU WALK BY, LURING YOU TO TRY THEIR DELICIOUS SWEET SPRING ROLLS, WHICH CAN BE SPRINKLED WITH SUGAR AND EATEN WITH THE FINGERS, OR SERVED AS A PUDDING WITH A CARAMEL SAUCE. TRADITIONALLY, THE FILIPINOS USE A SHORT FAT BANANA CALLED SABA AND JACKFRUIT (NANGKA), WHICH IS ONE OF THE LARGEST FRUITS IN THE WORLD, SMOOTH IN TEXTURE AND WITH A LOVELY SWEET AROMA. FOR THIS RECIPE USE ORDINARY BANANAS AND, IF YOU CANNOT FIND FRESH JACKFRUIT IN SOUTH-EAST ASIAN FOOD STORES, REPLACE IT WITH PINEAPPLE.

SERVES FOUR TO SIX

INGREDIENTS
    12 spring roll wrappers or
      lumpia wrappers
    2 firm, ripe bananas, thinly
      sliced diagonally
    175g/6oz jackfruit, thinly sliced
    30ml/2 tbsp palm sugar (jaggery) or
      muscovado (molasses) sugar
    1–2 eggs, beaten
    corn or vegetable oil, for deep-frying
    mint sprigs, to garnish (optional)
For the caramel sauce
    115g/4oz/1 cup sugar
    120ml/4fl oz/½ cup water
    250ml/8fl oz/1 cup coconut milk or
      coconut cream

1 For the sauce, in a heavy pan, heat the sugar and water until it caramelizes, shaking the pan occasionally.

2 When the mixture starts to turn a rich brown, remove from the heat and stir in the coconut milk or cream. Return the pan to the heat and continue stirring until the sauce thickens slightly. Remove from the heat and leave the sauce to rest.

3 Place a spring roll wrapper on a flat surface. Arrange, overlapping, 2–3 slices of banana with 2–3 slices of jackfruit 2.5cm/1in from the edge nearest to you. Sprinkle a little sugar over the fruit, then roll the nearest edge over the fruit, tuck in the ends and continue rolling into a loose log. (If it is too tight, the wrapper will split open when fried.)

4 Moisten the far edge with a little beaten egg to seal the roll so that the filling does not escape during the frying. Repeat with the remaining spring roll wrappers.

5 Heat enough oil in a wok or pan for deep-frying. Working in batches, deep-fry the spring rolls for 3–4 minutes, until golden brown all over. Using tongs, lift the spring rolls out of the oil and drain on kitchen paper.

6 Quickly reheat the sauce. Arrange the spring rolls on a serving dish, or in individual bowls, garnish with mint sprigs, if using, and serve with the caramel sauce drizzled over the top or on the side as a dip.

Per Portion Energy 246kcal/1043kJ; Protein 4g; Carbohydrate 47.3g, of which sugars 37.1g; Fat 5.9g, of which saturates 1.1g; Cholesterol 63mg; Calcium 55mg; Fibre 1.2g; Sodium 72mg.

INDONESIAN BLACK STICKY RICE PUDDING

OFTEN CALLED FORBIDDEN RICE, BLACK STICKY RICE IS USUALLY FLAVOURED WITH PANDANUS LEAVES BUT YOU CAN USE A VANILLA POD OR GINGER INSTEAD.

SERVES FOUR TO SIX

INGREDIENTS
  225g/8oz/1 cup plus 2 tbsp
    black glutinous rice
  300ml/½ pint/1¼ cups water
  60ml/4 tbsp palm sugar (jaggery)
  2–3 pandanus (screwpine) leaves,
    1 vanilla pod (bean) or 25g/1oz
    fresh root ginger
  400g/14oz can coconut milk
  a pinch of salt
  60ml/4 tbsp desiccated (dry
    unsweetened shredded) coconut

1 Put the rice in a large bowl, cover generously with cold water and leave to soak for 4 hours. Rinse the rice under cold running water and drain.

2 Put the rice in a pan, cover with the measured water and bring it to the boil. Stir in 45ml/3 tbsp of the sugar until dissolved, and then add the pandanus leaves, vanilla pod or ginger. Reduce the heat and simmer for 10–15 minutes, until the water has been absorbed. Remove from the heat, cover and leave to steam for 10 minutes.

3 Meanwhile, pour the coconut milk into a separate pan and bring to the boil. Stir in the remaining sugar and the salt until the sugar has dissolved. Keep warm.

4 In small, heavy frying pan, quickly dry-fry the coconut, tossing it all the time, until it gives off a lovely aroma and turns golden brown. Turn it into a bowl.

5 Remove the pandanus leaves, vanilla pod or ginger from the rice and spoon the pudding into individual bowls. Drizzle the hot coconut milk over the top and sprinkle with the coconut.

Per Portion Energy 249kcal/1044kJ; Protein 4g; Carbohydrate 42.5g, of which sugars 14.4g; Fat 7g, of which saturates 5.5g; Cholesterol 0mg; Calcium 33mg; Fibre 1.4g; Sodium 78mg.

FILIPINO FLAMBÉED BANANA FRITTERS

YOU CAN FIND DEEP-FRIED BANANA FRITTERS AT FOOD STALLS AND CAFÉS IN INDONESIA AND THE PHILIPPINES. THIS FILIPINO RECIPE HAS GRATED GINGER AND COCONUT ADDED TO THE BATTER.

SERVES THREE TO FOUR

INGREDIENTS
 6–8 small or 3 large ripe bananas
 corn or vegetable oil, for deep-frying
 15ml/1 tbsp sugar
 60ml/¼ cup rum
 coconut cream or ice cream, to serve
For the batter
 115g/4oz/1 cup plain
  (all-purpose) flour
 5ml/1 tsp baking powder
 pinch of salt
 2 eggs, lightly beaten
 400g/14oz can coconut milk
 15ml/1 tbsp palm sugar (jaggery)
 25g/1oz fresh root ginger,
  finely grated
 50g/2oz fresh coconut, grated, or
  desiccated (dry unsweetened
  shredded) coconut

1 First make the batter. Sift the flour, baking powder and salt into a large bowl. Make a well in the centre and drop in the beaten eggs. Gradually pour in the coconut milk, beating all the time with a whisk or wooden spoon, until the batter is smooth. Beat in the sugar, grated ginger and coconut. Leave the batter to stand for 30 minutes.

2 Cut the bananas in half and halve each again, lengthways. Beat the batter again, then drop in the bananas, making sure they are well coated.

3 Heat the oil in a deep pan until a cube of bread dropped into the oil browns and crisps.

4 Working in batches and using a pair of tongs, lift 2–3 banana pieces out of the batter and lower them into the oil. Keep them separate until the batter has cooked, to stop them sticking together.

5 Deep-fry the bananas until crisp and golden brown, then lift them out and drain on kitchen paper.

6 Arrange the deep-fried bananas in a wide, heavy pan and place over a medium heat. Sprinkle the sugar over the top and toss the bananas in the pan until they are sticky and slightly caramelized.

7 Lower the heat, pour in the rum and set alight. (Have a lid handy to smother the flames if necessary.) Spoon the rum over the bananas until the sauce has caramelized and the bananas are well coated. Serve immediately with coconut cream, or vanilla ice cream.

VARIATION
For a simpler version of this recipe, just dust the fritters with icing (confectioners') sugar or caster (superfine) sugar once they have drained, and eat warm.

Per Portion Energy 407kcal/1710kJ; Protein 7.8g; Carbohydrate 53.3g, of which sugars 29.7g; Fat 19.7g, of which saturates 8.8g; Cholesterol 95mg; Calcium 95mg; Fibre 3.4g; Sodium 151mg.

FILIPINO CRÈMES CARAMELS WITH ORANGE

A LEGACY OF THE SPANISH, THIS IS A VERY POPULAR SWEET SNACK IN THE PHILIPPINES. IT IS A HEAVIER VERSION OF A CLASSIC CRÈME CARAMEL, MADE WITH CONDENSED AND EVAPORATED MILK.

SERVES FOUR

INGREDIENTS
  2 x 400g/14oz cans evaporated milk
  150g/5½oz can sweetened condensed
    milk
  grated rind of 1 orange or a few
    drops of vanilla extract
  4 eggs
  2 egg yolks
  shredded rind of 1 orange, to
    decorate
  30ml/2 tbsp sugar
  30ml/2 tbsp water
For the caramel
  150g/5oz/¾ cup caster
    (superfine) sugar
  75ml/5 tbsp fresh orange juice

1 Preheat the oven to 160°C/325°F/ Gas 3. Put four 5cm/2in ramekins into the oven to warm.

2 To make the caramel, put the sugar and strained orange juice into a heavy pan and stir over a medium heat until the sugar has dissolved.

3 Bring the mixture to the boil and leave to bubble until dark golden in colour, resisting the temptation to stir. Do not let the caramel burn or become so thick that it sticks to the pan. It must be a thick pouring consistency.

4 Remove the ramekins from the oven and pour in the caramel, swirling it around so that it coats the bottom and sides. Put aside to let the caramel harden.

COOK'S TIP
If custard or gelatin-based desserts will not unmould or are not doing so neatly, dip the ramekins or moulds into a dish of very hot water for up to 5 seconds. This should allow the desserts to release from the moulds cleanly when inverted.

5 Meanwhile, put the evaporated milk, condensed milk and orange rind or vanilla extract into a heavy pan and heat until scalding but not boiling. Remove from the heat, cover and leave the milk to infuse for 15–20 minutes.

6 In a large bowl, lightly whisk the eggs and egg yolks together. Reheat the milk then strain into the egg mixture, whisking all the time. Strain into the ramekins.

7 Place the ramekins in a roasting pan and pour in boiling water until it comes halfway up the sides of the ramekins. Carefully transfer the roasting tin to the oven and cook for about 25 minutes until the crèmes caramels are set. (The mixture should be firm to the touch but with a hint of wobble, as it will continue to cook a little when removed from the oven.) Leave to cool, then chill in the refrigerator overnight.

8 To serve, press the edges of each dessert lightly to release it from the ramekin, then use a sharp, thin knife to ease it away. Place an individual serving plate over the top of each ramekin, hold both firmly and invert, giving a gentle shake to release the caramel.

9 Simmer the shredded orange rind with the 30ml/2 tbsp of sugar and water in a small pan over a low heat until they look syrupy and shiny, then spoon a little over the desserts, making a heap of caramelized rind on the top of each.

Per Portion Energy 398kcal/1678kJ; Protein 17.9g; Carbohydrate 54.8g, of which sugars 54.8g; Fat 13.5g, of which saturates 6.5g; Cholesterol 226mg; Calcium 461mg; Fibre 0g; Sodium 241mg.

COCONUT TARTS

In Mindanao, coconuts are plentiful and many desserts feature the meat of very young fruits, which is soft and jelly-like with a mildly astringent taste. It is not naturally sweet — quite different from the meat of older nuts that yield coconut milk. Commonly sold preserved as macapuno, it is available in jars in most Filipino stores.

MAKES ABOUT TEN TARTS

INGREDIENTS
100g/3½oz/¾ cup plain
   (all-purpose) flour
5ml/1 tsp caster (superfine) sugar
pinch of salt
65g/2½oz cold unsalted butter, diced
2 large (US extra large) egg yolks
1.5ml/¼ tsp vanilla extract
30ml/2 tbsp water
For the filling
6 egg yolks
75ml/5 tbsp sugar
60ml/4 tbsp plain (all-purpose) flour
45ml/3 tbsp melted butter
600g/1lb 6oz young coconut meat,
   finely grated
5ml/1 tsp lime juice

1 To make the pastry, mix the flour, sugar and salt in a large bowl until thoroughly blended. Put the cold butter into the bowl and rub it into the flour with your fingertips until the mixture resembles fine breadcrumbs. (Try to work in a cool place with cold hands when making pastry.)

2 Whisk the egg yolks with the vanilla extract and water. Mix this into the flour with a metal spoon or palette knife.

3 Stir the dough to blend thoroughly, then draw it into a ball. Knead lightly with your hands for a minute and divide into two portions. Wrap in clear film (plastic wrap) and chill for 1 hour.

4 Pinch off small balls of dough, roll out and press into the holes in a greased deep tartlet tin (muffin pan). Press the pastry firmly in and trim. Set aside.

5 Preheat the oven to 160°C/325°F/ Gas 3. Beat the egg yolks and sugar until the sugar is dissolved, then mix the flour and melted butter together and add to the egg yolks. Mix well.

6 Finally, add the grated coconut and lime juice. Stir to blend, then spoon some of the mixture into each tart case.

7 Bake for 15 minutes, then leave to cool slightly, before serving with vanilla or exotic fruit-flavoured ice cream.

Per portion Energy 460kcal/1911kJ; Protein 6.8g; Carbohydrate 23.3g, of which sugars 11.1g; Fat 38.5g, of which saturates 28.4g; Cholesterol 182mg; Calcium 58mg; Fibre 6g; Sodium 98mg.

SPICE ISLAND ICE CREAM

WITH SUCH A RANGE OF TROPICAL FRUIT AND SPICES, THERE IS ALMOST NO LIMIT TO THE FLAVOURS OF INDONESIAN ICE CREAM. IN THIS DELICIOUS DESSERT, WARMING SPICES, WHICH REFLECT THE REGION'S HISTORY OF INDIAN AND ARABIAN TRADERS, ARE COMBINED WITH COOL, SMOOTH AND RICH ICE CREAM TO MAKE A TRULY MEMORABLE, AND VERY INDONESIAN, DESSERT.

SERVES SIX

INGREDIENTS
    500ml/17fl oz/2 cups double
        (heavy) cream
    6–8 cloves
    6–8 cardamom seeds
    3–4 star anise
    3 cinnamon sticks
    90g/3½oz/½ cup caster
        (superfine) sugar
    150ml/¼ pint/⅔ cup water
    4 large (US extra large) eggs
    ground cinnamon or nutmeg,
        to decorate

1 In a heavy pan, heat the cream with the spices until scalding. Remove the pan from the heat and leave the cream to infuse until cool.

2 In a separate pan, heat the sugar and water together, stirring all the time, until the sugar has dissolved. Bring to the boil and boil for 2–3 minutes without stirring, then lower the heat and simmer for 5 minutes. Remove from the heat and leave to cool for 10 minutes.

3 Whisk the eggs together in a bowl. Gradually trickle in the hot syrup, whisking all the time, until the mixture becomes light and airy like a mousse. Strain the spice-infused cream into the mixture and whisk well together until thoroughly blended.

4 Pour the mixture into an ice cream maker and churn until frozen, according to the manufacturer's instructions. Alternatively, pour into a freezer-proof container and freeze, uncovered, for 1–2 hours until beginning to set around the edges. Turn into a bowl and beat to break up the ice crystals. Return to the freezer container, freeze and beat again, then cover and freeze until firm.

5 Decorate with a sprinkling of cinnamon and serve.

COOK'S TIP
This ice cream is very good served with warm apple or pear tart, or with flambéed bananas.

Per Portion Energy 522kcal/2157kJ; Protein 5.6g; Carbohydrate 17.1g, of which sugars 17.1g; Fat 48.5g, of which saturates 28.9g; Cholesterol 241mg; Calcium 68mg; Fibre 0g; Sodium 66mg.

FILIPINO MANGO ICE CREAM

Two of the most popular ice creams in the Philippines are made from fresh mangoes and coconuts. Ice creams are sometimes served as desserts in restaurants and at special feasts, otherwise they are enjoyed at any time of the day and in the evening at ice cream parlours and street stalls — perfect for a warm, tropical evening.

3 Mash the mango with a fork, or purée it roughly in an electric blender or a food processor.

4 Strain the cooled custard into a large bowl. Add the cream and whisk together. Beat in the mango purée until well mixed.

5 Pour the mixture into an ice cream maker and churn until frozen, according to the manufacturer's instructions. Alternatively, pour into a freezer container and freeze, uncovered, for 1–2 hours until beginning to set around the edges. Turn into a bowl and beat to break up the ice crystals. Return to the freezer container, freeze and beat again, then cover and freeze until firm.

COOK'S TIP
Serve the ice cream with thin slices of fresh mango to emphasize the flavours of this fruity treat.

SERVES FOUR TO SIX

INGREDIENTS
    6 egg yolks
    115g/4oz/generous ½ cup caster
      (superfine) sugar
    500ml/17fl oz/2 cups full fat (whole)
      or skimmed milk
    350g/12oz mango flesh (about
      3 mangoes)
    300ml/½ pint/1¼ cups double
      (heavy) cream

1 In a bowl, whisk the egg yolks and sugar together until light and frothy. In a heavy pan, heat the milk until scalding and then slowly pour the milk into the egg mixture, whisking all the time.

2 Strain the milk and egg mixture back into the rinsed pan. Heat, stirring all the time, until thickened but do not allow the mixture to boil. Remove the pan from the heat and leave to cool completely. Do not worry if a skin forms as you will strain the custard later.

Per Portion Energy 466kcal/1941kJ; Protein 7.2g; Carbohydrate 35.4g, of which sugars 35.2g; Fat 33.9g, of which saturates 19.2g; Cholesterol 275mg; Calcium 167mg; Fibre 2g; Sodium 59mg.

FRESH GINGER TEA

GINGER TEA IS A SPECIALITY OF THE HIGH-ALTITUDE REGIONS OF INDONESIA. OFTEN YOU WILL FIND AN OLD WOMAN MAKING THE TEA IN THE SMALL HILL SHELTERS MADE OF BAMBOO, WHERE PEOPLE STOP TO REST AND DRINK A GLASS OF THIS HOT AND SPICY BREW. GINGER TEA IS ALSO THE PREFERRED BREAKFAST BEVERAGE IN THE PHILIPPINES, AS IT IS WARMING AND STIMULATES THE DIGESTION.

SERVES FOUR

INGREDIENTS
1 litre/1¾ pints/4 cups water
40g/½oz fresh root ginger, peeled
  and sliced
1–2 cinnamon sticks
5ml/1 tsp black peppercorns
30ml/2 tbsp palm sugar (jaggery)
115g/4oz/¾ cup coconut flesh,
  finely shredded

COOK'S TIP
The tea improves with standing, so, if convenient, you can make it in advance and reheat it before serving.

1 Bring the water, ginger, cinnamon sticks, peppercorns and sugar to the boil in a pan, stirring until the sugar has dissolved. Boil rapidly for 2 minutes, then simmer for at least 15 minutes.

2 Divide the shredded coconut between four heatproof glasses and strain the hot ginger tea into the glasses. Serve immediately, with a spoon to scoop up the coconut.

Per Portion Energy 120kcal/500kJ; Protein 0.9g; Carbohydrate 8.8g, of which sugars 8.8g; Fat 9.3g, of which saturates 8g; Cholesterol 0mg; Calcium 8mg; Fibre 2.1g; Sodium 5mg.

ICED PRESERVED FRUIT AND BEAN DRINK

THIS IS THE FILIPINO VERSION OF VIETNAM'S FAMOUS RAINBOW DRINK. PACKED WITH FRUIT AND BEAN PRESERVES AND CHILLED WITH CRUSHED ICE, OVER WHICH SWEET CONDENSED MILK IS POURED, THE DRINK IS POPULAR WITH PEOPLE OF ALL AGES. KNOWN AS A 'WORKING MAN'S DRINK', IT IS FILLING ENOUGH TO BE CLASSED AS A SNACK AND SO REFRESHING THAT IS WELL WORTH SAMPLING ON A HOT SUMMER'S DAY.

SERVES TWO

INGREDIENTS
30ml/2 tbsp preserved sweet beans
30ml/2 tbsp preserved sugar
  palm fruit
30ml/2 tbsp preserved purple yam
30ml/2 tbsp preserved
  macapuno coconut
crushed ice
30ml/2 tbsp sweetened condensed
  milk
2 lychees, stoned (pitted)
4 slices mango, to decorate

1 Divide the preserved ingredients between two tall glasses, layering them in any order you want. Fill the rest of the glass with crushed ice to 2.5cm/½in from the top.

2 Spoon the condensed milk over the ice so that it runs down the inside of the glass.

3 Place a lychee on top of each drink. Make a small incision in the middle of each mango slice and use to decorate the glasses by securing them on the rim of the glass.

4 Serve immediately, with a long-handled spoon to reach down into the depths of the preserves.

Per Portion Energy 182kcal/775kJ; Protein 4.2g; Carbohydrate 39.4g, of which sugars 39.3g; Fat 2g, of which saturates 1g; Cholesterol 5mg; Calcium 94mg; Fibre 5.2g; Sodium 31mg.

FILIPINO MANGO AND LIME DRINK

THE TROPICAL ISLANDS OF THE PHILIPPINES ARE HOME TO A WIDE VARIETY OF DIFFERENT MANGOES, SOME OF WHICH YOU DO NOT SEE ANYWHERE ELSE. MOST OF THESE FRUITS ARE VARIETIES FOR EATING RAW, AND WHEN RIPE THEY ARE JUICY AND BUTTERY, MELTING IN THE MOUTH WITH AN EXQUISITE TROPICAL FLAVOUR. MANY MANGOES ARE USED TO MAKE EITHER MANGO ICE CREAM OR THIS DRINK, WHICH IS OFTEN ENJOYED AT BREAKFAST OR AS A SNACK IN THE HEAT OF THE DAY.

SERVES TWO

INGREDIENTS
4 very ripe mangoes, stoned (pitted)
15–30ml/1–2 tbsp sugar
crushed ice
juice of 1–2 kalamansi or
    ordinary limes
2 lime slices, to decorate

1 Purée the mango flesh in a blender or food processor. Sweeten with sugar to taste, then divide between two glasses.

2 Spoon some crushed ice over the top of the purée, then pour over the lime juice. Make a small incision in each lime slice and wedge them on the glass rims.

3 Serve with a straw or long spoon.

COOK'S TIP
The sweet-toothed Filipinos sometimes purée the mangoes with sweetened condensed milk, or pour the milk over the ice on top of the mango.

Per Portion Energy 230kcal/987kJ; Protein 2.2g; Carbohydrate 58g, of which sugars 57.1g; Fat 0.6g, of which saturates 0.3g; Cholesterol 0mg; Calcium 44mg; Fibre 7.8g; Sodium 7mg.

AVOCADO JUICE

ONE OF MANY UNUSUAL SWEET DELIGHTS FOUND AT STREET STALLS IN INDONESIA AND THE PHILIPPINES IS THIS THICK, SYRUPY AVOCADO JUICE, WHICH FALLS SOMEWHERE BETWEEN A SNACK AND A DRINK. ONCE AGAIN, THE SOUTH-EAST ASIAN PASSION FOR CONDENSED MILK DEFINES THIS DRINK. MIX THE DELECTABLE AVOCADO PURÉE INTO THE SWEET MILK AND ENJOY AT YOUR LEISURE.

SERVES TWO

INGREDIENTS
  30ml/2 tbsp sugar
  30ml/2 tbsp water
  2 ripe avocados
  a handful of ice cubes or crushed ice
  30ml/2 tbsp condensed milk

1 Put the sugar and water in a heavy pan and heat gently, stirring all the time, until the sugar has dissolved. Bring to the boil without stirring, then remove from the heat and leave to cool.

COOK'S TIP
As with any recipe that calls for them, use only properly ripened, seasonal avocados, as those available 'year round' do not have enough flavour.

2 When the sugar syrup is cold, put the flesh of the avocados in a large bowl or food processor, add the cooled sugar syrup and mash or blend until smooth.

3 Put the ice cubes into two tall glasses, spoon in the avocado mixture, then drizzle the condensed milk over the top. Serve immediately, with a long spoon so that the drinkers can mix the avocado with the condensed milk at their leisure.

Per Portion 324kcal/1353kJ; Protein 3.9g; Carbohydrate 30.1g, of which sugars 28.7g; Fat 21.6g, of which saturates 5.5g; Cholesterol 8mg; Calcium 84mg; Fibre 3.4g; Sodium 39mg.

WATER CHESTNUT AND LYCHEE SMOOTHIE

THIS DRINK HAS AN INTRIGUING CONTRAST OF CRUNCHY AND SMOOTH TEXTURES THAT MAKES A DELICIOUS END TO ANY SAVOURY MEAL. IT IS SO LIGHT IT CAN ALSO BE SERVED AS AN IN-BETWEEN-COURSES REFRESHER. WHEN SERVED VERY CHILLED, IT IS PERFECT AS A HOT-WEATHER THIRST QUENCHER BECAUSE IT IS LIGHTER THAN MOST SMOOTHIES WITH ITS WATER AND SYRUP BASE.

SERVES FOUR

INGREDIENTS

400ml/14fl oz/1⅔ cups
   iced water
10 canned water chestnuts
10 canned lychees and
   400ml/14fl oz/1⅔ cups of the syrup
2.5ml/½ tsp vanilla extract
lychees on cocktail sticks
   (toothpicks), to serve

1 Combine all the ingredients in a blender or food processor and blend into a thick smoothie.

2 Stir well and chill until required.

3 Pour the mixture into glasses filled with crushed ice, and decorate with a peeled lychee on a cocktail stick.

COOK'S TIP
Floating rose petals in the drink and serving it from a punch bowl make it a great choice for a party.

Per portion Energy 204kcal/868kJ; Protein 1.1g; Carbohydrate 52.8g, of which sugars 52.3g; Fat 0.2g, of which saturates 0g; Cholesterol 0mg; Calcium 7mg; Fibre 0.6g; Sodium 212mg.

SWEET BAKES

Filipinos enjoy sweet cakes and tarts hugely, and use their local fruits, palm sugar, nuts and rice flour to concoct some truly delicious treats. Indonesia, too, has a selection of special-occasion cakes and cookies that offer something quite different to familiar Western ones, such as a meringue-topped coconut pudding and crumbly Rice Flour and Coconut Milk Cookies. For anybody with a sweet tooth, this chapter is not to be missed!

FIESTA COCONUT RICE CAKE

THE SMALL QUANTITY OF SPRING ONIONS INCLUDED IN THIS RECIPE GIVES THE RICE CAKES AN INTERESTING TASTE, WHICH IS MUCH ENJOYED BY FILIPINOS. THE RICE CAKES CAN BE STEAMED IN BANANA OR PALM LEAVES, OR COOKED IN A HEAVY, NON-STICK PAN, AS IN THIS RECIPE.

4 Add the ginger, spring onion, vanilla extract and lime juice. Simmer until all the liquid has been absorbed. Remove from the heat, cover and leave to steam and cool.

5 Meanwhile, put the coconut in a small, heavy frying pan and dry-fry until it turns golden brown and gives off a nutty aroma.

6 When the rice has cooled and is fairly solid, cut it into a criss-cross pattern and lift out the diamond-shaped wedges with a spatula. Sprinkle a little of the coconut over the top and serve with lime wedges to squeeze over the cakes.

SERVES FOUR TO SIX

INGREDIENTS
  225g/8oz/1 cup plus 2 tbsp
    glutinous rice
  600ml/1 pint/2½ cups coconut milk
  225g/8oz/1 cup palm sugar (jaggery)
    or muscovado (molasses) sugar
  25g/1oz fresh root ginger,
    finely grated
  1 spring onion (scallion), white parts
    only, very finely chopped
  2–3 drops vanilla extract
  juice of 2 kalamansi or
    ordinary limes
  30ml/2 tbsp desiccated (dry
    unsweetened shredded) coconut,
    to decorate
  1 lime, cut into wedges, to serve

1 Put the rice in a sieve (strainer), rinse under cold running water until the water runs clear, then drain.

2 Put the rice and the coconut milk in a heavy, non-stick, shallow pan and bring to the boil, stirring to prevent the rice sticking to the bottom. Reduce the heat and simmer for 10 minutes, until the rice sticks to the back of a wooden spoon.

3 Add the sugar to the rice and stir gently with a wooden spoon until the sugar has dissolved completely.

COOK'S TIP
For an authentic touch, serve the cakes on banana or coconut palm leaves.

Per Portion Energy 323kcal/1365kJ; Protein 4.1g; Carbohydrate 76g, of which sugars 44.1g; Fat 1g, of which saturates 0.2g; Cholesterol 0mg; Calcium 56mg; Fibre 0g; Sodium 114mg.

YOUNG COCONUT PUDDING

PODENG (FROM THE DISH'S NAME OF PODENG KELAPA MUDA) IS THE INDONESIAN TRANSLITERATION OF THE 'PUDDING', AND THIS ONE IS ALMOST WESTERN IN CONCEPT BUT FOR THE COCONUT. IT IS SOMETHING LIKE QUEEN OF PUDDINGS, BUT WITH A COCONUT RATHER THAN LEMON AND JAM FILLING.

SERVES FOUR

INGREDIENTS
  6 egg yolks
  115g/4oz sugar
  ¼ tsp vanilla extract
  65g/2½oz/9 tbsp plain
    (all-purpose) flour
  90ml/6 tbsp sweetened
    condensed milk
  120ml/4fl oz/½ cup warm water
  250g/9oz young coconut meat,
    finely chopped
For the meringue
  6 egg whites
  15ml/1 tbsp caster (superfine) sugar
  pinch of salt
  65g/2½ oz flaked (sliced) and
    toasted almonds

1 Preheat the oven to 200°C/400°F/
Gas 6. Put the yolks, sugar and vanilla
extract in a large bowl and whisk until
slightly frothy.

2 Gradually add the flour to the
condensed milk and water in a medium
pan, mixing constantly to blend well.

3 Mix the coconut meat into the flour
mixture, then stir in the egg yolk and
sugar mixture. Cook over a low heat,
stirring with a wooden spoon, until the
mixture thickens, about 5 minutes. Pour
into a greased ovenproof dish.

4 Put the egg whites in a clean, grease-
free bowl and whisk until white and
stiffening, using an electric whisk if you
prefer. Add the sugar and salt and
continue to whisk until stiff peaks form.

5 Spread the meringue over the coconut
mixture, and bake for 15–20 minutes,
until the topping turns pale golden. Top
with the flaked and toasted almonds
and serve at room temperature.

Per portion Energy 668kcal/2791kJ; Protein 17.2g; Carbohydrate 58.4g, of which sugars 45.6g; Fat 42.3g, of which saturates 24.1g; Cholesterol 308mg; Calcium 169mg; Fibre 6.9g; Sodium 141mg.

CASHEW TARTS

THESE DELICIOUS TARTS ARE REMINISCENT OF EUROPEAN PATISSERIE, YET ARE UNIQUELY FILIPINO. VERY MORE-ISH AS A TEA-TIME TREAT OR SNACK, THESE CRUNCHY BITES ARE A FAVOURITE BAKE DURING FESTIVE SEASONS. THEY CAN BE MADE IN ADVANCE AS THEY STORE WELL.

MAKES ABOUT 10 SMALL TARTS

INGREDIENTS
225g/8oz ready-rolled shortcrust pastry
3 large (US extra large) eggs, separated
100g/3½oz/½ cup sugar
200g/7oz/generous 1 cup unsalted cashew nuts, coarsely chopped
2.5ml/½ tsp vanilla extract
30ml/2 tbsp evaporated milk
65g/2½oz/⅓ cup butter, melted
5ml/1 tsp lemon juice
cream or ice cream, to serve

1 Preheat the oven to 160°C/325°F/Gas 3. Cut the pastry and press into 10 x 7cm/2½in fluted tartlet tins (muffin pans). Chill.

2 Beat the egg yolks a little and add the sugar. Continue to beat until the mixture is creamy and well blended.

3 Add the chopped cashews, vanilla extract, milk, butter and lemon juice.

4 Whisk the egg whites in a clean, grease-free bowl with an electric whisk until they form stiff peaks. Fold into the yolk mixture. Fill the chilled tartlet tins and bake for 25 minutes, until golden.

5 Allow the tarts to cool and serve with whipped cream or vanilla ice cream.

VARIATION
If you want just one large tart, use the pastry to fill an 18cm/7in fluted tart tin (pan) and bake for 35 minutes, or until set.

Per portion Energy 337kcal/1403kJ; Protein 7.6g; Carbohydrate 25.1g, of which sugars 12.1g; Fat 23.6g, of which saturates 7.9g; Cholesterol 75mg; Calcium 49mg; Fibre 1.1g; Sodium 212mg.

PALM FRUIT PIE

IN THE FILIPINO PROVINCE OF LAGUNA, BUKO PIE (COCONUT PIE) REIGNS SUPREME AS A DESSERT. HOWEVER, COOKS CAN ADAPT AND TWEAK FAVOURITE RECIPES, COMING UP WITH FRESH IDEAS. HERE IS A NEW TAKE ON THE PIE, WHICH IS FINISHED OFF WITH A DELICIOUS COFFEE ICING.

SERVES SIX TO EIGHT

INGREDIENTS
    350g/12oz ready-rolled shortcrust
        pastry
    400g/14oz can palm fruits, drained
For the coffee icing
    115g/4oz/½ cup butter
    200g/7oz/1 cup caster
        (superfine) sugar
    250ml/8fl oz/1 cup thick double
        (heavy) cream
    1 heaped tsp instant coffee granules
    20ml/2 tbsp evaporated milk
    icecream, to serve

1 Preheat the oven to 180°C/350°F/ Gas 4. Roll out the pastry until 5mm/¼in thick and use to line an 18cm/7in fluted tart tin (pan). Press down gently on the base and sides and trim away any excess pastry. Chill for at least 30 minutes.

2 Chop the palm fruits very finely and put into the chilled tart case. Bake for about 20 minutes. Allow to cool.

3 To make the coffee icing, place the butter in a bowl and beat with a wooden spoon or electric mixer until creamy and pale in colour. Gradually add the sugar and cream, whisking with an electric blender for 3–5 minutes until thick and smooth.

VARIATION
If you prefer little tarts, use 12 x 7cm/ 2½in fluted tartlet tins (muffin pans) and bake for about 20 minutes.

4 Dissolve the coffee in the evaporated milk in a small pan over a low heat, then add to the butter mixture.

5 Beat until the mixture has the consistency of thick cream and is a uniform tan colour. Chill until ready for use.

6 Spread the icing on top of the tart and smooth with a palette knife. Chill thoroughly before cutting the tart into wedges and serving with a generous helping of ice cream.

Per portion Energy 493kcal/2060kJ; Protein 5.9g; Carbohydrate 50.4g, of which sugars 30.3g; Fat 31.2g, of which saturates 15.7g; Cholesterol 58.3mg; Calcium 166.3mg; Fibre 1.3g; Sodium 331mg.

ROLLED WAFER COOKIES

BARQUILLOS ARE A FAVOURITE SNACK COOKIE OF FILIPINO CHILDREN, AND ALL OVER THE ISLANDS YOU CAN FIND THESE READY-MADE WAFERS, WHICH ARE DELICIOUS ON THEIR OWN OR WITH ICE CREAM. THEY ARE EASY TO MAKE, AND AT THEIR BEST WHEN EATEN WARM, FRESH FROM THE OVEN, AS A QUICK TREAT WITH A MID-AFTERNOON CUP OF TEA.

2 Add the sugar, vanilla extract and lemon zest, and stir well until the sugar has dissolved.

3 Ladle 15–30ml/1–2 tbsp of the batter into the lightly greased indentations of two tartlet tins (muffin pans).

4 Bake for 15 minutes until the wafers are golden brown. Remove from the oven to cool and harden.

COOK'S TIP
If you haven't got a tartlet tin (muffin pan), place some lightly greased baking parchment on a baking sheet and ladle the batter to make rounds of about 8cm/3in in diameter. Bake as above.

MAKES ABOUT 20 WAFERS

INGREDIENTS
   75ml/5 tbsp milk
   6 egg yolks, lightly beaten
   65g/2½oz/9 tbsp plain
    (all-purpose) flour
   200g/7oz/1 cup sugar
   1.5ml/¼ tsp vanilla extract
   15ml/1 tbsp grated lemon zest

VARIATION
You can alter the flavouring by adding a fruit extract such as banana or pandanus.

1 Preheat the oven to 180°C/350°F/ Gas 4. Mix the milk with the egg yolks in a bowl and slowly add the flour, continually whisking until it is all incorporated to give a smooth batter.

Per portion Energy 71kcal/298kJ; Protein 1.4g; Carbohydrate 13.2g, of which sugars 10.7g; Fat 1.8g, of which saturates 0.5g; Cholesterol 61mg; Calcium 21mg; Fibre 0.1g; Sodium 5mg.

RICE FLOUR AND COCONUT MILK COOKIES

THESE MAY BE OF INDONESIAN ORIGIN BUT AS A FESTIVE TREAT THEY ARE DE RIGUEUR AMONG THE NONYAS THROUGHOUT SOUTH-EAST ASIA DURING THE LUNAR NEW YEAR. THE LITTLE CRUMBLY BITES ARE MADE FROM A BLEND OF RICE AND TAPIOCA FLOUR, AND MAY BE CUT INTO PRETTY SHAPES WITH SPECIAL CUTTERS. A FINE TOUCH IS TO SPRINKLE THEM WITH SESAME SEEDS.

SERVES SIX TO EIGHT

INGREDIENTS
    400g/14oz/2 cups tapioca flour
    200g/7oz/generous 1 cup rice flour
    200g/7oz/1 cup sugar
    250ml/8fl oz/1 cup thick coconut milk
    3 egg yolks
    1 egg white
    1 tsp baking powder
    1 egg, beaten
    sesame seeds (optional)

1 Mix both flours and dry in a wok over a very low heat. This is an important step to remove any moisture that is still in the flour. In Indonesia, it is simply dried in the sun for a few hours.

2 Mix the sugar and coconut milk and simmer for 5 minutes on low heat. Remove from the heat and allow to cool.

3 Beat the egg yolks and egg white separately until frothy and add to the coconut milk mixture. Whisk for a few minutes but do not over-beat, as the cookies should not be full of air.

4 Sift the dry flour and baking powder into a large bowl. Make a well in the centre and pour in the egg and coconut milk mixture. Stir well, then knead into a soft dough. If the dough is too wet, add a little more tapioca flour. It should be dryish but not falling apart, and come away from the bowl easily.

5 Roll out the dough on a floured board to about 1cm/½in thick. Use cutters to make different shapes or make little rounded cookies by hand, each about 2.5 cm/1in in diameter.

6 Dust a baking sheet with a little tapioca flour. Place the cookies on the sheet, brush with a little beaten egg and sprinkle with sesame seeds, if desired.

7 Preheat the oven to 180°C/350°F/ Gas 4 and bake each batch for about 12–15 minutes until pale golden but not brown.

8 Cool on a rack and store in an airtight jar, where they should stay crisp for up to 2 weeks.

Per portion Energy 410kcal/1737kJ; Protein 4.3g; Carbohydrate 95.2g, of which sugars 27.7g; Fat 3.1g, of which saturates 0.8g; Cholesterol 99mg; Calcium 45mg; Fibre 0.7g; Sodium 59mg.

INDEX